Winning with One-Liners

3,400 HILARIOUS
LAUGH LINES TO
TICKLE YOUR
FUNNY BONE
& SPICE UP
YOUR SPEECHES

Compiled by
Pat Williams

Health Communications, Inc.
Deerfield Beach, Florida

www.hci-online.com

Library of Congress Cataloging-in-Publication Data

Williams, Pat, 1940–
    Winning with one-liners : 3,400 hilarious laugh lines to
tickle your funny bone & spice up your speeches / compiled
by Pat Williams.
        p. cm.
    ISBN 0-7573-0057-X (tp)
        1. American wit and humor.   I. Title.

PN6165 .W55 2002
818'.5402—dc21

                                        2002068689

©2002 Pat Williams
ISBN 0-7573-0057-X

Publisher: Health Communications, Inc.
            3201 S.W. 15th Street
            Deerfield Beach, FL 33442-8190

R-10-02

Cover and inside book design by Larissa Hise Henoch
Inside book formatting by Dawn Von Strolley Grove

What People Are Saying About
Winning with One-Liners . . .

"The best way to enjoy this book is 'one-liner' at a time—it will make you smile."

—**Betty White**
actress, author

"As a veteran of over fifty years of political wars, I can tell you with certainty that politics is a funny business. Just consider all the jokers who have held office in my lifetime! And speaking of funny business, *Winning with One-Liners* gets my vote as one of the funniest joke collections I have ever seen. If you elect to buy this book, your candidacy for really big laughs will improve immeasurably."

—**Bob Dole**
former U.S. Senator

"I love one-liners and I love to laugh. This book is packed with both. I loved it!"

—**Jeff Foxworthy**
comedian

"Pat Williams is a comedy genius. Granted, he stole all this material, but the people he stole it from are very, very funny."

—**Dave Barry**
humor writer

"For a man who never took a shot he didn't like, I just love this book! It's filled with over 3,400 'shots' and these jokes are guaranteed to score with your audience. The room will rebound with laughter."

—**Charles Barkley**
retired NBA great

"My teachers used to warn me that if I kept telling those silly jokes I was going to end up a bum. Well, might I suggest you throw together a couple dozen of these 3,400 very amusing jokes, find yourself a little retirement home full of old folks where you can try them out, and who knows, you could end up a bum like me. Actually this 'bum' life isn't all that bad."

—**Tim "the Bum" Conway**
comedian

"If you have to make a speech, this is the book to have. If you don't have to make a speech, this is the book to have. Pat Williams finally hit a homerun."

—**Joe Garagiola**
former MLB player and broadcaster

"*Winning with One-Liners* is an amazing compilation of one-liners that will be used by comedians and toast masters for decades to come—I know I will!"

—Monty Hall
host of *Let's Make a Deal*

"A laugh riot. Ba dum bum!"

—Mary Tyler Moore
comedienne

"This book is a must for every amateur performer and every beginning speaker for one very important reason: The longer a joke is, the harder it is to be funny! Most people can't even *remember* a long joke, much less *tell* it properly. This is a superb collection—enjoy it, use it—and be popular in your group.

—Art Linkletter
lecturer, author, entertainer, and star of
two of the longest running shows in broadcasting history

"Any basketball player knows it's important to dribble before you shoot. Any great speaker knows you need ammunition before you speak. Pat Williams' *Winning with One-Liners* contains 3,400 great 'shots' that will hit the target with any audience."

—Tom Tolbert
NBA TV analyst

"If, as I believe, laughter is the WD-40 of life, then this book is the Kevlar vest of the speaking business. Audiences can be tough, but these one-liners will soften them up."

—Mike Veeck
baseball executive

"*Winning with One-Liners* should be required reading for anyone in need of a good laugh. For those on the speaking circuit it's an absolute must! It's like having flash cards to learn math or the ABC's to learn to read. Read the book, use the lines, enjoy the laughter."

—Larry Andersen
broadcaster, Philadelphia Phillies

"As an authority in hitting, I got to where I could tell the difference between a fast ball and curve ball in total darkness. A fast ball will raise a welt on your body about three inches and a curve ball about an inch. Speaking of hitting, Pat Williams' *Winning with One-Liners has* thousands of jokes that are bound to be hits with you and your audiences."

—"Mr. Baseball" Bob Uecker
broadcaster, Milwaukee Brewers

"Why wrestle with frustration when it comes to finding heavy-weight humor? If you are looking to govern audience laughter, check out this body of work. This fabulous book earns my seal of approval."

—Jesse Ventura
governor of Minnesota

Dedicated to
ROBERT ORBEN
line-for-line the
best and most prolific
one-liner writer
of all time,
and to
KEN HUSSAR
a funny, funny friend
and my partner in joke collecting
for more than twenty-five years.

Contents

-D-

-E-

-F-

-G-

-H-

-I-

-J-

-K-

-L-

-M-

-T-

-U-

-V-

-W-

-Z-

Acknowledgments

I would like to thank Bob Vander Weide, president and CEO of RDV Sports, COO John Weisbrod, and the RDV Sports family; Melinda Ethington, my invaluable assistant; Hank Martens of the mailroom at RDV Sports; Ken Hussar, for his friendship and his thorough proofreading of this book; Peter Vegso of Health Communications, Inc., and his fine staff, including Christine Belleris, Allison Janse, Lisa Drucker, Susan Tobias, Larissa Hise Henoch, Lawna Patterson Oldfield, Dawn Von Strolley Grove, Anthony Clausi, Terry Burke, Kim Weiss and Kelly Maragni; and my wife, Ruth, and our children, who have been so supportive of this project.

Introduction

"Faster than a speeding bullet. More powerful than a locomotive. Able to leap tall buildings at a single bound." Oh, the wondrous powers of the superheroes of our childhood! Well, this book will not transform you into a superhuman being, but it does contain one of the most important powers one can possess—the power of great jokes that produce mighty laughs.

I first became aware of the impact of humor as a high-school student at Tower Hill School in Wilmington, Delaware, where students attended required chapels twice a week. Of the numerous speakers I heard, I best remember the ones who made me laugh.

Chapels were also mandatory at Wake Forest University, Winston-Salem, North Carolina, where I did my undergraduate studies. Many days students could be seen sleeping or reading newspapers as speakers droned on. This was not the case, however, on the occasions when basketball coach Bones McKinney commanded the platform. Bones packed the house and loaded his messages with hilarious down-home humor. The audiences came filled with anticipation and were never disappointed, because they knew it wouldn't be long before "Ole Bones" would make the house rock with laughter.

As one who has been in the professional sports arena for over forty years, I have come to respect and be influenced by the wit of Abe Lemmons, Lefty Gomez, Joe Garagiola, Bill Veeck, Pete Carlesimo, Bob Vetrone, Bob Uecker, Tommy Lasorda, Frank Layden, and others.

I was in a banquet audience when Frank (Layden) was speaking, and watched his audience mastery enviously as he delivered one explosive laugh line after another. That evening was an epiphany for me, as I hungered for the skill he had, and it was then that I became serious about humor.

In 1976, I met Ken Hussar, a Lancaster, Pennsylvania, comedian, and we became instant friends, bound by our love for superior, clean material. For over twenty-five years we have researched, studied, and collected jokes, purchasing hundreds and hundreds of books, subscribing to the best humor services, watching the late-night talk show hosts and comedians, combing the Internet, and in the process compiling an enviable and voluminous collection. The jokes that are found on the pages that follow are the best-of-the-best from that collection, and have all been battle-tested in live action from the podium.

Robert Orben, to whom this book is dedicated, is in my opinion the best joke writer of all time, and has been a major influence, not only to me, but to countless speakers and comedians.

I have read that one hundred thousand speeches are given daily in the United States, and know from experience that the vast majority of speakers crave material that will draw laughs. The best speakers are aware of the contagious power of laughter that unites and entertains an audience, and at the same time gives the speaker an adrenaline rush. Oh, what a feeling!

This book offers you the winning material you need and want. I emphasize that I am a collector and not the creator of these wonderful jokes—the best ever written and spoken.

As this book was in the final stages of preparation, Mr. Televison, Milton Berle, dubbed by columnist Walter Winchell as "The Thief of Bad Gags," died at age ninety-three. In response to such accusations. Berle would respond, "I wish I had said that, and don't worry, I will," and "I laughed so hard [at that joke] I nearly dropped my pencil and paper."

Brilliant comedy writer, Larry Gelbart, at Uncle Miltie's farewell service, described Berle's eclectic style, saying, "He had a propensity for giving other people's material a new home." In the Berle tradition, I am giving the jokes in this book a new address.

Tonight Show host Jay Leno says, "You can't stay angry at someone who makes you laugh."

A century ago, Mark Twain noted, "Against the power of laughter, nothing can stand."

Actor Hal Holbrook claims, "When you laugh away something, you've used the most powerful instrument you can to surgically remove it and keep it from hurting you."

American humor icon and author Garrison Keillor says, "Jokes are democratic. Telling one right has nothing to do with having money or being educated. It's a knack, like hammering a nail straight. Anyone can learn it, and it's useful in all situations."

You are holding the finest collection of funny, clean jokes ever. Read 'em and reap!

Accountant

My accountant started my day off badly by calling me. "I'm leaving the firm to go to work for the government."
I asked, "What are you going to do?"
He answered, "I'll be making license plates."

• • •

He got an erector set for Christmas and the first thing he built was a tax shelter.

• • •

He used to be the company accountant, but his idea of not filling in check stubs so that the company would always have money in the bank just didn't work out.

• • •

He's such a financial genius that the American Association of Accountants just named a loophole after him.

• • •

He's a highly respected accountant—a ledger in his own time.

• • •

My accountant said that he was leaving to pursue an MBA. I later found out that that meant Mexico, Brazil and Argentina.

• • •

Our firm has an accountant who's shy and retiring. He's about four hundred thousand dollars shy. That's why he's retiring.

• • •

Our new accounting firm is Kool and Laidback. I'm a little concerned. Their motto is, "Hey, pal, close enough!"

• • •

Sign in an accountant's office: "In God We Trust. All Others We Audit."

• • •

ADAGES

"Oh give me a home where the buffalo roam," and I'll show you a home that really needs carpet cleaning.

• • •

A chrysanthemum by any other name would be easier to spell.

• • •

Beauty is only skin deep, but ugly goes clear to the bone.

• • •

If the pen is mightier than the sword, in a duel, I'll let you have the pen.

• • •

If you think that it's a small world, you've never run out of gas on a country road.

• • •

It's a small world, but I wouldn't want to paint it.

• • •

It doesn't matter whether you win or lose—until you lose.

• • •

It is better to give than to receive, and besides, you don't have to send thank-you notes.

• • •

Let a smile be your umbrella and you'll get a mouthful of rain.

• • •

Lightning never strikes twice in the same place, but it seldom has to.

• • •

The reason that lightning doesn't strike twice in the same place is the same place usually isn't there a second time.

• • •

Like the little skunk said when the wind changed, "Now it all comes back to me."

• • •

Live each day as if it were the first day of your marriage and the last day of your vacation.

• • •

Live each day as if it were your last and someday you'll be right.

• • •

Most people can't stand prosperity . . . but then again, most people don't have to.

• • •

Nothing in life is "fun for the whole family."

• • •

Nothing is impossible, with the possible exception of twirling a baton in a modular home.

• • •

One good turn gets most of the blanket.

• • •

People who say, "I slept like a baby," usually never had one.

• • •

Practice makes perfect? Have you ever heard a child taking piano lessons?

• • •

Praise is something that someone tells you about yourself that you've suspected all along.

• • •

Progress may have been all right once, but it's gone on too long.

• • •

Remember, a journey of a thousand miles begins with Dad saying, "I know a shortcut."

• • •

Remember, today is the tomorrow you worried about yesterday—but not nearly enough.

• • •

Show me a man who doesn't know the meaning of the word fear, and I'll show you a man who gets beaten up a lot.

• • •

Show me a man who has both feet firmly planted on the ground and I'll show you a man who can't get his pants on.

• • •

Show me a man who walks with his head held high, and I'll show you a man who hasn't gotten used to his bifocals.

• • •

Spend each day as if it were your last and you'll be broke by sunset.

• • •

Sticks and stones may break my bones, but words can never hurt me—unless someone throws an unabridged dictionary at me.

• • •

Teach a man to fish and he'll eat fish for the rest of his life; teach a fish to learn, and pretty soon fish will be running around in schools.

• • •

The happiest days of your life are the school days, providing your children are old enough to attend.

• • •

The man who said, "Talk is cheap," never said, "I do."

• • •

The pen is mightier than the sword, although it better be a really huge pen.

• • •

The severity of the itch is inversely proportional to the length of the reach.

• • •

The trouble is that when someone tells you to "Have a nice day," it puts all the pressure on you.

• • •

There is more than one way to skin a cat, none of which I want to hear about.

• • •

There's no fool like an old fool, but some teenagers can offer some pretty stiff competition.

• • •

Things improve with age? Did you ever attend a class reunion?

• • •

Those who say, "Good things come to those who wait," have never had a slow waitress in a restaurant that serves lousy food.

• • •

Today is the first day of the rest of your life. But relax. So is tomorrow.

• • •

Two can live as cheaply as one—if one has lockjaw.

• • •

We should beat our swords into plowshares, because if you hit a guy with a plowshare, you've really hit him hard.

• • •

You can't fool all the people all the time, but those turnpike signs come pretty close.

• • •

You can't fool all the people all the time, but if you can do it once every four years, you'll have a promising career ahead of you in politics.

• • •

You can't take it with you. If you could, hearses would come with roof racks.

• • •

You know that you're doing something wrong when you try to seize the day and you keep missing it.

• • •

Advertising

A businessman displayed a hostile attitude toward advertising. I asked why. He said, "I tried advertising once when I owned a store. It was a disaster. People came from all over, even from the next county, and they bought everything I had in stock. Why, they nearly put me out of business."

• • •

Advertising can be very expensive, especially if your wife can read.

• • •

Do you know what happens to kids who take two hours to eat lunch? They grow up to be advertising executives.

• • •

Headache commercials are always talking about fast relief. Fast? It takes twenty minutes just to get the cotton out of the bottle!

• • •

I met a guy at a party who's in subliminal advertising, but I only got to meet him for a split second.

• • •

Advice

Never hire an electrician with no eyebrows.

• • •

"It's a small world after all"? Try touring it by bus sometime.

•   •   •

A key chain is a device that allows you to lose several keys all at once rather than one here and one there.

•   •   •

Advise your children to get you quality gifts. After all, they don't want to inherit junk.

•   •   •

Be suspicious if you discover that your auto mechanic has clean fingernails.

•   •   •

Beware of a chiropractor who wears a neck brace.

•   •   •

Beware of bargains in life preservers, parachutes, and heart transplants.

•   •   •

Breakfast is the most important meal of the day. If you're not home by that time, you're in trouble.

•   •   •

Cross-country skiing is great—that is, if you live in a small country.

•   •   •

Despite what you read in the papers, people do not usually die in alphabetical order.

•   •   •

Don't think that the world is against you. Some smaller countries may be neutral.

• • •

Don't attempt to search for an albino in a blizzard.

• • •

First impressions are important. That's why you should never send a résumé postage-due.

• • •

For healthy teeth and bones, drink lots of milk, eat plenty of foods high in calcium and stay away from NFL linebackers.

• • •

Give your kids violin lessons. That way they won't need haircuts.

• • •

If lightning strikes, make sure that you're walking next to a tall person.

• • •

If you want to forget all your troubles, wear tight shoes.

• • •

If you want your shoes to last longer, take bigger steps.

• • •

In an underdeveloped country, don't drink the water. In a developed country, don't breathe the air.

• • •

Live life one day at a time. After all, isn't that why they were put in consecutive order?

• • •

Look over the top of your glasses so you don't wear out the lenses.

• • •

Misers aren't fun to live with, but they make wonderful ancestors.

• • •

Most yacht owners object to being referred to as boat people.

• • •

Never answer the phone and call to your wife, "It's your mother—long distance—thank goodness."

• • •

Never argue with your wife when she's tired or rested.

• • •

Never attempt to put on a pullover sweater while eating a caramel apple.

• • •

Never bet on a horse whose jockey rides sidesaddle.

• • •

Never buy a portable TV on the sidewalk from a man who is out of breath.

• • •

Never buy glue if you notice the label is peeling off the bottle.

• • •

Never buy Q-Tips at the Nearly-Nu Shop.

• • •

Never drop your contact lens during tap dancing class.

• • •

Never entrust your life to a surgeon who has more than two Band-Aids on his fingers.

• • •

Never fall in love with a tennis player. To him, love means nothing.

• • •

Never get a tattoo during an earthquake.

• • •

Never get into a fight with an ugly person. He has nothing to lose.

• • •

Never give up on life, unless a three-hundred pound person is stepping on your windpipe.

• • •

Never go mountain climbing with a beneficiary.

• • •

Never go on a long trip with anyone who is learning to play the harmonica.

• • •

Never go to a brain surgeon whose nickname is Jitters.

• • •

Never promise a farmer that you'll water his plants and feed his animals while he's on vacation.

• • •

Never take a memory course from a man who has his shirt on backwards.

• • •

Never wave to a friend at an auction.

• • •

Never wear flip-flops unless your toes are all pointed in the same direction.

• • •

On a slow weekend, put your pet chameleon on a plaid cloth.

• • •

One advantage of living in a mobile home is that if it catches on fire, you can meet the fire company halfway there.

• • •

Remember the first rule in chemistry class: Don't lick the spoon!

• • •

Remember when you buy gas at the self-service pump to thank yourself and tell yourself to have a nice day.

• • •

Remember, when you go to court, you're putting your fate in the hands of twelve people who weren't smart enough to get out of jury duty.

• • •

Ride subways during the rush hour and get your suit pressed free.

• • •

The best cure for insomnia is to get lots of sleep.

• • •

The best place to be during an earthquake is bungee-jumping.

• • •

The best way to give advice to your children is to find out what they want and advise them to do it.

• • •

The best way to locate the slowest moving line at a bank or supermarket is to get in it.

• • •

The best way to look young is to hang around with very old people.

• • •

The easiest way to find something lost around the house is to buy a replacement.

• • •

The easiest way to refold a road map is in a ball.

• • •

The first rule of administering CPR is to make sure that the victim hasn't been chewing tobacco.

• • •

The law of heredity is that all undesirable traits come from the other parent.

• • •

The nice thing about wearing boots is that your socks don't have to match.

• • •

The perfect gift for the man who has everything is a burglar alarm.

• • •

The problem with giving advice is that people feel obliged to repay you.

• • •

The quickest way to get absolutely wealthy in real estate is to inherit some.

• • •

Three rules for successful living: Never play cards with a man named Slim, never eat at a place called Mom's, and never call a Sumo wrestler Fatty.

• • •

To bring more harmony into your life, invite a barbershop quartet over to your house for the weekend.

• • •

To prevent injuring your thumb while hammering, have your wife hold the nails.

• • •

Today is a good day to overcome obstacles. Try a steeplechase.

• • •

Today is also a good day to learn patience. Spend some time teaching your pet turtle to play fetch.

• • •

Today is an excellent day for revenge. Pay the paper boy with a wet check.

• • •

Today is an excellent day to find yourself. I suggest you start with the phone book.

• • •

Today is National Individuality Day, so let's join the millions of people nationwide who are celebrating.

• • •

Today, why not dial a few wrong numbers just to keep people on their toes?

• • •

Use the last key in the bunch because that's the one that will unlock the door.

• • •

We'd all accept good advice if it didn't interfere with our plans.

• • •

When in an elevator, surprise fellow travelers by saying, "For those of you who just got on, let me review my first three points. . . ."

• • •

When someone gives you a lemon, make lemonade. Well, in your case, when you lay an egg, make an omelet.

• • •

Women like silent men. They think they're listening.

• • •

You know that you're overworked when your driver's license photo looks better than you.

• • •

You will enjoy amusement parks particularly if your hobby is waiting in lines.

• • •

AFTERSHAVE

He smells like an explosion at an Old Spice factory.

• • •

I can always tell when the boss is going to arrive. His aftershave makes it from the parking lot to the office door about five minutes before he does.

• • •

AIR-CONDITIONING

I have a theory that room air conditioners really don't cool a room. Their annoying rattle takes your mind off the heat.

• • •

One thing slower than molasses in January is an air-conditioner repairman in August.

• • •

We've got some tough economic problems to solve, like what do we do with the tremendous concentration of wealth in the hands of air-conditioning repairmen?

• • •

We made the best of a bad situation. While we waited for the air-conditioner repairman to come, we toasted marshmallows over the air conditioner.

• • •

AIRLINE

"How often do jumbo jets crash?" asked the nervous passenger. "Generally, only once," replied the flight attendant.

• • •

A tightwad got off the plane and complained, "Well, there's another $2.50 in flight insurance wasted."

• • •

Airfares are so low that some airlines are in danger of going under. One was forced to raise millions by holding a used luggage sale.

• • •

An old-timer was asked if he enjoyed his first flight. He replied, "It wasn't as bad as I expected, but I never did put all my weight down."

• • •

I asked the flight attendant on the small airline what the two dinner choices were. She said, "Take it, or leave it."

• • •

Astronauts are the only people who take off in Florida and don't have to change planes in Atlanta.

• • •

Did you ever realize that serving coffee on an airplane causes turbulence?

• • •

Do you realize that if the Wrights hadn't invented the airplane, we'd have had to find another way to lose our luggage?

• • •

Flight attendants always tell you the name of the pilot. As if anyone's going to say, "Oh, he's good. I just love his work!"

• • •

Flying is the second greatest thrill known to man. Landing is first.

• • •

He was once involved in an airline disaster. But he'll eat anything that's put in front of him.

• • •

His plane was flying through a terrible storm. The flight attendant said, "Do something religious." So he took up a collection.

• • •

I complained at the desk about my lost luggage, and the guy behind the counter was wearing my clothes.

• • •

I didn't finish the dinner I was served in the first-class section. The flight attendant said to me, "Finish what's on your tray. Think of all those people who are starving in tourist."

• • •

I flew fifty thousand miles last year, which really isn't that impressive when you consider that my luggage flew one hundred thousand.

• • •

I flew on a very small airline. Even their flight between Minneapolis and St. Paul wasn't nonstop!

• • •

I just had a terrible thought. What if the people who prepare airline food are the same ones who fix the planes?

• • •

I knew I was on a budget airline. Before take-off, the flight attendant announced that the meat loaf could be used as a flotation device.

• • •

I now own property in Paris. That's where the airline sent my luggage.

• • •

I took one of those budget flights. They made me put on goggles and a scarf before boarding.

• • •

I was on a no-frills airline. The flight attendant walked over to me and said, "Get your own meal."

• • •

If it weren't for airlines we'd be up to our ears in honey-roasted peanuts.

• • •

I'm sorry I had to dress like this, but it's the airline's fault. They didn't realize that my luggage and I were traveling together.

• • •

I've been flying too much lately. I went to the movies with my wife, and when we sat down in the theater I tried to buckle my seatbelt.

• • •

Our local library lists airline schedules under light fiction.

• • •

The captain announced, "The meals today are roast chicken, pot roast and tortellini. If you don't get your first choice, don't be disappointed, because they all taste the same anyway."

• • •

The pilot's voice came over the speaker, "The good news is that we're safely on the ground. The bad news is, we never took off."

• • •

The speaker in the cabin came on: "This is your pilot speaking. If you look out the starboard or right side of the plane, you will notice that the engine is on fire. If you look out the port or left side of the plane, you'll notice a bright orange dinghy bouncing about on the waves. I am speaking to you from that dinghy!"

• • •

The flight attendant announced, "It is now time for food service. Since you selected our no-frills flight, please take just one bite before passing the sandwich along."

• • •

The unwritten law of airlines is that if you have the middle seat, the people on either side of you have elbows that could spear olives.

• • •

There are two types of luggage—carry-on and lost.

• • •

You know that the airline is in trouble when prior to take-off, the pilot walks down the aisle handing out copies of his résumé.

• • •

A guy walks up to the ticket window and says, "I'd like to buy two chances on your next flight to Orlando."

• • •

A plane was going up and down and sideways. A nervous lady suggested, "Everybody pray."
A guy said, "I don't know how to pray."
The lady said, "Well, then do something religious."
So the guy starts a bingo game.

• • •

I flew on Crashlandia Airlines. They have no in-flight movie, but every now and then your life would pass before your eyes.

• • •

If you look like your passport photo, you're not well enough to travel.

• • •

They had mistletoe hanging at the airport baggage center so you could kiss your luggage good-bye.

• • •

What's with a nonstop flight? Call me old-fashioned, but I want my flight to stop—preferably at an airport!

• • •

When I fly, I think of three things: faith, hope and gravity.

• • •

AMTRAK

One never needs to be bored. If you have three or four hours to spare, there are many things you can do to occupy your time—like making a phone call to Amtrak to make reservations.

• • •

ANIMALS

The lion and the lamb will lie down together, but the lamb won't sleep much.

• • •

Two cows were watching as a milk truck passed. On the truck's side was written, "Homogenized, Pasteurized, with Vitamin A added."

One cow remarked, "Kind of makes you feel inadequate, doesn't it?"

• • •

ANTIQUES

The frustrating thing about getting old is seeing expensive antiques and remembering items just like them that you threw away.

• • •

When you think about it, ten years from now many antiques will be made of plastic.

• • •

Apartments

It's a strange building. If someone upstairs flushes the toilet, my water bed drops two inches.

• • •

I went to the county health department to purchase five hundred cockroaches. I promised the landlord that I'd leave the apartment the same way that I found it.

• • •

Cryogenics is nothing new. My landlord has been freezing bodies every winter for years.

• • •

Tour guide: "This building has been here for over three hundred years. Not a stone has been touched, nothing has changed, nothing has been replaced."
Tourist: "They must have the same landlord we do."

• • •

I don't want to complain about the way our landlord is maintaining the building, but yesterday I slipped on the ice—in front of our bathtub.

• • •

Army

He was a really quick thinker. During the war, when things got bad, he volunteered to go back to the states for reinforcements and supplies.

• • •

The first thing that I learned in the army is that it's a lot harder to catch grenades than it is to throw them.

• • •

He went into the service in spite of a bad heart murmur. His heart kept murmuring, "I don't want to go . . . I don't want to go."

• • •

During World War II, he was saved by an Italian family that hid him in a basement for two years. The family lived in Brooklyn.

• • •

I just tried on my old army uniform, and the only thing that fits is the tie.

• • •

One great thing about being in the army—you never have to worry about what to wear.

• • •

You've got to worry about some of the guys that show up to enlist. Especially the ones who attempt to pronounce the eye chart.

• • •

He used to fire on his own troops just to confuse the enemy.

• • •

He learned some things in the army that have sustained him throughout his entire adult life. For instance, little potatoes are easier to peel than big potatoes.

• • •

You have no idea what the food was like. For punishment they gave you seconds.

• • •

What does an army cook do when he retires? Every recipe he knows concludes with, "Serves 3,000."

• • •

Our drill sergeant was a tough one. Tough? He wore a toupee that he kept on with a nail!

• • •

Being in the army was tough; somebody was always telling me what to do, where to go, what to wear, what to say. Civilians can experience the same feeling in another institution—marriage.

• • •

The sergeant instructed, "This bullet can penetrate two feet of solid wood. So remember, keep your heads down."

• • •

I was classified 5-F. That meant that if the United States was invaded, the army would send me overseas.

• • •

He blew up six ammo dumps, seven factories and one ball bearing plant, and then the army shipped him overseas.

• • •

In the army, he was always where the bullets were thickest—at the ammo depot.

• • •

ART

Modern artists sign their names at the bottoms of paintings so that we'll know how to hang them.

• • •

Understanding modern art is like trying to figure out the plot in a bowl of alphabet soup.

• • •

Someone asked Picasso how one could tell the importance of a painting. "Is it the style, the history, or is it the master who painted it?" they asked the master.

Picasso replied, "They are all very important, but for a painting to be truly important, it must first be expensive."

• • •

I need a lot of light to paint. It's tough to read those tiny numbers.

• • •

All he knows about art is that if it hangs on a wall, it's a painting, and if he has to walk around it, it's sculpture.

• • •

AUDIENCE REPARTEE

I knew this was going to be a good day when I walked into the supermarket and found a shopping cart with all the wheels going in the same direction.

• • •

Why are you so grim? You people are looking at me as if I were your daughter's first date.

• • •

"Testing, one, two, three. Had this been an actual speech, you'd have been asleep by now."

• • •

(after generous applause) I am glad to see that we both appreciate the finer things in life.

• • •

(after long intro) Do you realize that if I were one of those speakers who needed no introduction, we'd all be getting in our cars and going home now?

• • •

(as a late arrival edges toward a seat) Wow, I'm only five minutes into the program and someone is already starting the standing ovation!

• • •

(award) Thank you for this award. I consider it a first step toward my goal of world domination.

• • •

(bad microphone) Can you hear me? You know, I've spoken to more dead mikes than an Irish undertaker.

• • •

(convention closing) And as we head home with a bounce in our step, faith in our hearts, new ideas in our minds, bills in our pockets and towels in our suitcases . . .

• • •

(dead mike) I know that this is the Christmas season, but I think that this is carrying "Silent Night" a little too far.

• • •

(heckler) I remember you. Where's your clown suit and seltzer bottle?

• • •

(heckler) I wasn't expecting you here tonight. The moon isn't full.

• • •

(heckler) Isn't she sweet? She has all the charm of a meter maid with a quota.

• • •

(joke dies) Here's another one you might not care for.

• • •

(joke dies) And I was expecting so much more from that one . . .

• • •

(long banquet) I didn't realize anything could last this long without Saran Wrap or Tupperware.

• • •

(long banquet) This reminds me of a similar experience I had when I read the Sunday New York Times from cover to cover. My suit went in and out of style four times tonight.

• • •

(no immediate questions during Q&A) I'm asking for questions, not pledges!

• • •

(people get up to leave) Now that's what I like. A moving standing ovation!

• • •

(people leaving early) Was there an accident? Are you lawyers?

• • •

(receiving a gag gift) All my life I've wanted something like this . . . which kind of gives you an idea of the kind of life I've had.

• • •

(receiving an award) Getting this plaque is an enlightening experience. Up until now I didn't know that Wal-Mart (or other discount chain) did engraving.

• • •

(receiving an award) I don't deserve this award. But then again, I have arthritis, and I don't deserve that either.

• • •

(sip from water glass) Wow! I've got to get that recipe!

• • •

(someone leaving) Now you know why they call me a motivational speaker.

• • •

(someone sneezes) Wow, that one blew the monogram right off the handkerchief.

• • •

(someone takes flash picture) Wow! With a flash like that you could charge for tanning sessions.

• • •

(someone walks in late) Glad you could join us. Where have you been? You're lucky. I almost marked you absent.

• • •

(struggling to raise microphone) The ironic thing is that I became a speaker because there was no heavy lifting.

• • •

(to an audience of doctors) This is the first time I have ever addressed an audience of doctors, so I've tried to do some of the things my mother told me before going to the doctor. Put on clean underwear . . . try to look poor . . .

• • •

(to bearded man) Get a load of that beard! Were you born or trapped?

• • •

(to heckler) Look, buddy, pretend I'm your wife and ignore me for awhile, okay?

• • •

(to man in tux) I like your outfit. Did you mug a penguin?

• • •

(tray falls) Where was I? I lost my place about the same time the waitress lost her job.

• • •

(umpire or referee in audience) Can everyone hear me all right? (to referee) Can you see me all right?

• • •

(when a joke dies, tear up an index card and say:) "That's the last time I'll ever buy a joke from (emcee)."

• • •

(when flowers are at head table) I've died before many audiences before, but this is the first group that has been thoughtful enough to send flowers.

• • •

(when someone precedes you with a great opening) Wow! I wouldn't give this spot to the cleaners.

• • •

(when you forget something) This is awful. Every year General Motors is recalling more and more, and I'm recalling less and less.

• • •

A man of letters, he is considered second only to that woman of letters—Vanna White.

• • •

After such a great meal, let me remind you that thunderous applause burns up seventeen calories per minute.

• • •

All my jokes are ad-libbed. You don't think I do this stuff pre-meditated, do you?

• • •

All those in favor of taking a break, please signify by raising your eyelids.

• • •

Always keep a smile on your face because it looks silly on other parts of your body.

• • •

And as Henry VIII said to each of his wives, "I won't keep you very long."

• • •

And now I will close, before you realize that I don't know what I'm talking about.

• • •

And now I'm turning the program over to _____, which is a lot like asking (famous fat person) to watch your lunch for you.

• • •

As Mason used to say to Dixon: "We've got to draw the line somewhere."

• • •

Audiences compare me to Jay Leno. They say, "Compared to Jay Leno, you stink."

• • •

Be honest now. What do you think of our chef? Really, what this man doesn't know about cooking, you could put in a stomach pump.

• • •

Before I go any further, I'd like my wife to stand so you can greet her. (pause and look around the room) You know, I thought it was awfully quiet after we stopped at the last service station.

• • •

Can those of you way in the back hear me? If not, please don't holler. Just wave your binoculars.

• • •

Don't worry. Loud applause doesn't frighten me.

• • •

Don't be embarrassed to ask the simplest, most basic question, because that's the only kind I'll be able to answer.

• • •

Drive carefully, folks. There's a shortage of good audiences out there.

• • •

Dullness is directly proportional to the number of brown suits in the crowd.

• • •

During the middle of my last performance, a member of the audience stood up and said, "Is there a Christian Scientist in the audience?"
"I'm a Christian Scientist," a lady replied.
"Would you mind changing places with me?" said the man. "I'm sitting in a draft."

• • •

Every time I write a new joke, some guy uses it the year before.

• • •

First, I'm going to promise you a very short message. There's something wrong when pizzas are delivered in thirty minutes and speeches aren't.

• • •

First, let me thank you for allowing me to be a part of an evening that will live forever in my memory. How often do you see five hundred people come into a place, sit down and order the same meal?

• • •

He knows how to make a long story short. He always forgets the ending.

• • •

He is looking for diversion, so he enrolled in a painting class. The class ran overtime this afternoon, so he rushed straight to this banquet. He didn't even have the time to wash the paint off his fingers.

• • •

He'll be selling some of his books here tonight . . . a few of his Perry Masons, the Time-Life Home Improvement series, and some hardly opened college textbooks. . . .

• • •

Here's a speaker who's an inspiration to people everywhere. They figure if he can make it to the top, anybody can!

• • •

As we close tonight's program, why don't we stroll out to the parking lot and watch our cars depreciate?

• • •

He escaped serious injury two weeks ago while horseback riding. He slipped off the saddle, his foot got caught in the stirrups, and he escaped unhurt when a quick-thinking manager from Kmart came out and pulled the plug.

• • •

He was up until 4 A.M. with a great book. Once he starts coloring, he finds it hard to stop.

• • •

He's a speaker whose words have a lingering effect. The last group he spoke to is still sleeping.

• • •

He's been to more banquets than green peas.

• • •

He's from Gary, Indiana. When he goes to the big city, he can't sleep unless he has a burning tire in the middle of his room.

• • •

He's not too hip. He once had an audience with the pope and said, "Hey, this has been fun. Next time we get together, bring your wife and kids."

• • •

His hobby is collecting antiques, which comes as no surprise to those of us who just heard his jokes.

• • •

His next selection will be performed a cappella, an Italian expression which means, "The band just left."

• • •

I always remember that wooden chairs have produced as many standing ovations as speakers have.

• • •

I always wanted to be a stand-up comedian. I felt confident in knowing that if I failed, at least no one would laugh at me.

• • •

I am pleased to announce that I have been named the Rotary Club's Man-of-the-Year for my ability to talk in circles.

• • •

I am pleased to be here tonight. If you live in New Jersey (or city), you're glad to be anywhere.

• • •

I appreciate the wonderful reception I was given. When I arrived at the airport, there was a cab waiting for me.

• • •

I asked him why he was removing his name tag. He said, "I don't need it now. I've memorized it."

• • •

I asked the chairman how long I should speak at the Kiwanis Club. He replied, "Well, speak as long as you want. The luncheon starts at 1:15 and we all leave at 1:45."

• • •

I ate breakfast in my car on my way to work this morning. The only tough spot was pouring syrup on the pancakes.

• • •

I believe in audience participation. So, when I finish talking, you applaud.

• • •

I believe my time is up, and from the looks on your faces, I believe you realized it before I did.

• • •

I can tell that this is a high-class neighborhood. All the graffiti is spelled correctly.

• • •

I can't remember the last time I had such a great show. Not that tonight's show was so special. I just have a lousy memory.

• • •

I can't tell you how much I enjoy speaking to an attractive and intelligent audience. And I know I'll enjoy speaking to this group, too.

• • •

I did a Catholic benefit last night. I knew that it was a Catholic benefit, because I left my car in front of the hotel and they raffled it off.

• • •

I didn't get any sleep preparing my speech last night, and I sincerely hope that you didn't get any sleep while I was making it.

• • •

I do my best thinking in the morning, and right now I think I'd like to go back to bed.

• • •

I don't think I'll need the microphone. After all, with a wife, three children, a dog and mother-in-law in the home, I'm used to talking loudly.

• • •

I don't worry when people walk out on me. It's when they walk toward me that I worry.

• • •

I don't deserve to be on this dais with such a distinguished group—of course, I don't deserve kidney stones, either, but I've got them, too.

• • •

I don't know how you enjoyed your meal, but it's nice to know that Trigger didn't die in vain.

• • •

I don't know whether to have a short prayer and then have the treasurer's report, or to have the treasurer's report followed by a long prayer.

• • •

I frequently have balanced audiences. Half take notes while the other half take naps.

• • •

I got seven hundred fan letters this week, and I would have gotten more if I hadn't developed writer's cramp.

• • •

I have some bad news for those of you who gave your cars to the guys outside. This place doesn't have valet parking.

• • •

I hope the good Lord will forgive my introducer for overpraising me, and me for enjoying it so much.

• • •

I have three kids, none of whom pay any attention to me. Could it be that they're in training to become an audience?

• • •

I haven't had this much fun since I saw a rerun of the Waltons sorting cranberries.

• • •

I hope you can see me back there. If you can't, I'm six-three, have rugged good looks and look like (handsome celebrity).

• • •

I hope you enjoyed your meal. I asked the chef what that unusual flavor was in the soup, and he said, "With the terrible lighting in this kitchen, who knows?"

• • •

I know that you have a lot of questions, and I have a lot of answers. Let's just hope that they match.

• • •

I know that you'd rather have Jay Leno addressing you, but don't worry. You're still getting his material.

• • •

I know that you're nervous tonight. After all, this is the first time that you've ever appeared before me as an audience.

• • •

I once made the mistake of telling the audience to hold their applause, and they're still walking around with it to this day.

• • •

I only hope that you enjoy showering praise half as much as I enjoy receiving it.

• • •

I possess a rare comedy magic. Just last night, I made an entire audience disappear.

• • •

I practiced that joke in front of the mirror and got the same response.

• • •

I promise to be brief, unless, of course, I remember where I put my notes.

• • •

I really feel badly for the 175 chickens and 7,000 peas that have given their lives to make this dinner possible.

• • •

I request that you hold your questions until I get to my car.

• • •

I saw his coat in the cloakroom. I knew it was his when I noticed the mittens were sewn to the sleeves.

• • •

I see a lot of smiling faces in the audience. I can always tell when the kids are back in school.

• • •

I see that some of you have given up laughter for Lent.

• • •

I sense that this is an intelligent, experienced audience and that you are saving your thunderous standing ovation for the conclusion of my presentation.

• • •

I sought the advice of a consultant to improve my appearance. He suggested low-wattage lighting.

• • •

I want to thank you. This audience has made me feel right at home—which gives you an idea of the kind of family life I have.

• • •

I was almost in an accident on my way here. I pulled off the side of the road to let an ambulance pass and almost forgot to let two lawyers get by.

• • •

I was going to sprinkle my speech with ad-libs, but unfortunately, I left them at home.

• • •

I went into a store and said to the clerk, "Can you help me?" The clerk said, "No, sir. I've heard you entertain before."

• • •

I'll keep my remarks to fifteen minutes due to throat trouble. Your program chairman told me he'd choke me if I spoke longer than fifteen minutes.

• • •

I'm as confused as a termite in a yo-yo.

• • •

I'm going to close now, because I only have two minutes left of my allotted speaking time—and I usually need that for applause.

• • •

I'm like a cross-eyed discus thrower. I may not set a lot of records, but I do keep the crowd alert.

• • •

I'm not going to be long tonight. I've only got this jacket rented out until 9 P.M.

• • •

I'm sorry that I'm late. I locked a coat hanger in my car. It's a good thing I had my keys.

• • •

I'm sorry, but I've forgotten your first and last name.

• • •

I'd like to start off with a few words about myself. You all look like you could use a little sleep.

• • •

If laughter is the best medicine, then this man is a wonder drug.

• • •

If you allow me to look at my notes during my speech, I'll permit you to look at your watches.

• • •

If you don't understand a joke, just raise your hand and we'll discuss it.

• • •

If you found anything that I said tonight to be enlightening or beneficial, you need help!

• • •

If you had all been listening to that incredible introduction you wouldn't still be sitting there, you'd all be kneeling.

● ● ●

I'm as frustrated as a dog at a whistlers' convention.

● ● ●

I'll keep my remarks brief, for I know that many of you only have time for a short nap.

● ● ●

I'll make a deal. I'll stop talking if you start applauding.

● ● ●

I'll open the floor for questions. And since they so seldom get a chance to speak, let's start with the married men.

● ● ●

I'm not going to bore you with a lot of facts and figures. I'll bore you without them.

● ● ●

I'm one of Jay Leno's joke writers. Every time Jay tells a joke, I write it down.

● ● ●

I'm sorry I'm late, but I fell asleep proofreading my speech.

● ● ●

I'm sorry I'm late. I made a U-turn in front of a doughnut shop and fourteen policemen gave me a ticket.

● ● ●

I'm sorry I'm late. It takes my wife forever to change a flat.

• • •

I'm sorry that I'm late. I know that "there's a time and place for everything," and I got them mixed up.

• • •

In closing, I ask those of you who are still awake to leave quietly, so as not to disturb the others.

• • •

In closing . . . I just love that phrase. It's sort of like a wake-up call for the audience.

• • •

In conclusion, let me end my program with these fitting words: WAKE UP!

• • •

In conclusion, please take these suggestions home and sleep on them. I see that some of you already have a head start.

• • •

Incidentally, I'm hard of hearing, so if your applause is not very loud, I won't be able to hear you.

• • •

It is obvious that you have not heard of my reputation as a speaker. Otherwise, more of you out there would be dressed in pajamas.

• • •

It was a really tough audience last night. Everyone in it looked as if they knew where Jimmy Hoffa was buried.

• • •

It wasn't easy doing the show. The seats faced the stage.

• • •

It's been more than a borderline thrill to be here—it's been a major inconvenience.

• • •

It's certainly nice to be in your town. The last time I was here it was closed.

• • •

It's difficult to speak after a brief, witty introduction. Thank you for not putting me in that position.

• • •

It's been a long evening. Permit me to make it longer.

• • •

It's nice to see that so many empty seats were able to make it.

• • •

I've been known to hold audiences in the palm of my hand, which gives you an idea of the size of my audiences.

• • •

I've started my own fan club, and right now my son and I are trying to talk my wife into joining.

• • •

I've talked so much tonight, I think my lips have lost weight.

• • •

Just picture that this room is a big popcorn maker and that you are all kernels. I promise that I will supply all the hot air.

• • •

Ladies and gentlemen, honored guests. Well, that takes care of my formal remarks. And now, for the informal part, "Hey, what's happenin', dudes?"

• • •

Last night when I performed, the audience sat there with their mouths open. It was amazing to see a crowd that size all yawn at once.

• • •

Last night's audience was so rowdy that one guy yelled, "Louder!" during the silent meditation.

• • •

Let's dispense with the minutes of last month's meeting and we'll move right to the treasurer's report as soon as the sergeant-at-arms removes the handcuffs from our treasurer.

• • •

Listening to him will make you change your belief that time flies.

• • •

My act was so bad that people kept shouting, "Up in front!"

• • •

My audience last night was rough. They threw vegetables at me . . . in cans!

• • •

My fee tonight will cover a very large part of my vacation budget—tollbooths with exact change lanes.

• • •

My first thought when I was invited here was that the evening would be a real bore. That's my current thought, too.

• • •

My last audience gave me a nice basket of fruit—one piece at a time.

• • •

My last show opened with great difficulty. The curtain was up.

• • •

My most recent appearance was at the grand opening of a salad bar where I threw out the first crouton.

• • •

My parents warned me in my early days about hanging out with the wrong crowd, but I decided to speak tonight anyway.

• • •

My show was so bad last night that half the empty seats got up and left.

• • •

People have been somewhat indifferent to my performances

lately. Last night an audience gave me a shrugging ovation.

• • •

Please hold your applause until everyone has been introduced. If someone applauds we'll have to start over again.

• • •

Please hold your questions until I'm finished, but feel free to break into enthusiastic applause at any time.

• • •

Someone told me that I gave a dynamite performance, but not in those exact words. What they said was that I really bombed out there.

• • •

That remark makes about as much sense as an ashtray on a motorcycle.

• • •

That's a great question, sir, and I'll probably think of a great answer while I'm shaving tomorrow morning.

• • •

The audience was so quiet that not only could you hear a pin drop, you could hear it on the way down.

• • •

To make a long story short, nothing beats seeing your audience yawn.

• • •

Tonight's program was produced by Ron Meedy and Jeremy Oaker. This has been a Meedy/Oaker production.

• • •

We all drew straws to see who'd emcee, and my drawing looked least like a straw.

• • •

We have a lengthy program tonight, and, let me say, if you're an insomniac, this may be your lucky night!

• • •

We weren't sure our speaker would be able to be with us today, but, fortunately, due to a hole in the prosecution's case . . .

• • •

We will now take a look at the instant replay so you can get a close-up look of that joke dying.

• • •

We'll be out of here faster than a fat kid in dodge ball.

• • •

When I got off the plane I was greeted by my fan club. Mother never looked better.

• • •

When I started in this business I had only twenty-five cents in my pocket. Now I'm seventy-five thousand dollars in debt.

• • •

When my show opened, the mayor gave me the key to the city. The next day, the city changed the locks.

• • •

While driving here tonight, my wife and I saw a very long funeral procession. I said, "I wonder who died?"
She said, "The one in the first car."

• • •

Would the owner of the tan sedan with plate number RO2-765 and the headlights on, please report to the parking lot? We'd like to hold a memorial service for your battery in ten minutes.

• • •

Yesterday I met the president. It's not easy to meet a person of power and importance, but he handled it well.

• • •

You did a great job tonight. Every roast should have a serious speaker.

• • •

You know that you've been on the road too long when you come home and dial a nine to get an outside number.

• • •

You look like you could all use a little shut-eye, so I've invited Bill up here to say a few words.

• • •

Your train of thought, sir, does it have a caboose?

• • •

We've now come to the part of the program that any man who has ever tiptoed into the house at three in the morning is familar with—it's the question-and-answer period.

• • •

Baby-Sitter

When the father returned home, he found the baby-sitter lying motionless on the floor, with his six-year-old son standing in a corner holding a toy gun.

"What's going on?" the dad asked.

The sitter said, "Oh, I'm all right. This is the only way I get any rest."

• • •

Baby-sitter: That's a teenager you pay $6.50 an hour to eat $20 worth of snacks.

• • •

Happiness is hiring a baby-sitter who is on a diet.

• • •

The kids are such terrors that they can only get baby-sitters through the Teamsters union. The last sitter they got was named Rocco.

• • •

The worst part about spending seventy-five dollars on an evening out is that when you get home the baby-sitter looks like she had a better time than you did.

• • •

We've discovered a foolproof way to make sure the sitter watches our kids. Right before she arrives at the house we put the kids in the refrigerator.

• • •

Bachelor

He wanted to cook Thanksgiving dinner but he has trouble with the turkey recipes. Everyone he looks at starts out with, "Take a clean pan."

• • •

I stopped by to visit a bachelor friend, and it was really touching. There he was standing in front of the sink doing the dish.

• • •

One drawback of being a bachelor is doing the dishes and making the bed, and knowing that you're going to have to do the same thing over again next month.

• • •

When a single guy buys a place setting for eight, he's not getting set to entertain. He's thinking, "Eight consecutive meals without having to do dishes."

• • •

Bald

(sight gag) Walk over to a bald man, lean over, look carefully at the top of his head and straighten your tie.

• • •

A lot of people don't know this, but last week he quietly switched from Head & Shoulders to Mop & Glo.

• • •

Being bald has its advantages. You can walk into a room and immediately know where the air-conditioning is coming from.

• • •

He almost had a tragic experience this week when a California condor tried to hatch his head.

• • •

He asked for an Oriental rug for his birthday, and his wife got him a toupee that was made in Hong Kong.

• • •

He bought some Grecian Formula and was really disappointed. He said, "Not only doesn't it work, but it tastes horrible."

• • •

He has a receding hairline which has receded all the way back to his neck.

• • •

He keeps his hat on with a suction cup.

• • •

He suffers from split hairs. His split a long time ago.

• • •

He washed his hair this morning and forgot where he put it.

• • •

He went to a stylist who parted the remaining hair he has horizontally across his head. The style looks great, but people keep coming up to him and they whisper in his nose.

• • •

He's so bald that his head keeps slipping off the pillow when he sleeps.

• • •

He's having a bad hair day. The right one keeps getting tangled with the left.

• • •

He's not bald. He just happens to have a very wide part.

• • •

He's wearing a recycled toupee. If you look very closely, you can see where it used to say Welcome.

• • •

His toupee looks like a flattened road squirrel.

• • •

His toupee looks so natural except for the price tag dangling behind his left ear.

• • •

His wife reasons that she can spend a lot of money on hairdos since he doesn't have to spend any money on his hair.

• • •

I always say, "They don't put marble tops on cheap furniture."

• • •

I am really proud. Yesterday I was guest speaker at the National Hair Restorers' Convention and I got to throw out the first toupee.

• • •

I don't care what you say about baldness. At least it's neat.

• • •

I first met him on a Philadelphia street corner. There he was in that tan trench coat, his hair blowing in the wind . . . and him too proud to run after it.

• • •

I saw him down at the barber shop today . . . reminiscing.

• • •

I won't even attempt to tell him a hair-raising story.

• • •

I won't say that he's bald. He just has a part that won't quit.

• • •

If bald is beautiful, how come Willard Scott just gets letters from women who are one hundred years old?

• • •

If there is a tooth fairy for hair, can you imagine what (bald person) would be worth today?

• • •

Life can be cruel. As a child, I didn't have enough money to go to a hair stylist. Now I have the money, and I don't have the hair!

• • •

Life is unfair. Take shaving. How is it that we never get bald on the face?

• • •

Medical research clearly shows that there is just one thing that will prevent baldness—hair!

• • •

My hair's getting thin, but then again, who wants fat hair?

• • •

New Schmell Hair Conditioner is not guaranteed to grow hair, but what it will do is shrink your scalp to fit what hair you've got.

• • •

One of the nice things about being bald is that when company comes over, all you have to do is straighten your tie.

• • •

Sure he's getting bald. People were certainly right when they said he'd come out on top.

• • •

There are three ways a man can wear his hair: parted, unparted and departed.

• • •

This new hair restorer is really something. Last week I spilled some on my comb, and now it's a brush.

• • •

We read in the Bible that the very hairs on our heads are numbered, and in this case, each year it gets easier for the Lord to take inventory.

• • •

When he said that his right ear was warmer than his left ear, I knew his toupee was on crooked.

• • •

When the Lord makes something good, he doesn't cover it up.

• • •

Banks

Loan officer: "Your assets seem to be in good shape. Tell me about your liabilities."
Applicant: "No problem. I can lie with the best of them!"

• • •

"I'd like to borrow fifty thousand."
"That's a lot of money, sir. Can you give us a statement?"
"Yes. I am very optimistic."

• • •

A teller was held up three times by the same man.
The investigating officer asked, "Have you noticed anything different about the man?"
The teller said, "Come to think of it, each time he comes in, he's a little better dressed."

• • •

(loan applicant) "I'd like to consolidate my debts into one back-breaking loan."

• • •

His wife entered the bank and said, "I'd like to open a joint account. A checking account for me and a deposit account for my husband."

• • •

I don't know how much money I have in the bank. I haven't shaken it recently.

• • •

I know that my bank is in trouble. I went in and applied for a loan, and the loan officer said, "Funny, we were just about to ask you the same thing."

• • •

I saw a sign in our bank that read, "Deal with a bank you can trust. Trust your neighbor." And then I noticed that they had all their pens on chains.

• • •

I went to one of those talking auto-teller machines and it said, "Wait, before I turn over the money; weren't you the guy who kicked my cousin, the Coke machine?"

• • •

I went to the bank for a home improvement loan and they gave me two thousand dollars to move out of the neighborhood.

• • •

I would like to open a joint account with someone who has money.

• • •

I've never been overdrawn at the bank, just underdeposited.

• • •

My bank has no confidence in me. They print three things on my checks: my name, my address and "Insufficient funds."

• • •

One of the bank employees was so ambitious that he took his work home with him.

• • •

Sad news today. Three more banks went under and they took two toaster companies with them.

• • •

Some bank! Before I could make a withdrawal, I had to wait until someone came in and made a deposit!

• • •

Sure, electronic banking is a fast way to transfer money. But I know a faster way—marriage!

• • •

The bank just threw me out of their Christmas club. They said I wasn't coming to their meetings.

• • •

The bank turned down his vacation loan. To retaliate, he bought a five-pound fish, wrapped it, put it in a safe deposit box, borrowed vacation money from another bank, and then left town for three weeks.

• • •

We have a joint account. I put my money in, and my wife takes it out.

• • •

Why can't the people who write the bank advertising copy be the same persons who approve the loans?

• • •

You know that your bank is on shaky financial ground when they give their calendars out one month at a time.

• • •

Teller: "I can cash your check if you can identify yourself."
The woman pulls a mirror from her purse, looks in it and says, "That's me, all right."

• • •

Banquets

(after audience has been seated for a long time) Let's all stand up and fluff our pillows.

• • •

(after intro) Now I know what a stack of pancakes must feel like after the syrup is poured on.

• • •

(opening) As my Dad used to say . . . (long pause). My Dad wasn't much of a talker.

• • •

(to guest who dresses casually) I can tell that he's taking this banquet seriously. His socks match.

• • •

First, I'd like to compliment the chef on this marvelous dinner. I didn't even know that Black and Decker made steaks (or specific meat entree).

• • •

I've been introduced by people of rank before, but this was the rankest.

• • •

I've been to so many chicken dinners that when I go home, I no longer sleep—I roost.

• • •

Barber

A patron was telling his barber that he was going to the Vatican and that he was going to get a private audience with the pope.

The barber said, "You're crazy! In the first place, don't go to Italy. It's a poor country to visit, the weather stinks and you won't even come close to seeing the pope."

When the patron returned to the barber shop the next month, the barber asked, "How was your vacation?"

"Great!" said the customer. "The trip was fantastic. Rome was beautiful, the weather was spectacular and I had a private audience with the pope."

"You did!" exclaimed the barber. "Did he say anything to you?"

"Yeah," replied the customer. "When I knelt to kiss his ring, the pope asked, 'Hey, where did you get that lousy haircut?'"

• • •

A man walked into the barber's and said, "I'd like to have my hair cut like Tom Cruise's."

The barber started clipping away like crazy.

"Are you sure you know what Tom Cruise looks like?" asked the customer.

"Of course I do!" snapped the barber. "I saw him twice in *The King and I.*"

• • •

"Haven't I shaved you before?"

"No, sir. I got that scar on my neck during the Vietnam conflict."

• • •

I switched barbers when I saw him ordering supplies: two bottles of hair tonic, two bottles of shaving lotion and sixteen bottles of iodine.

• • •

After being cut six times by the barber, the customer said, "May I have a razor?"

"Why?" said the barber. "Do you want to shave yourself?"

"No, just defend myself," the customer replied.

• • •

Baseball

"Sure we're behind in the game, guys, but six runs here, and another eight runs there, and we'll be right back in it."

• • •

A billboard on the left-field fence read: "The Phillies use Arid Extra-Dry." A fan spray painted underneath, "And they still stink!"

• • •

A fan yelled to the catcher: "Hey, the only thing that you know about pitching is that you can't hit it!"

• • •

A father watched his young son practice baseball in the back-yard by throwing the ball up and swinging at it. Time and time again the bat missed contact. The boy noticed his father watching, and said, "Wow, Dad! Aren't I a great pitcher?"

• • •

After five consecutive hitters nailed the pitcher's first pitch for hits to open the ball game, the manager called the catcher to a mound conference and asked, "What kind of stuff does he have today?"

The catcher replied, "I don't know. I haven't caught anything yet."

• • •

Owner to manager: "I don't know how we're going to get along without you, but starting tomorrow, we're going to try."

• • •

One player on a cellar-dwelling baseball team wanted to play all the games on the road because: "We get to hit more than any other team. We always get to bat nine innings, and they only get to bat eight."

• • •

After watching a 450-foot homer disappear out of the stadium, the manager said to the pitcher, "Anything hit that high and far should have a stewardess and an in-flight movie."

• • •

A Little League coach consoled his team which had just been whipped: "Boys, don't get down on yourselves. You did your best and you shouldn't take the loss personally. Keep your chins up. Besides, your parents should be very proud of you boys. In fact, just as proud of the parents of the girls on the team that beat you."

• • •

The Cubs' highlight film for the past season has been nominated for an Oscar as the best short feature of this year. It runs one minute and twelve seconds.

• • •

April is the month for showers, and the Phillies pitching staff is living proof of that.

• • •

As a pitcher, I never had much of a fastball. I hurled one, and it fell to the ground halfway between the mound and home plate. Turns out it collided with a mosquito.

• • •

He has the quickest bat in the league. He can take his bat from the rack, go to the plate and make an out, come back to the dugout and put the bat back in the rack faster than anyone I've ever seen.

• • •

Have you noticed how many major league teams are using mascots to give their fans a laugh? The Phillies have the Phanatic. The Pirates have the Parrot. The (losing team) have their starting lineup.

• • •

Baseball can be so confusing to a child. I saw one game where the coach yelled, "Hold at third," and his mother was yelling, "Come home this instant!"

• • •

Baseball fans are an odd lot. They sing "Take Me Out to the Ball Game," and they're already there.

• • •

He gets to first base faster than an ambulance-chasing lawyer gets to the scene of an accident.

• • •

He has all the tools, and it's a good thing. By the all-star break he'll be a carpenter.

• • •

He's been in such a slump that when he finally hit the ball through the infield, he had to call AAA and ask for directions to first base.

• • •

He's been working on a new pitch. It's called a strike.

• • •

He's in the twilight of a very mediocre career.

• • •

His scouting report read, "He may not be big, but he's slow."

• • •

I could have been a professional athlete. My problem in baseball is that I can never hit a curve ball. My problem in golf is that I always do.

• • •

I've seen better swings on a condemned playground.

• • •

I wanted to be a big league umpire, but I kept passing the eye exam.

• • •

I was a nonviolent baseball player. I could go for weeks at a time without hitting anything.

• • •

I was watching a baseball game on TV and my wife said,

"Speaking of high and outside, the grass needs mowing."

● ● ●

In his job he doesn't come in contact with many people. He's (losing team's) third-base coach.

● ● ●

It's a good idea that kids in Little League are exposed to umpires that are never wrong and always win arguments. It helps prepare them for marriage.

● ● ●

(losing team) They couldn't sweep a series if they hired nine all-pro janitors with corked brooms.

● ● ●

My friend said, "I know I'm a loser. I lost my wallet. My wife is very sick. I lost my job. The Phils lost to the Dodgers. It's unbelievable—leading by three in the eighth, and the Phils lost to the Dodgers!"

● ● ●

Our team finished in last place because our batters never got to hit against our pitchers.

● ● ●

Some find their place in the sun and become rich and famous. Others can't even find a baseball in the sun, and they become outfielders for the (losing team).

● ● ●

Someone asked him why he switched from a thirty-four ounce bat to a twenty-nine ounce bat. He said, "Well, when I strike out, it's lighter to carry back to the bench."

● ● ●

That team has been in the cellar so long, their team insignia is a mushroom.

• • •

The (losing team) are at it again this season. The only thing that stays in the cellar longer is a furnace.

• • •

The best thing about playing for the Cubs is that you never have to worry about anyone stealing your World Series ring.

• • •

The coach lacked confidence in his starting pitcher. On the lineup card he penciled in, "Miller and others."

• • •

The team's manager was not made to feel too secure. The name on his locker was written in pencil.

• • •

To give you an idea of the kind of season that we've had, the person who handled our side of the scoreboard was sick for three weeks and nobody noticed.

• • •

We lost fifteen games in a row. One day we had a rainout, and the team threw a victory party.

• • •

Who can say that our team lacks depth? Three of them were philosophy majors in college.

• • •

You know that you're pitching badly when the fifth inning rolls around and the ground crew is dragging the warning track.

• • •

You know you've been cut from the team when you arrive in the locker room and the manager snaps, "Hey, man, no visitors allowed!"

• • •

Watching the (team) play is relaxing. There are no disturbing loud noises, like the sound of a bat hitting the ball.

• • •

I lacked confidence as a Little League pitcher. Instead of a baseball cap, I wore a shower cap to the mound, and instead of the rosin bag, I carried Soap-on-a-Rope.

• • •

He wasn't much of a hitter. In fact, the only time he ever broke a bat was when his car ran over it in the driveway.

• • •

BASKETBALL

A basketball coach bumped into an old lady while leaving the arena. He looked at her and said, "No offense."

The old lady snapped, "You can say that again. And no defense either!"

• • •

The coach screamed at his center to get defensive rebounds.

"I am," said the center. "It's not my fault that they're all going through the net first."

• • •

(Losing team) are like opossums. They play dead at home and get killed on the road.

• • •

The preseason predictions were correct. We were the team to beat—and everybody did!

• • •

(short player) He won't be playing tonight. He injured himself when he fell off a ladder while he was picking strawberries.

• • •

(short) He got a new advertising contract acting as a spokesman for a chain of miniature golf courses.

• • •

(short) His best sport is the limbo. He's so good he can limbo under a rug.

• • •

(short) He's so short he needs to stand on a stool while showering. Otherwise, the water would be cold by the time it reached him.

• • •

(during a season plagued by poor attendance) A guy walked up to our ticket window and woke up the ticket seller. He said, "I'd like four tickets for tonight's game. By the way, what time does the game start?"

The agent said, "For four tickets, what time would you like the game to start? For four tickets, we'll come over to your place and play."

• • •

A winning streak for this team is back-to-back off days.

• • •

Answers found on our team questionnaire:
Best position: Crouched over.
Church preference: Red brick.
Father's alma mater: Always do your best.
Favorite color: Plaid.
Favorite seafood: Salt water taffy.
Have you lived in Orlando all your life: Not yet.
Mother's alma mater: A winner never quits, and a quitter never wins.
Who to notify in case of accident: A good doctor.

• • •

At the beginning of the year we had a booster club, and by the end of the season it had turned into a terrorist group.

• • •

Coach after a big loss: "Their players put their pants on the same way as our players do. It just takes them longer to pull them up."

• • •

(coach, after a physical game) "I haven't seen so much pushing and shoving since the day I got on a school bus by mistake."

• • •

Coaches who listen to the fans wind up sitting next to them.

• • •

He accounted for three thousand points during his career. He scored one thousand and gave up two thousand on the defensive end.

• • •

He eats, sleeps and dreams basketball, but he only looks like he eats them.

• • •

This year our basketball team plans to run and shoot. Next season we hope to run and score.

• • •

We have a great bunch of outside shooters. Unfortunately, we play all our games indoors.

• • •

He knew his career was over when he was driving down the lane and he was called for three seconds.

• • •

He sank three baskets in a row and then made three consecutive turnovers. What a player! He keeps both teams in the game!

• • •

He was so tall that when he was born his birth certificate read, "June 1, 2 and 3."

• • •

He's one of the finest officials money can buy.

• • •

He's so kind to the refs. He helps them feeling their way into the gym before the games.

• • •

He's a disciplined offensive player. If he has the shot, he takes it. If he doesn't have the shot, he takes it.

• • •

He's the kind of player who improves as the season goes along. So the coach told him yesterday afternoon that we had played nine games already.

● ● ●

I asked one of the players on the employee questionnaire, "Where was the Declaration of Independence signed?"
He said, "On the bottom!"

● ● ●

I can tell you what it's like working in an NBA front office. Picture a nervous breakdown with paychecks.

● ● ●

I don't mean to be critical, but this guy is such a poor foul shooter that if he crossed himself at the free throw line, he'd miss his forehead.

● ● ●

I play in an over-fifty basketball league. You can't start a fast break without a note from your doctor.

● ● ●

I play in the over-fifty basketball league. We don't have jump balls. The ref just puts the ball on the floor, and whoever can bend over and pick it up gets possession.

● ● ●

I wanted to take my family to a Knicks game, but the bank wouldn't approve my loan.

● ● ●

I was invited to a masquerade party and I won first prize. I stuffed my pockets full of money and went as a free agent.

• • •

I won't say how bad our team is, but I've seen more baskets made by occupational therapy groups.

• • •

I won't say he's overweight, but his stomach crosses mid-court three steps before he does.

• • •

I'm involved in a long-term relationship—watching the NBA play-offs.

• • •

Last season we couldn't win on the road, and this year we can't win at home. My failure as a coach is that I can't think of anywhere else to play.

• • •

My career ended abruptly. My team retired my jersey while I was still in it.

• • •

My days with the team are numbered. I was recently sent on a scouting trip to the Bermuda Triangle.

• • •

My wife doesn't follow basketball very closely. She doesn't know whether the ball is stuffed or inflated.

• • •

One of our recruits thought that Sherlock Holmes is a housing development and that Henry Cabot Lodge is a resort in Virginia.

• • •

Our center is a yoga master. He learned yoga trying to fit into airline seats.

• • •

Our center never crayoned on walls as a kid, but you should have seen the ceiling!

• • •

Our center's gut is so large, he's given new meaning to the term "expansion team."

• • •

Our coach loves the refs. He sends them cards every Christmas—in Braille.

• • •

Our first-round draft choice spent the off-season working as a lifeguard. He can't swim, but you should see him wade!

• • •

Our number-one draft choice just learned his first three words in French—Coupe De Ville.

• • •

Our team doesn't need more shooters. It needs more makers.

• • •

Our team is so bad that the cheerleaders stay home and phone in the cheers.

• • •

Our team was really bad. We lost nine straight and then we went into a slump. On our day off we had a victory celebration.

• • •

Our team was so slow on the fast break that they reran the game tapes on a View Master.

• • •

Q: What do basketball players do in the off-season?
A: Sit in front of you at the movies.

• • •

(skinny player) He looks like he went to a blood drive and forgot to say when.

• • •

(skinny player) He looks like the advance man for the famine!

• • •

Talk about turnovers. My high-school team was called so often for traveling that we were sponsored by AAA.

• • •

The coach is preparing the team for the crowd noise that they'll hear during the season. He runs practices with a laugh track.

• • •

The NBA game is spectacular. You see millionaires running all over the floor. It's like watching the Senate on C-SPAN.

• • •

The NBA season is so long that the players seldom get time to spend at home with their butlers and chauffeurs.

• • •

The referee called so many fouls against us in last night's game that the pea in his whistle caught on fire.

• • •

The team was in a slump, so the coach thought he had better review the basics. He picked up the ball and said, "This is the basketball."

One player said, "Not so fast, coach."

• • •

One of our players was recently asked what the biggest detriment to an NBA player is: ignorance or apathy.

He replied, "I don't know and I don't care."

• • •

They're a team in transition. They're going from bad to worse.

• • •

This is the first year for our church basketball team. We haven't raised enough money for uniforms, so we have to play our games in choir robes. It really slows down our fast break. And the choir smells funny on Sunday mornings, too.

• • •

We've had so many injuries on our team this year that the cheerleaders are nurses and the team bus is an ambulance.

• • •

We have a minor scheduling problem. This year the last game of the play-offs conflicts with the home opener.

• • •

We traded for him and he turned the team around. We had a winning record when he came to us.

• • •

B IBLE CHARACTERS

Bible Characters' Greatest Hits:

Noah: "Raindrops Keep Falling on My Head"
Adam and Eve: "Strangers in Paradise"
Lazarus: "The Second Time Around"
Job: "I've Got a Right to Sing the Blues"
Moses: "The Wanderer"
Samson: "Hair"
Daniel: "The Lion Sleeps Tonight"
Joshua: "Good Vibrations"
Elijah: "Up, Up and Away"
Methuselah: "Stayin' Alive"

• • •

B IRTHDAY

I got my son a bicycle for his birthday, and I hid it where he'll never find it—in the bathtub.

• • •

When it comes to birthday parties it's easy to divide mothers into two groups: those who think that a birthday party for twenty-four five-year-old kids can be organized, educational and fun—and those who have had one.

• • •

You can always tell the experienced parents at a children's birthday party. They don't hand the kids napkins—they give 'em dropcloths.

• • •

Body Building

Every day my wife bends over and touches the floor seventy times. It's not exercise. She's picking up the kids' clothes.

• • •

Every morning I get up, bend over and touch my toes. The trouble is—I touch my toes with my stomach.

• • •

Books

Just a word to those of you who bought the book, *Skydiving Made Easy*. There is a correction on page nine, paragraph seven. The words "State zip code" should be changed to "Pull rip cord."

• • •

I joined the new condensed book club. Some of the titles they are offering this month are: *The Hardy Boy; A Tale of One City; Dr. Jekyll; For Whom the Chime Dings; A Few of the King's Men; Snow White and Grumpy;* and *The Brother Karamazov.*

• • •

A man came to my door and said, "I'd like to read your gas meter."
I said, "Whatever happened to the classics?"

• • •

"Your manuscript is both good and original. But the part that is good is not original, and the part that is original is not good."

• • •

(huge volume) This book is a coffee-table book. That is, if your coffee table has industrial-strength legs.

• • •

After the show, he'll be autographing copies of his latest book, *Winning Through Irritation.*

• • •

Did you ever notice that in bookstores you'll find the diet and exercise books right between humor and fiction?

• • •

He took two months off from work to finish a novel he was working on, which gives you some sort of idea as to what a slow reader he is.

• • •

He hasn't chosen a pen name yet, but he's considering Papermate or Bic.

• • •

He's a really slow reader. By the time he finishes reading a murder mystery, it doesn't matter who did it. The statute of limitations has run out.

• • •

Some of my latest books are:

How I Turned $500,000 into Half a Million
Money Can Make You Rich
How to Become Best Friends with Yourself Without Becoming Emotionally Attached
How to Create Airline Food at Home

• • •

I asked the clerk to show me the self-help section and she said, "If I did, that would defeat the whole purpose."

• • •

I asked what the best-paid writers write and he told me, "Prescriptions."

• • •

I bought a book on obsessive-compulsive disorders. It's great. I've already read it 523 times.

• • •

I bought a self-help video, *How to Handle Disappointment*. When I got it home, the box was empty.

• • •

I bought the book, *1,001 Ways to Avoid Consumer Rip-offs*, and there were only five hundred ideas in it.

• • •

I just finished writing *Personal Victory Through Self-Confidence*, but I don't think that anybody will publish it.

• • •

I just read an anti-self-help book entitled *Your Crummy Life Will Never Change*.

• • •

I just wrote a best-seller. Now all I have to do is find some best-buyers.

• • •

I know how the library can cut down on overdue books. Instead of hitting you with a fine, they can make you *do* a book report!

• • •

I made a mistake by having the local library research my roots. The librarian discovered that one of my ancestors had an overdue book, and I had to pay a $910 fine on it.

• • •

I purchased Hugo's *Hunchback of Notre Dame* at the bookstore's bargain table. The spine was bent.

• • •

I'm not saying he's dense, but it's safe that his autobiography will not be called *The Man Who Knew Too Much.*

• • •

My latest book was so dull that they had to recall the Braille version. Blind people's fingers kept falling asleep.

• • •

No one who can read is ever successful at cleaning out an attic.

• • •

One reviewer said of his book, "Its chief fault is that the covers are too far apart."

• • •

Some of the greatest contributions to literature have been made by people who have threatened to write a book but have never gotten around to it.

• • •

Someone gave me the book *Being a Powerful Decision Maker*, but I can't decide whether or not I want to read it.

• • •

Talk about egos. His latest book is *Famous Men Who Have Known Me*.

• • •

The annoying thing about Chinese mystery books is that you know who the murderer is on the first page.

• • •

The best way to become a successful writer is to read good writing, remember it, and then forget where you remember it from.

• • •

The boss just finished his autobiography. It's called *I Came, I Saw, I Criticized*.

• • •

The chief attribute of his latest book is the wide margins.

• • •

Writing has its ups and downs. One day you're writing a column and the next day you're painting one.

• • •

You've heard that old question about what two books you'd like to have on a desert island? My choices would be practical titles like *Thirty Easy-to-Prepare Recipes for Sand*, or *How to Gut a Coconut*.

• • •

As our publisher once said to Tolstoy, "Make up your mind, Leo, do you want to write a book about war or peace?

• • •

I just love the book you wrote. I've been reading it night and day, and I'm now on page ten.

• • •

Novice to author: "I'm interested in writing a book. What's the best way to start writing?"

Author: "I suggest from left to right."

• • •

I just read the book *The Miracle of Helium*. I couldn't put it down.

• • •

I've written several children's books. I didn't mean to. They just turned out that way.

• • •

The boss tells me I can read faster if I don't stop to color the pictures.

• • •

I wrote something last week that was accepted by Simon and Schuster. It was my check to join the Book-of-the-Month Club.

• • •

This book is dedicated to my wife, without whose charge cards it might not have been necessary.

• • •

I just finished writing a book. One critic stated, "Once you put it down, you just can't pick it up again."

• • •

I asked a reviewer, "Did you read my last book?"
He answered, "I certainly hope so."

• • •

I was going to title my next book *Being Decisive*, but then I changed my mind.

• • •

I wasn't overly sensitive when the publisher returned my manuscript, but I was hurt when he sent it by junk mail.

• • •

I am writing a book that will be in a class by itself. It's for people who want to be unpopular, maladjusted, unsuccessful, and fat, with low self-esteem.

• • •

I was in a used bookstore the other day and found *How to Hug*. I thought it was a romantic how-to book, but when I got it home I discovered that it was volume six of the World Book Encyclopedia.

• • •

A rare book is one that has been borrowed and returned.

• • •

An Eskimo in an igloo was reading to his youngster, "Little Jack Horner sat in a corner. . . ."
The child interrupted, "Daddy, what's a corner?"

• • •

Boss

"As I see it, Fornby, you have two major problems. First of all, you take no pride in your work. The second is you have absolutely no reason to."

• • •

"Boss, for twenty years I've been doing the work of three men. How about a raise?"
"Well, I can't afford to give you a raise, but tell me who the other two guys are and I'll fire them."

• • •

"I know that you can't afford to get married on the money that I'm paying you, young man," said the boss. "And someday you'll thank me for it."

• • •

The boss said, "I want you to be happy here. If there's anything you need I'll show you how to get along without it."

• • •

One morning I arrived fifteen minutes late for work. The boss asked, "Why are you late?"
I said, "I fell down a flight of steps."
"It doesn't take fifteen minutes to fall down a flight of steps!" growled the boss.

• • •

(secretary to boss) "Are you still grouchy from yesterday, or did something new happen?"

• • •

(to employee) "It's not important that we understand each

other, Johnson, just that you understand me!"

• • •

(to employee) "Feel free to interrupt any time you consider your job security irrelevant."

• • •

I asked the boss why he is in such a good mood today. He said, "I scored 121." I replied, "Great, your golf game's improving." "I was bowling!" he snapped.

• • •

"Don't think of this as a firing. Think of it as an exit-level position."

• • •

A rumor spread through our office that the boss had been diagnosed as "temporarily insane." Half of the office questioned the word "insane", while the other half questioned the word "temporarily."

• • •

Ability is what you need to get ahead on the job if the boss doesn't have any daughters.

• • •

After months of urging, the boss put in a suggestion box. One of these weeks he says he's going to put a slot in it.

• • •

Boss: "My philosophy has always been, 'Doing things excellently and wholeheartedly brings greater satisfaction than money.'"
Reporter: "Is that the philosophy that made you rich?"
Boss: "No, I became rich when I convinced the people who work for me of that philosophy."

• • •

Crime doesn't pay, and working for my boss doesn't either.

• • •

Boss: "I notice that you come to work late every morning."
Employee: "Yes, but you'll also notice that I leave early every afternoon."

• • •

He is rather patronizing to the boss. I overheard him say, "I agree with everything you've ever said or thought in your life."

• • •

The boss's favorite pastime was stapling popcorn to the ground and watching the pigeons go crazy.

• • •

I told the boss that I'd be in bright and early tomorrow morning. He said, "Good! Either one will be an improvement."

• • •

I told the boss I wanted more personal recognition and he told me to wear a name tag.

• • •

I wanted to give the boss something that would be representative of the years that I have worked for him, but you can't frame an ulcer.

• • •

My boss just showed me how to cut my taxes in half. He reduced my salary 50 percent.

• • •

My boss says that I'm inconsistent. Well, maybe once in awhile, but not all the time.

• • •

Sign on the boss's desk: "Do you like to travel? Do you enjoy meeting new people? Do you want to free up your future? All this can be yours if you make one more mistake."

• • •

The boss has a sign on his desk that reads, "Indecision Is the Key to Flexibility."

• • •

The boss is a charitable man. He almost single-handedly turned this business into a nonprofit organization.

• • •

The boss is always late and comes to work at 12:30. One day he arrived at 8:30 A.M. and the guards immediately began to eat lunch.

• • •

The boss is so cheap that he thinks that volunteers are overpaid.

• • •

The boss just gave me a raise. Last time I saw something that small I was looking at the *Sports Illustrated* swimsuit issue.

• • •

The boss said, "Your resume is the best collection of exaggerations I've ever seen. We need a man like you in our advertising department."

• • •

The boss says that he's grooming me for a new executive position in the company. By the way, what is a scapegoat, anyway?

• • •

The boss says that I'm a good person to bounce ideas off of because nothing ever sinks in.

• • •

The boss says that what constitutes a living wage is whether you are giving it or getting it.

• • •

The boss says that when it comes to buying Christmas gifts, money is no object, as long as they don't cost that much.

• • •

The boss tells me he's on my side. Yeah, so is appendicitis.

• • •

The boss thinks he's right 100 percent of the time—sometimes more!

• • •

The boss treated me to lunch today. It was great. I got the Happy Meal.

• • •

The boss won't replace me with a computer. Where could he find a computer that grovels?

• • •

The doctor gave the boss a shot of venom. Now he's feeling like his old self again.

• • •

When you're climbing the ladder of success at work, take time to notice the boss's son on the escalator.

• • •

You can tell when it's payday at the office. The boss goes around wearing a black armband.

• • •

You might say the boss is stubborn. Even as a kid, when he went sledding, he had an Inflexible Flyer.

• • •

Office worker: "This is great weather we've been having, isn't it?"
Boss: "We? Who made you a partner all of a sudden?"

• • •

Until further notice, do not use the suggestion box. The handle is broken and it won't flush.

• • •

The boss said, "I don't know how we could ever get along without you around here. But starting tomorrow, we're going to try."

• • •

The boss said, "Listen, stupid . . ." He always calls me "Listen."

• • •

Boss: "This is my son, Frank. He's going to start at the bottom for a few days."

• • •

Employee: "I wasn't going to ask you for a raise, but some snitch told my kids that American children eat three meals a day."

• • •

His relationship with the boss is based on more than respect and trust. It's based on fear.

• • •

In business circles he has been called a Renaissance man. And that's because most of his ideas come from the fifteenth century.

• • •

Once the boss thought he was wrong, but he was mistaken.

• • •

Contrary to popular belief, he is not a yes man. When the boss says no, Bill says no, too.

• • •

When the boss called to offer me the job, I was almost too excited to tell the operator that I'd accept the charges.

• • •

The boss says, "I always quote myself. I like to add spice to the conversation."

• • •

The boss told me that I'm more like a son to him than an employee. So I said, "In that case, how about an increase in my allowance?"

• • •

There was a slight problem at the office today. The boss accidentally smiled and got a charley horse in his face.

• • •

The boss's new book is called *The Joy of Cheap*.

• • •

Someone must be asking the boss for a raise. I'd know that laugh anywhere.

• • •

I knew right away that the boss was going to talk to me about my salary when he began, "It's the little things that count."

• • •

My boss is so generous. He read that you could feed a family of four in India for ten dollars a year, so he sent his whole family there.

• • •

Someone asked my boss, "How many people work here?"
He said, "Oh, about four out of six."

• • •

This is America's traditional time for turkeys, fruitcakes and surprises. But enough about my boss. Let's talk about Christmas.

• • •

The boss and I get along great. I laugh at all his jokes and he laughs at all my suggestions.

• • •

The boss said, "In a way, I'd hate to lose you. You've been just like a son to me . . . surly, impertinent, insolent, unappreciative. . . ."

• • •

He said, "You're fired!"
I said, "Fired? I thought slaves had to be sold!"

• • •

The boss and I are friends, pure and simple. I'm pure, and he's . . .

• • •

Thanks to our boss, this Christmas was a learning experience. I never knew that the Salvation Army sold gift certificates.

●　●　●

The boss returned from the suggestion box, shaking his head. "Why can't they be more specific? Which lake? What kind of kite?"

●　●　●

"Boss, will you like me as much if my plan loses money for the company?"

"Sure, I'll like you as much. I'll just miss having you around."

●　●　●

Let's put things in perspective. All the boss wants from me is perfection—although he'll settle for more.

●　●　●

The boss gave me a bonus that made it possible for my mother to work for the rest of her life.

●　●　●

The boss just signed me to a multiday contract.

●　●　●

The boss had us out on his yacht this weekend. It was beautiful to see all twelve employees rowing in unison. The boss then told the guys, "I've got some good news and some bad news for you. The good news is, take a fifteen-minute rest. The bad news is that when the fifteen minutes are up, I want to go waterskiing."

●　●　●

Rich? He got a check back from the bank marked "insufficient funds," with a sticky note attached to it that explained, "Not yours—ours."

• • •

He said, "But, boss, if I got here on time it would be such a long day!"

• • •

My boss told me that he was going to make a change in my department, which didn't bother me until I remembered that I was the only one in my department.

• • •

The boss said to one of the guys in the office, "You're the most useless person I ever saw. You don't do an hour's work in a month. Tell me one single way the firm benefits from employing you."

The clerk replied, "When I go on vacation, there's no extra work thrown on the others."

• • •

Our boss is what you would call conservative. He still thinks an obscene gesture is reaching for your paycheck.

• • •

The boss says that he's going to write his autobiography as soon as he can figure out who the main character should be.

• • •

We're all congratulating the boss on his new book, *The Fear of Spending.*

• • •

This morning I had a long talk with my boss. Actually, he had a long talk. I had a long listen.

• • •

The boss always says that anything goes. And this morning he called me "Anything."

• • •

The boss is so easygoing. Just yesterday he told me, "Don't think of me as the boss. . . . Just think of me as a friend who's never wrong."

• • •

The boss is such a modest, unassuming man. He doesn't even demand that we call him "sir." He says that kneeling and kissing his hand is sufficient.

• • •

The boss was examining the petty cash fund yesterday. He calls it the petty cash fund. We employees call it the payroll.

• • •

My first boss was eighty years old. He said, "I'm signing you to a lifetime contract."
I asked, "Yours or mine?"

• • •

As a holiday treat, the boss told us he was taking us to a fancy French restaurant—Jacque in the Box.

• • •

I told the boss, "I have to take my paycheck to the bank because it's too little to go by itself."

• • •

Bowling

Interest your kids in bowling. It's a great way to get them off the streets and into the alleys.

• • •

One advantage of bowling over golf is that you very seldom lose the ball.

• • •

He's such a celebrity in his hometown that the local bowling alley named a gutter after him.

• • •

If you can't hear a pin drop, there is something definitely wrong with your bowling.

• • •

If our town didn't have bowling, there would be no culture at all.

• • •

Boxing

A fighter was taking a terrific beating. When the bell rang, he staggered to his corner. His manager said, "Let him hit you with his left for awhile. Your face is crooked."

• • •

He's the only boxer in the history of the sport to be knocked out while shadow boxing.

• • •

I quit because I had a problem with my hands. The refs kept stepping on them.

• • •

The boxer had written on his tombstone: "You can stop counting. I'm not getting up."

• • •

When he fought, the ring announcer would say, "In this corner, wearing blue trunks and an expression of panic . . ."

• • •

At the end of the second round, my corner told me, "Keep it up. You've got a no-hitter going."

• • •

By the sixth round, I had my opponent covered with blood—mine.

• • •

I swung with a crushing left hook, but I was backpedaling so fast that it never got there.

• • •

I used to feint with my nose and lash out with my chin.

• • •

I was knocked out so many times that I sold advertising space on the soles of my shoes.

• • •

If you wanted to see me fight, you had to get there early.

• • •

"Just think of it," said the boastful boxer to the manager, "tonight I'll be fighting on TV before millions of people."

"Yes," answered the manager, "and they'll all know the results of the fight at least ten seconds before you do."

• • •

You've been learning for seven years now, and you can only count to ten. What will you become in life if you continue this way?

A boxing referee!

• • •

Bumper Stickers

Change is inevitable, except from a vending machine.

• • •

If we're not to eat animals, why are they made of meat?

• • •

Business

A downtown merchant advertised a vacuum cleaner at $49.95, with the ad, "Hurry down. At this price, they won't last long." I bought one, and the ad was right. It didn't!

• • •

A go-getter, working his way up the corporate ladder, was at a business luncheon. The boss approached him and said, "Hartman, I notice that you are not wearing the company logo pin on your lapel."

"Oh, no," said the eager one, "I left it on my pajamas."

• • •

An employee told his boss, "I need a raise. There are three companies that are after me right now."

The boss said, "Really? Which ones are they?"

The employee said, "Gas, water and electric."

• • •

Businessmen can be divided into two types: those who don't take tranquilizers—the nervous wrecks—and those who do—the calm wrecks.

• • •

During the summer, employees learn how to deal with stress, while their managers are attending seminars to learn how to create it.

• • •

Every morning I get up, have breakfast, look at the *Forbes* list of the four hundred wealthiest people in America, and if I'm not on it, I go to work.

• • •

Federal Express had a terrific obstacle to overcome. First they had to convince people that anything with the word "federal" in it could be speedy.

• • •

He made his fortune early in life by selling matches to impatient Boy Scouts.

• • •

He made so many mistakes at his last job that the government tried to hire him as a consultant.

• • •

His first resume didn't get him a job, but it did win him the Pulitzer Prize for fiction.

• • •

His last business venture wasn't very successful. In fact, the only difference between Bill's last company and the Titanic was that the Titanic had a band.

• • •

How does the personnel manager assign newly hired individuals? He leaves them in the interview room for a few minutes. When he returns:

- if they don't look up, they're assigned to security;
- if they start staring blankly out the window, they go to the finance department;
- if they've disassembled the table they're sent to engineering;
- if they're screaming and waving their arms, they're assigned to manufacturing, and
- if they're not there, they go to sales.

• • •

I finally got my own office. Sure it's small and cramped, but it's mine and it's private—except when another employee barges in to ask for a broom.

• • •

I just read a how-to book that explains how to get along with your boss, administrators and other office executives, while staying fit and trim. It's called *Aerobic Groveling*.

• • •

I often ponder, "Which came first—the CEO memo or the wastebasket?"

• • •

I started to worry about our chief financial officer when he asked me how often our annual report came out.

• • •

I went to an unfinished furniture store and they sold me a tree.

• • •

If all is said and nothing is done, the committee meeting is finally over.

• • •

If he could be in two places at the same time, both would lose money.

• • •

If we painted a picture of last month's sales, it would be a still life.

• • •

I'm addicted to our office coffee. When I get to work, the first thing I do is grab a cup. Nothing beats that rich mellow flavor of Styrofoam.

• • •

In the business world, an executive knows something about everything, a technician knows everything about something and the switchboard operator knows everything.

• • •

Life is what you make it, which could explain a lot of resumes.

• • •

My son wants to be an entrepreneur; you know, a person who starts with nothing, creates an idea, raises money, works seventy hours a week, and becomes wealthy. And my boy's off to a good start, too. He already has the nothing.

• • •

Our business school had a baseball team. We never stole second. We embezzled it.

• • •

Our company has a sophisticated system for executive decision making. This morning I overheard the boss saying, "Eenie, meenie, miney, mo . . ."

• • •

Our company's dental plan is "chew on the other side."

• • •

Sign in office: "In case of fire, leave the building with the same reckless abandon that you do at quitting time."

• • •

Since three out of four small businesses fail, my recommendation is to start a large business.

• • •

Some coffee makers are disguised as filing cabinets, which corresponds with some coffee drinkers who are disguised as office workers.

• • •

The question on the application card read, "Length of residence at present address?" and the prospective employee wrote, "About forty feet, not counting the garage."

• • •

The second law of business: Be wary of any company whose annual report is done in pencil.

• • •

Two lions escaped from a zoo and decided to split up to avoid capture. They agreed to meet three weeks later.

When they reunited, the first said, "I'm hungry, frightened, cold and wet. I'm headed back to the zoo. How are things going with you?"

The second replied, "I'm great. I'm hiding out at (large corporation's) headquarters. I'm safe and well fed. Each week I eat one of their vice-presidents, and that gives me my sustenance."

The other asks, "You eat a vice-president every week? How do you get away with that?" "Easily," the other responds. "As long as I'm quiet and clean up my mess, nobody seems to notice."

• • •

A colleague lost his job and reported, "They told us it was a merger, and it was—in the sense that the Titanic *merged* with the iceberg."

• • •

There are certain clues as to when a company is in trouble. For instance, when the annual report lists the soda machine as a profit center.

• • •

They knew that they had found the right man to be their bill collector. They discovered him in the office waiting room reading *Jaws*, and he was rooting for the shark.

• • •

They reached the ultimate in cost reduction . . . they went out of business.

• • •

Two 7–Elevens merged and became a 14–Twenty-two.

• • •

Two large companies are pursuing him—VISA and MASTERCARD.

• • •

We have a tough sick leave policy. There is no time off for illness or surgery. Death is accepted, but you have to give three weeks' notice.

● ● ●

We have one of those cheap fax machines in the office. The pictures don't look bad after you connect the dots.

● ● ●

We need a secretary at business meetings to take minutes. That gives us the assurance that at any given moment, at least one person is paying attention to what is being said.

● ● ●

You know that the contract is one-sided when they refer to one of the parties as the "stuckee."

● ● ●

You know that your business has problems when your right-hand man is a guy named "Lefty."

● ● ●

You know that your business is in trouble when . . .

- the CEO walks by your desk and says, "Hey, watch those staples!"
- the corner Dairy Queen threatens a hostile takeover
- the former conference room is now a chinchilla ranch
- you say, "See you tomorrow," and the night watchman laughs uncontrollably
- you start receiving memos in Japanese
- the boss asks you if you know anything about starting fires

● ● ●

You might say that we have a religious problem in our office. We have to convince our employees that Sunday is the day of rest.

• • •

At our last board meeting a phone call interrupted the proceedings. The secretary announced, "The treasurer wants to give the financial report, and he's calling long distance."

• • •

His business is really doing well. They've had two fires and only needed one of them.

• • •

Two partners were fishing and their boat tipped. One started swimming for shore, while the other floundered helplessly. The swimmer called, "Bob, can you float alone?"
Bob replied, "Here I am drowning, and you want to talk business."

• • •

The boss said, "I'm sorry, but if you take two hours for lunch today, I'll have to do the same for every man whose wife gives birth to quintuplets."

• • •

I made two mistakes this year. The first was starting a brand-new business. The second was starting it in a fireproof building.

• • •

A management team came into my office to find out what our workers were best suited for. They learned that most of the employees were best suited for unemployment.

• • •

My former business had nothing to do with football, but it did wind up in the hands of a receiver.

• • •

Work is really important. If it wasn't for work, where would most people rest up from their vacation?

• • •

The boss is all business. I saw him on the beach wearing a three-piece, pin-striped bathing suit.

• • •

An executive interviewing a lady applicant asked, "I see your birthday is May 17. What year?"

"Every year," she replied.

• • •

Creative writing is something that you often find in magazines, and almost always in résumés.

• • •

How independent can you get? I know an exterminator who doesn't make house calls. Did you ever try to get one thousand cockroaches in a cab?

• • •

I won't say how our company's doing, but to give you an idea, they played "Taps" at our yearly business meeting.

• • •

Business wasn't really thriving at that place. I walked in and asked for change for a twenty and they made me a partner.

• • •

My son is a born executive. He's only five, but already it takes him two-and-a-half hours to eat lunch.

• • •

One of our employees is very bright. He starts thinking the moment he gets up in the morning and doesn't stop until he gets to his desk.

• • •

Our business is so bad that yesterday I went to my favorite lunch spot and they refused to serve me the businessman's lunch.

• • •

I'm very proud of the way I became general manager. I started out as president.

• • •

Our organization is really aggressive. Ours is the only office I know where Musak plays Sousa marches.

• • •

Every piece of equipment in our office is covered by insurance . . . except the clock. And our employees are always watching that.

• • •

He goes to the airport, plunks down his airline credit card on the counter and says, "Give me a ticket to anyplace. I've got business everywhere."

• • •

The boss started a large men's clothing store in Tokyo. It went great, but he went broke on the alterations.

Calculator

I was using my new talking calculator at the supermarket. When I totaled up the money I had spent on junk food, my calculator said, "Have a nice day, Fatso!"

• • •

California

A thief robbed the First National Bank of Los Angeles and escaped into thick air.

• • •

On a clear day if you look out your hotel window UCLA.

• • •

I just love living in Los Angeles, where I can see the air I breathe.

• • •

He's been married to the same woman for sixteen years, which is like eighty-something in California years.

• • •

In California, they don't throw their garbage away—they turn it into TV shows.

• • •

Camps

An angry bear approached our picnic site, looking for food. My wife asked me, "Shall I give him some of my potato salad?"
I said, "No, he's angry enough already."

• • •

As he went off to summer camp, his mother advised him, "Now, Billy, remember to put on a clean pair of socks every day."

When Billy came home from camp three weeks later, he was a foot taller.

• • •

You know that summer camp is going to be pricey when it lists the weenie roast as "frankfurter flambé."

• • •

A tearful child called home from camp. "Are you homesick?" asked his mother.

"No, I'm heresick," sobbed the child.

• • •

They sent their children to a camp for stockbrokers' kids. At the campfire, the kids told merger stories.

• • •

Summer will soon be here, and here's a little tip to make your vacation days seem longer. Go camping.

• • •

It has now been reliably determined that sushi was first discovered by a camper with a fish and wet matches.

• • •

Camping? His idea of roughing it is slow room service!

• • •

He sent his kids to a camp that takes them back to nature and keeps them there.

• • •

I'm not the outdoor type. Don't misunderstand me. I love Mother Nature. I just don't want to move in with her.

• • •

Scout leader: "Remember, fellows, if you get lost in the woods at night, get your bearings from the sky. A glow will indicate the nearest shopping center."

• • •

The outdoor life is not for me. Too many animals work the night shift.

• • •

There's a new, exclusive Yuppie camp, Camp Gimmee Gucci. It has an indoor lake, and late at night the campers all sit around and tell ghost stories in front of the microwave.

• • •

Were it not for camping the world would be full of malnourished mosquitoes.

• • •

Whoever said, "Money can't buy happiness," never sent his children to a summer camp.

• • •

This has been one of the most restful and relaxing summers we've ever had. I realized that when I said, "Tomorrow the kids come home from camp."
And my wife said, "Who?"

• • •

The swimming instructor was so sick one day that they sent the golf pro to take his place. I almost drowned. He kept telling me to keep my head down.

• • •

Summer camps are places that are staffed by seventeen-year-old counselors, which is amusing. You wouldn't trust them with your car, but with your kids it's okay.

• • •

We're trying something new this summer. We're sending the dog to camp and the kids to obedience school.

• • •

Summer camp is where the parents spend a thousand dollars so their daughter can learn to make a fifty-cent potholder.

• • •

It's a time of real adjustment when you send your kid to camp. The first morning he's away, you awaken and think, "Where's Billy?" By the third week you're wondering, "How's Billy?" Best of all is the fifth week when you wake up and think, "Who's Billy?"

• • •

Fear is zipping up your sleeping bag and that itch in your big toe starts to move.

• • •

When their son returned from camp they thought he had grown four inches. Then they washed his feet and he returned to his normal height.

• • •

A child sent his parents a letter from camp with the request, "Send food. All they serve here is breakfast, lunch and dinner."

• • •

Cars

He's so proud of his new truck. He didn't get the trendy kind—he bought a UPS truck. As he claims, "Laugh if you will, but I can now park anywhere I want!"

• • •

An irate speeder said, "Why don't you people get organized? First you take away my driver's license and the next day you ask to see it!"

• • •

Whenever he picks up a hitchhiker, he likes to say, "Buckle up. I want to try something I saw in a cartoon."

• • •

What do you call a guy who's missed ten car payments?
A pedestrian.

• • •

A policeman stopped me and said, "How come you're driving so fast?"
I told him, "Well, I had my accelerator to the floor."

• • •

A woman parked her car on a hill and it rolled away, crashing into several vehicles. The officer at the scene of the accident said, "Why didn't you put on your emergency brake?"
The lady replied, "Since when is mailing a letter an emergency?"

• • •

Salesman: "Buy this car and you won't make another payment until March."
Customer: "Oh, did the credit union tell you about me?"

• • •

I asked a friend, "How often do you rotate your tires?"
He said, "Every time I drive."

• • •

A driver at an accident scene was overheard, "But it can't be my fault. I have no-fault insurance."

• • •

A great musician can bring tears to a person's eyes. But, then again, so can an auto mechanic.

• • •

A mechanic related, "Today I worked on a Mustang, a Colt and a Cougar. I feel more like a veterinarian than a mechanic."

• • •

Do you want to know what becomes of people who flunk their driver's tests? They become parking valets.

• • •

Few things have a shorter life span than a clean garage.

• • •

Have you noticed how much more courteous the police have become? Yesterday I went through a red light and a cop pulled me over, walked back to my car, tipped his cap and said, "Good afternoon. My name is Bill and I'll be your arresting officer today."

• • •

Here's some advice that will help you avoid a speeding ticket. Buy a CB radio, get a good radar detector, and in the event you are pulled over, always have a bag of fresh doughnuts on the front seat.

• • •

I feel great tonight. I don't have to make car payments anymore. I got a letter from the bank this week that read, "This is the last letter we will be sending you about your car payments."

• • •

I get six miles per gallon with my new car. My son gets the other twenty.

• • •

I know how to eliminate all the city's traffic problems. Have all the lights turn red and keep them that way.

• • •

I own a compact car that can stop on a dime, and that's because it doesn't have the power to go over it.

• • •

I took the road less traveled, and now my car needs front-end alignment.

• • •

I was in a horrible traffic jam. An Amway salesman collided with a Jehovah's Witness and it took them four hours to exchange information.

• • •

If you need help getting back on your feet, just miss two car payments.

• • •

If you think that no one cares that you are alive, just try missing a car payment sometime.

• • •

My car can pass anything on the road, provided that it's going in the opposite direction.

• • •

My car has an antitheft device—it's appearance.

• • •

Never lend your car to someone to whom you have given birth.

• • •

The best safety device in a car is a rearview mirror with a policeman in it.

• • •

My car breaks down so often, I bought the perfect second car—a tow truck.

• • •

Service station washrooms are places where it takes you ten minutes just to clean the soap.

• • •

Sign at a gas station: Courteous and Efficient Self-Service.

• • •

If Rolls Royces are so great, why don't you see more people driving them?

• • •

When buying a used car, always check to see if the hood latch is worn out.

• • •

CHILDHOOD

As a child, I was deathly afraid of heights. My dad built me a tree house on a stump. When someone sneezed I only said, "Gesund."

• • •

Dad was a great procrastinator. I was eight years old before he named me.

• • •

He set his home on fire when he was a kid and his parents immediately sent him to his room.

• • •

He was so big when he was born that the doctor was afraid to slap him.

• • •

His parents were overprotective. When he played badminton, they made him wear a helmet.

• • •

His parents were very poor. His father ran a paving business in Venice.

• • •

Instead of bedtime stories, his father used to read him bus schedules.

• • •

I told my mom I was running away from home. She said, "On your mark . . ."

• • •

As a kid, he stood in the corner so much in school that he developed a triangular forehead.

• • •

As a child, his parents moved a lot, but he always found them.

• • •

His parents used to take him for long walks in the woods, but he always found his way home.

• • •

Our family was so large that Mom made Jell-O in the bathtub.

• • •

He had a nasty disposition. As a kid, he had an imaginary friend who wouldn't even play with him.

• • •

My parents were a little overprotective. I had the only tricycle on the block with training wheels.

• • •

He was a precocious child. At four months he was already eating solids . . . pencils, crayons, books. . . .

• • •

When he was lost he said to the cop, "Do you think we'll find my parents?"

The cop replied, "I don't know. There are so many places they could hide."

• • •

He told his father, "Nobody likes me."

His dad said, "Don't say 'nobody.' Everyone hasn't met you yet."

• • •

My great-grandpa recalls his childhood: "In 1850, the bathtub was invented, and the telephone in 1875. I was able to sit in the bathtub for twenty-five years without the phone ringing once."

• • •

I always wanted to spend more time with my kids. Then one day, I did!

• • •

I always wondered why babies spend so much time sucking their thumbs. Then one day I tasted the baby food!

• • •

CHILDREN

How far apart should children be spaced?

Oh, I'd say about a mile and a half.

• • •

Nurse to father waiting in maternity ward: "Well, did you want a boy or a girl?"

"A boy."

"Well, I'm afraid it's a girl."

"That's okay. That was my second choice."

• • •

Babies are Nature's way of telling people what the world looks like at two o'clock in the morning.

• • •

CHINA

When I was in China, I found the language very difficult. One hundred thousand words and none of them in English!

• • •

CHINESE RESTAURANT

While in a Chinese restaurant, I saw an item on the menu, Pork Rice Almond Ding. I asked the waiter, "What's that?"

He said, "We take some pork, rice and almonds and put them in the microwave."

I said, "Well, what's the ding?"

He said, "That's the timer!"

• • •

CHRISTMAS

Remember, hang on to your youth for as long as you can. The minute you stop believing in Santa Claus, you get socks and underwear for gifts.

• • •

The three great holiday gift lies are, "Easy to assemble," "Unbreakable" and "One size fits all."

• • •

I don't think I'll be getting my wife anything this year. She still hasn't used the snow shovel I got her last Christmas.

• • •

I just hope that this Christmas my wife will give me some presents that I can afford.

• • •

I thought that my friends would like to know that I wear a size-sixteen shirt, a size-nine shoe, and if you are considering a cash gift, I take an extra large.

• • •

I went shopping last night and my VISA card overheated.

• • •

I'd love to get my wife everything she wants for Christmas, but I just don't know how to gift wrap Bloomingdale's.

• • •

Just think, if Christmas was canceled this year, Wisconsin would be stuck with 3 million tons of cheese.

• • •

My wife is getting ready to do some serious Christmas shopping. She took her credit cards out for a tune-up.

• • •

My wife was out Christmas shopping. When she got home, I had to give her Mastercard mouth-to-mouth resuscitation.

• • •

My wife's idea of Christmas cards: Visa/Mastercard/Discover.

• • •

The boss doubled our Christmas bonus. This year we get two fruitcakes.

• • •

The boss's favorite expression is, "Be grateful for little things," which he always says while he's handing out the Christmas bonuses.

• • •

The perfect Christmas gift for the person who has everything is a burglar alarm.

• • •

My mother-in-law gives really exciting gifts for Christmas. Last year she gave me a gift certificate good for four hours of free advice.

• • •

Now today's consumer Christmas tip for kids, brought to you by the mall merchants' association. Remember, kids, if Santa brings everything you ask for, you're not asking for enough.

• • •

This Christmas, give the teenage doll that's so realistic it doesn't walk, it slouches.

• • •

Note on a Christmas package: Fragile, throw underhand.

• • •

Last Christmas I got my wife a gift certificate and she went right out and tried to exchange it for a larger size.

• • •

My mother-in-law came to visit last Christmas, and she's such a comic. Gave us a set of towels marked HERS and ITS.

• • •

Batteries are very important. They make things work. That's why I'm giving a dozen to my brother-in-law.

• • •

Every Christmas I have this terrible decision to make. Whether to pay my son's tuition at the university or buy a Christmas tree.

• • •

Christmas cookies in my house last about as long as a ceasefire in the Middle East.

• • •

I get such delight watching my children hanging up their stockings Christmas Eve. It's not that it's Christmas Eve, it's just such a thrill to see them hang anything up!

• • •

If we look realistically, the Christmas presents of today are the garage sales of tomorrow.

• • •

For Christmas, his wife wanted a car of her own, but he bought her furs and jewels instead. He said he didn't know anyone who made imitation cars.

• • •

Do you realize that if it wasn't for Christmas we would never get to know our wife's sizes?

• • •

Businesses say that this will be the greatest Christmas ever. I thought the first one was!

• • •

I don't mind getting money for Christmas. It's always just the right size.

• • •

For Christmas, his father got a puppy for him, and we all agreed that that was a pretty fair trade.

• • •

I'd like to remind you all that there are only nine shopping days left 'til Christmas. I take a size fifteen shirt, size-eleven socks, I like club ties—and my hand grip fits the steering wheel of a Porsche.

• • •

CHURCH

A pastor said, "We welcome all denominations, especially tens and twenties."

• • •

I think that the next time there is a new pope, they should elect a Southern Baptist. Catholics have been in there a long time.

• • •

Pastor describing his congregation: "We have 300 members, all active; 150 working for me, and 150 working against me."

• • •

The pastor promised him a two-week break from tithing if he promises not to participate in congregational singing.

• • •

The last time I sang in church the pastor told me it would be okay for me to play golf next Sunday.

• • •

Pastor, I've got some terrible news. Someone broke into our church last night and stole ninety thousand dollars worth of pledges.

• • •

Does a good beginning and a good ending make a good sermon? Yes, if they're close enough together.

• • •

A new pastor preached a stirring sermon on gossip but then made a fatal error by closing the service by singing "I Love to Tell the Story."

• • •

The preacher was dickering with the salesman to lower the price on the new car. "Remember," he said, "I'm just a poor Baptist preacher."

"I know," said the salesman. "I've heard you preach!"

• • •

He got up to leave during a long sermon. The minister said, "Where are you going?"

John replied, "To get a haircut."

The minister said, "You should have gotten one before you came."

John replied, "When I came in, I didn't need one!"

• • •

A lady said to her pastor, "Something that puzzles me. Exactly how old was Hezekiah?"

The pastor answered, "Well, he was different ages at different times."

"Oh," said the lady, "I never thought of it that way."

• • •

Did Moses wander in the wilderness because God was testing him, or do you think it was because, like most men, Moses refused to stop and ask for directions?

• • •

CITY

He's been appointed to the city's Beautification Committee. His job is to stay out of sight.

• • •

In school he never could find the shortest distance between two points, so he became a taxi driver.

• • •

Our garbage collectors in the city are so considerate. They always leave a little to start out with again.

• • •

"Is this bench taken?"
"Not yet. It isn't even dark."

• • •

I asked a city dweller, "Do you know where the post office is?"
He said, "Yes," and kept right on walking.

• • •

They say that if you drink water from the Fountain of Youth you will never get a day older. The same is true of Lake Erie.

• • •

Clothes

He's a real trendsetter. He was the first one in the office to wear brown and white shoes.
Then he lost the brown one.

• • •

His clothes are so old that if he were a history teacher he could dress for the part.

• • •

I saw his suit featured in a national magazine—*Field and Stream.*

• • •

I underwent acupuncture this morning. I tried on a new shirt.

• • •

What a wardrobe! No wonder people call him the Prince of Polyester.

• • •

I love that formal wear. I didn't know Fruit-of-the-Loom made tuxedos.

• • •

He has a tough time buying clothes. There aren't many stores that stock medium dumpy or 42 droopy.

• • •

He has a suit of clothes for every day of the year, and I see that he is wearing it tonight.

• • •

He's worn that suit so many years it's been in and out of style five times.

• • •

He said. "Whenever I'm down in the dumps I buy new clothes." I was wondering where he got his clothes.

• • •

Colds

A sure cure for the flu that will get you back to work the next day is to watch eight hours of daytime television.

• • •

Remember, a cold medicine can't be much good if you can stand the taste.

• • •

Remember, germs are carried in the air. So avoid breathing air, unless you know where it's been.

• • •

When you get the flu, doctors recommend that you drink plenty of liquids, which is certainly sound advice when you consider it's so tough to drink anything else.

• • •

College

(parent sending son to college) "Look at it this way. We're not losing a son. We're losing a savings account."

• • •

He had the worst study habits in the history of college until he found out what he was doing wrong. He was highlighting his texts with a black Magic Marker.

• • •

A philosophy degree is helpful in a lot of ways. It gives you the background you need in order to fill out an unemployment form in Latin.

• • •

A teen decided not to go to college. He convinced his parents to give him the money that it would have cost to send him to college for four years. He then took the money and retired on it.

• • •

At graduation time, millions of graduates go out to seek their fortunes, while millions of parents try to rebuild theirs.

• • •

College prepares the young adult for the business world. It teaches one how to sit and look interested for fifty minutes.

• • •

College prepares you for real life. Right off, it puts you in debt.

• • •

He attended college and did poorly. He couldn't make his eight o'clock class, and he was going to night school.

• • •

He majored in communication and minored in philosophy. Now he can wonder out loud.

• • •

He was a fast learner and a quick forgetter.

• • •

I took Introduction to Shakespeare, but I was terribly disappointed. He never showed up the whole semester.

• • •

My grade point average was so low that the dean appointed a football player to tutor me.

• • •

People mockingly call it a drive-in college, and say that cars just drive through and they throw a diploma through your window. That's not true. You have to stop first.

• • •

There are many ways to go bankrupt, but it's hard to beat having a child in college.

• • •

They gave up water polo at (local college). The horses kept drowning.

• • •

To be successful in business, graduates need an M.B.A., Master in Business Administration, or an M.B.I., Mighty Big Inheritance.

• • •

Why do (college's) graduates hang their diplomas from the rear-view mirrors of their cars?

So they can park in handicapped spaces.

• • •

The government is getting tougher on the collection of student loans. The new secretary of education is Vito Corleone.

• • •

June is when college graduates take their diplomas in hand and go out to conquer the world. July is when the world counterattacks.

• • •

We really had some tough teams at my alma mater. I'll never forget guys like Moose, Crusher, Bronco and Tiger. And that was just the chess team!

• • •

He played hooky from correspondence school. He sent in empty envelopes.

• • •

I went to junior high, senior high and college in the same community, which was a very convenient arrangement. That way I could use the same textbooks all the way through.

• • •

Many people haven't heard of my alma mater, but let me assure you, it's one of the goodest colleges in the United States.

• • •

There is only one way to cope with the rising costs of putting a kid through college. When they're very young, start an education fund for them and every year add to it. Then, just when they're ready to enter college, rob a bank.

• • •

Statistics show that 90 percent of people who actually listen to commencement speeches are parents who are making one last attempt to get something for their money.

• • •

He went to public school on a scholarship and is educated beyond his intelligence.

• • •

He took an aptitude test his senior year in college. The examiner told him, "You have a bright future in any field where a close relative holds a senior management position."

• • •

A wealthy graduate, talking to a college president, said, "Well, now that I've made a lot of money, I'd like to do something for the good old alma mater and donate a building. Let's see, in what subject did I excel?"

After looking over his transcript, the president told the philanthropist, "I suggest you build a dormitory. Judging from your records it looks like you slept most of the time."

• • •

What do tornadoes and graduates of (name university) have in common?

They both end up in trailer parks.

• • •

COMPUTERS

I don't need a computer that has all the answers. I have a wife.

• • •

I know computers are smarter than people. I've never seen one jogging.

• • •

Someone asked me if I know anything about word processors. Know anything? I married one!

• • •

CONVENTIONS

I attended the Plumbers' Convention in Flushing, New York . . . the Hot Dog Manufacturers' Association in Frankfort, Kentucky . . . Parents of Twins in Minneapolis/St. Paul . . . Weight Watchers' Convention in Gainesville, Florida, and the National Contortionists' Convention in South Bend, Indiana.

• • •

COWS

If milk builds strong bones and healthy bodies, why do cows have such lousy posture?

• • •

CRIME

I live in a high-crime area. It doesn't have a doughnut shop.

• • •

I read a sad story about a kid who decided on a life of crime and made the mistake of trying to pull his first heist at a doughnut shop.

• • •

My friend decided to become a police officer after his first doughnut. . . .

• • •

Latest statistics reveal that robbery in the city is down, but that's because all the good stuff has already been taken.

• • •

Some people leave their radios on when they're not home to give the impression that their house is occupied. Burglars have a special name for this. They call it background music.

• • •

A gunman pointed his pistol at me and said, "Congratulations!"
I asked, "Why?"
He said, "Because you are about to enter a lower tax bracket."

• • •

The counterfeiter's last words to the judge before sentencing were, "Are you sure Bob Hope's picture isn't on the hundred-dollar bill?"

• • •

As the blindfold was being put into place, a criminal was asked if he had any last requests.
The convict said, "I sure do! Use blanks!"

• • •

A guy was sent to Leavenworth because he was making big money. About a third of an inch too big.

• • •

Crime is so bad in the United States that the Statue of Liberty is holding both arms in the air!

• • •

The trouble with opportunity knocking on the door in these days of high crime rates is that by the time you unhook the chain, push back the bolt, turn two locks and shut off the burglar alarm, it's gone.

• • •

Why are pictures of criminals displayed in post offices? Are we supposed to write to them? I think they should be printed on postage stamps. That way mail carriers can be on the lookout for them while they're out delivering the mail. Better yet, when the police take the photos of the criminals, they should lock them up right there.

• • •

Dating

A girl applied to a computer dating service and reported that she liked water sports and formal wear, and the computer matched her with a penguin.

• • •

Dad to daughter's date: "She says she'll be right down. Care for a game of chess?"

• • •

Father answering phone: "No, this is not your dreamboat. This is her supply ship."

• • •

He told her that he was taking her to a restaurant that had a Netherlands motif, which was his way of saying that they were going Dutch.

• • •

He took her to the Tunnel of Love, and she made him wait outside.

• • •

I took my date horseback riding. We had a great time until I ran out of quarters.

• • •

I went to a computer dating service and they gave me the number for Dial-a-Prayer.

• • •

"You look like my first husband."
"How many times have you been married?"
"None."

• • •

I took her to my favorite dinner spot, but it was awfully hard to hold a conversation. Maybe our table was too close to the automatic pinsetters.

• • •

She dated a guy who said that he didn't want to get involved too seriously. In fact, when they were playing tennis, he wouldn't say, "Fifteen-love." He would say, "Fifteen-I-really-like-you-but-I-want-to-see-others."

• • •

"If you give me your phone number, I'll give you a call."
"It's in the book."
"Good, what's your name?"
"It's in the book, too."

• • •

He heard that it was always proper to flatter his date. One night he went out with a girl who was rather plump. When he took her to the door, he was stumped for something nice to say. Finally, he sputtered, "You know, for a fat girl you don't sweat much."

• • •

I took her to a restaurant and asked her, "How do you like your rice—baked or fried?"
She said, "Thrown!"

• • •

He took her to an amusement park and I asked, "Did you take her through the Tunnel of Love?"
He said, "Yeah, but I didn't like it. It was dark and damp, and we got all wet."

I said, "Was there a leak in your boat?"
He replied, "There's a boat?"

• • •

He took a girl horseback riding, and when they stopped to rest, the horses rubbed their necks against each other affectionately. The guy said to the girl, "Ah, me, that's what I'd like to do."
His girl responded, "Well, go ahead, it's your horse."

• • •

When I said to my future wife, "I'm not much to look at," she said, "That's okay, you'll be at the office most of the day anyway."

• • •

The couple was strolling along the beach, lost in love. The young beau looked out to the sea and eloquently said, "Roll on, thou deep, dark, blue ocean—roll."
His girl looked at him with admiring eyes and spoke, "Oh, Herman. You're wonderful. It's doing it!"

• • •

She threw out subtle hints. On hot summer days she used to fan me with a marriage license.

• • •

The older gentleman approached the young lovely and asked, "Where have you been all my life?"
She answered, "Well, for the first forty years, I wasn't even born!"

• • •

At the restaurant she said, "I'll have the oysters Rockefeller, the pressed duck and baked Alaska, unless, of course, you're saving for a ring or something. . . ."

• • •

I went to a party where I was to meet a blind date. I walked up to the girl and said, "Hi, are you Mary Beth?"

She asked, "Are you Pat?"

I said, "Yes."

She said, "I'm not Mary Beth!"

• • •

Daughters

My daughter has no luck at all. Last year a fella asked if he could change her name to his and she said yes. And ever since he's been calling her Bruce.

• • •

Daylight Savings Time

We move our clocks ahead an hour Saturday night but I don't mind losing an hour's sleep. I get it back Sunday morning during the minister's sermon.

• • •

I could never figure out that when we set our clocks back an hour, the sun goes down an hour earlier. How does the sun know to do that?

• • •

Deejays (Disc Jockeys)

The time is now twenty after twelve. And for those of you attending (local college) that means the short hand is on the twelve and the big hand is on the four.

• • •

Dentists

I go to the dentists, Drillem, Fillem and Billem.

• • •

It's tough to get an appointment with a dentist these days. My dentist requires that you plan a toothache three months in advance.

• • •

My dentist had his office redecorated. Now all he's waiting for is a shipment of old magazines.

• • •

I go to a budget dentist. His examining room doesn't have a spit sink. When he's through with you he just says, "Now rinse and swallow."

• • •

Orthodontists are magicians. They can remove a person's life savings through a kid's mouth.

• • •

My dentist told me that artificial sweeteners cause cavities in false teeth.

• • •

Throughout history, there have been great names that have struck terror in hearts: Alexander the Great, Attila the Hun, Ivan the Terrible and Weinberg the Orthodontist.

• • •

With all the gold and silver in his teeth, the dentist advised him never to smile in bad neighborhoods.

• • •

If you want to keep your teeth in good condition, brush your teeth after every meal and mind your own business.

• • •

"How much will it cost to have this tooth pulled?"
"Twenty dollars," said the dentist.
"Twenty dollars for thirty seconds of work?"
"Well, if you like," said the dentist, "I can work more slowly."

• • •

The dentist told me, "I have some good news and bad news for you. The bad news is you have seven teeth that must come out, you need a lot of root canal work and your gums are all diseased."
I asked, "What's the good news?"
He said, "I broke 80 on the golf course yesterday."

• • •

Diet

It's time to diet if you think gravy is a beverage.

• • •

It's time to diet when you can pinch an inch—on your forehead.

• • •

A man succeeded to get his wife to diet by telling her, "Do you realize that there are forty pounds of you that I'm not legally married to?"

• • •

Cottage cheese must be the most fattening food around. Everywhere I go, I see fat people eating it.

• • •

He really carries his weight well, but it takes two trips.

• • •

He stepped on one of those new computerized talking scales. The scale went clang, bang, and a voice in the machine said, "One at a time, please."

• • •

Here's today's dieting tip: Low-fat pastries taste better if you smear a lot of butter on them.

• • •

Here's a tip to help you get more fiber in your diet—eat the tablecloth.

• • •

I'm on the BBC Diet—Buy bigger clothes.

• • •

He's starting to get serious about his diet. He dunks his dough-nuts in Slim Fast.

• • •

His idea of burning off fat is to eat a pizza in a sauna.

• • •

I discovered that I can't lose weight because my fat cells are all shaped like tiny boomerangs.

• • •

I eat a well-balanced diet. My problem is that I eat it too often.

• • •

I just couldn't keep on my diet. So I did the next best thing. I became jolly.

• • •

I just got off a ten-day diet, and I lost about a week and a half.

• • •

I tried dieting once, but it didn't work. Cottage cheese makes lousy hot fudge sundaes.

• • •

I tried dieting once. It was the worst six hours of my life.

• • •

I tried the high-fiber diet. The first meal I didn't know whether I should eat it or weave a basket.

• • •

I tried to diet, but it's tough. Three fast-food chains have sued me for nonsupport.

• • •

I try to watch what I eat. I need quicker eyes, though.

• • •

I would do better on diets, but eating makes me hungry.

• • •

I'm trying to get back to my original weight—eight pounds, eight ounces.

• • •

If you drink a diet soda with a candy bar, they cancel each other out.

• • •

I'm on two diets. I just don't get enough food on one.

• • •

I'm really serious about my diet this time. I'm using a salad dressing called Six Hundred Islands.

• • •

Inside every fat person is a thin person crying to get out—to order a chocolate sundae.

• • •

It would be easy for me to lose weight if replacement parts weren't so easily available at the refrigerator.

• • •

Lose some weight if someone calls you fat and all you can do is turn the other chin.

• • •

More diets start in dress shops than in doctors' offices.

• • •

My cholesterol tests came back and they indicate that I have honey-glazed arteries.

• • •

My doctor gave me a choice: "Either lose fifty-five pounds or grow six inches taller."

• • •

My doctor suggested that I cut back on red meat, so I've stopped putting ketchup on my hamburgers.

• • •

People wouldn't be buying so many diet books if they hadn't bought so many cookbooks in the first place.

• • •

Remember, the famous response as to why something was done—"because it was there"—was meant for mountain climbing, not eating.

• • •

The diet doctor told me that I can't have ice cream for dessert anymore, so now I have it as an appetizer.

• • •

The only way that I could lose seventy-five pounds would be to get mugged in London.

• • •

The second day of a diet is always easier than the first—by the second day you're off of it.

• • •

You know that it's time to diet when your doctor tells you that that mysterious rash on your stomach is steering wheel burn.

• • •

You know that it's time to diet when your kids try to bury you at the beach and they run out of sand.

• • •

You're overweight if the couch gets up when you do.

• • •

Doctors

"Did the doctor find out what you had?"
"No, he charged me thirty-five dollars, but I had forty-five dollars in my wallet."

• • •

(before an operation) "Would you like some sodium penathol to put you out, or would you just like a peek at your bill?"

• • •

(to patient) "Your tests are back. Don't come any closer."

• • •

A cirrhosis specialist and podiatrist married and they hung out a shingle that said Liver and Bunions.

• • •

A doctor will take care of poor people, even if it means making you one.

• • •

A doctor, walking through his waiting room to move his double-parked car, turned to his patients and said, "Now in the meantime, don't anyone get better until I return."

• • •

A fool and his money are soon parted. However, if you go to a doctor, it's surgically removed.

• • •

A hold-up man broke into a medical center, and the doctor charged him for an office visit.

• • •

The doctor said to his patient, "There's really nothing unusual about your condition, Mr. Thomas, except that it seldom occurs in a person who's still living."

• • •

(overheard in the doctor's office) "I've been in this waiting room so long, I think I've recovered."

• • •

Do you know what doctors write to pharmacists in Latin on those prescription pads? "I got mine, now you get yours!"

• • •

He's a great doctor. Most of his patients are older than his office magazines.

• • •

He's recovering from major surgery. The surgeon just separated him from his wallet.

• • •

How is it that the same doctors that can't cure the common cold are doing artificial heart transplants?

• • •

I always wanted to be a doctor, but I found that I was allergic to tax shelters.

• • •

I asked my doctor for a second opinion, so he billed me twice.

• • •

I asked my doctor how my body compared to other men my age. He replied, "Living or dead?"

• • •

I asked the podiatrist what the fastest cure for an ingrown toenail is and he said, "A power lawn mower."

• • •

I bought a great, low-mileage used car from a doctor who had only used it to make house calls.

• • •

I complained to my doctor that my nose was sore. He said, "Stay off of it for a couple of weeks."

• • •

I had walking pneumonia and my doctor charged me by the mile.

• • •

I have a doctor's appointment for eight thirty, which is ten o'clock doctor-time.

• • •

I just found out what MD means—Many Dollars!

• • •

I just got my bill for my stay in the hospital. Now I know why surgeons wear masks.

• • •

I saw an interesting sign at an optometrist's office: Eyes Examined While You Wait.

• • •

I told my doctor I had shingles and he tried to sell me aluminum siding.

• • •

I told my doctor that I was feeling better and asked for his bill. The doctor said, "You're not strong enough for that yet."

• • •

I wasn't feeling very well and my doctor cured me in just one visit. He told me my insurance wouldn't cover it.

• • •

I went to the doctor Wednesday afternoon and he charged me double for making him work on a holiday.

• • •

If there was any justice in this world, there would be a waiting room where doctors would have to sit to get paid.

• • •

Medical school dean to student: "You can be proud of your academic achievement, but you must learn to write a little less clearly."

• • •

My doctor advised me that I had plenty of good years left if I eat sensibly, get regular exercise and if I stay away from natural causes.

• • •

My doctor advised me, "Do everything in moderation, except when it comes to paying my bill."

• • •

My *doctor* doesn't believe in fancy machines. He just has you sit in his waiting room for two hours, and that takes care of the stress test.

• • •

My *doctor* is a cholesterol expert. He removed the fat from my wallet.

• • •

My *doctor* is so upset by the increase in malpractice insurance premiums that he can hardly putt.

• • •

My *doctor* never mentioned to me that one of the side effects of the medicine that he prescribed for me was poverty.

• • •

My *doctor* told me that eggs aren't good for the heart, but did you ever see a chicken with a pacemaker?

• • •

My *doctor* told me to cut back on two food groups—liquids and solids.

• • •

My *doctor* told me, "The nice thing about older patients is that it is easier to find their veins."

• • •

My *doctor* took my pulse and said he wouldn't give it back until I had paid him for an office visit.

• • •

My doctor's home was burglarized, and was he shocked! He didn't know that anyone made house calls anymore.

• • •

My physician suggested that I turn my body over to someone who will exercise it.

• • •

My sister used to date a doctor, but every time he sent her a love letter, she had to take it to the druggist to read it.

• • •

One hospital has a new operating room with a sand trap, so that the doctors can operate in familiar surroundings.

• • •

Patient to doctor: "I arrived early for an appointment and you took me right away. You spent time with me. I can read your prescription. Are you sure that you're a real doctor?"

• • •

Patient to doctor: "I don't need a stress test. I have a wife, three daughters and one bathroom."

• • •

Patients' Rule Number One: "Never get sick on a Wednesday, unless you plan to get sick on a golf course."

• • •

The doctor said, "You need constant medical attention. I suggest you become a greenskeeper at your local golf course."

• • •

The doctor said, "I'll have to wait to examine you. My stethoscope hasn't been in the freezer long enough."

• • •

The doctor said, "Now don't worry. We'll have you up and complaining about my bill in no time."

• • •

The doctor told the patient, "Just pay me when you can. In the meantime, I'll just keep your liver."

• • •

The medical profession is under attack today, but I am proud that I have a doctor who still makes house calls. Every day he calls his houses in Honolulu, Palm Springs and Monaco.

• • •

The only thing the doctor found encouraging about my test results was they weren't his.

• • •

Think how much higher medical costs would be if physicians had new magazines in their waiting rooms.

• • •

Here are some medical tips: Never go to a doctor whose office plants are dead. Never go to a chiropractor who wears a neck brace.

• • •

Why is it that you can never read the doctor's prescriptions, but the bills are always legible?

• • •

I told my doctor, "When I touch my chest it hurts. When I touch my knee it hurts. When I touch my throat it hurts. What's wrong with me?"

He said, "You've got a broken finger."

• • •

I said, "Doc, can you cure me?"
He answered, "Not on your salary."

• • •

An obstetrician had worked his way through medical school by working part-time at a deli. This was quickly noted when he made his first delivery, held it aloft for the proud father to see, and asked, "It's a little over seven pounds. Is that okay?"

• • •

"What's the difference between an allergy and an itch?"
"Oh, about three hundred dollars."

• • •

Doctor: "I'm upset. This skin ointment that I prescribed for you hasn't been doing the job. You've been using it, haven't you?"

Patient: "No, doc. The directions say, 'Apply locally,' and I've been out of town on business all week."

• • •

I keep telling my doctor, "I'm not mature enough."
He dismisses the whole idea and says, "That's silly."
And I guess he should know. After all, he's one of the finest pediatricians around.

• • •

The patient asked the doctor, "Can you treat me?"
The doctor answered, "No, you'll have to pay like everyone else."

• • •

(to patient) "Do you always stutter?"
Patient: "N-N-N-o, d-d-d-oc. Only when I s-s-s-peak."

• • •

(panicky parent to doctor) "My daughter just swallowed a razor blade. What should I do?"
"Use your electric razor until I get there."

• • •

"You're a very lucky man, Mr. Gabriel," said the doctor. "You have a very inexpensive disease."

• • •

The doctor said, "Now I want you to take this medicine after every meal."
Patient: "But, doc, I haven't been able to eat anything for four days!"
Doctor: "Well, in that case, the medicine is going to last a lot longer."

• • •

A doctor chastised a patient for letting his condition become so bad.
"I know I should have seen you sooner, doc, but I was stuck in the waiting room."

• • •

"Doc, you've got to help me. I've lost my memory."
Doctor: "When did it happen?"
Patient: "When did what happen?"

• • •

Our local med school has a new, practical course for students: "How to Wedge Out of Sand Traps."

• • •

"Doc, I have a trick knee. What shall I do?"
"Join the circus," said the medic.

• • •

The eye doctor said, "Can you read the last three numbers on the chart?"
I said, "Yes. 1-8-5."
He said, "That's fine, because that is the price of your new glasses."

• • •

A doctor was visiting a friend who was carving a roast for dinner.
"How do you like those cuts, doc? I'd make a pretty good surgeon, wouldn't I?" bragged the host.
"Yeah," said the doctor. "Now let me see you put it together again."

• • •

What do you take when you have that run-down feeling?
The license plate number of the vehicle that hit you!

• • •

A woman came to her doctor with a new complaint every week. "I'm so hard of hearing, I can't even hear when I cough," she whined.
The doctor proceeded to write her a prescription.
"Will this help me hear better?" inquired the hypochondriac.
"No," said the doctor. "But it will help you to cough louder."

• • •

I told my doctor, "I want a second opinion."
He said, "Sure, as soon as you pay for the first one."

• • •

Do you know what the longest wait in the world is? It's when the nurse tells you, "Go into room B, take off your clothes and the doctor will be with you in a moment."

• • •

"Doc, how can I avoid falling hair?"
"Step to one side."

• • •

I called the doctor's office for an appointment. They said, "The doctor can see you next Thursday at 4 P.M." I said, "But I've had an accident and I'm bleeding profusely!"
The secretary replied, "Well, in that case, make it 3:45."

• • •

Doctor: "I recommend that you eat less, don't go on vacation and work longer hours."
Patient: "Okay, doc, if it'll make me feel better."
Doctor: "I'm not saying that it'll make you feel better, but at least you'll be able to pay my bill."

• • •

He told me that he'd have me on my feet in less than a month, and he was right. When I got his bill, I had to sell my car.

• • •

He went to the doctor, and the doctor told him he had six months to live. He went to another doctor who told him the same thing. So now he has a year. . . .

• • •

A recent survey shows that of all jobs, caddies live the longest. They get plenty of fresh air and exercise, and if there's ever a medical emergency, a doctor is always nearby.

• • •

I was born on a Wednesday, and the way that I remember is that the doctor slapped me with a putter.

• • •

This May, my son will fulfill his lifelong dream to associate himself with the great doctors, surgeons and medical researchers of our time, when he graduates from Harvard. He's going to be a caddy.

• • •

My ophthalmologist doesn't exactly inspire confidence. He sends out his bills in Braille.

• • •

"You're coughing more easily this morning," the doctor said.
"I should be," replied the patient. "I've been practicing all night."

• • •

"Don't forget," the lady told the doctor, "when my Melvin made lots of money for you by giving measles to the entire fifth grade."

• • •

Nurse: "That man to whom you just gave a clean bill of health just dropped over dead in the office as he was leaving, doctor. What should I do?"
"Turn him around," said the doctor, "so it looks as if he was walking in."

• • •

Never trust a doctor who stores his hypodermic needles on a dartboard.

• • •

Nurse to patient: "You have an appointment in two weeks."
Patient: "But I could be dead in two weeks!"
Nurse: "Well, in that case, you can cancel your appointment."

• • •

After the doctor operated, he discovered he left a sponge in me. I don't have any pain, but I really get thirsty.

• • •

I asked the doctor, "What kind of shape am I in?"
"Let's put it this way," said the doc, "from now on I want you to pay me in advance."

• • •

The doctor gave me something to raise my low blood pressure. His bill!

• • •

My doctor said, "Let me start with your medical history. Do you pay your doctor bills promptly?"

• • •

An apple a day keeps the doctor away. Sure, but so do golf and European vacations.

• • •

My eye doctor said, "Close one eye and tell me what you see."
I said, "Half of a bad suit."

• • •

Doesn't it always bug you how people talk about doctors *practicing* medicine? What—do they *practice* it until they get it right?

• • •

A doctor is someone who acts like a humanitarian and charges like a plumber.

• • •

My *doctor* asked me if I ever had a stress test. I said, "Yeah, when I got your last bill."

• • •

He had an injury and the doctor told him, "Take a pill every day and walk a mile each day. Call me at the end of the month."

At the end of the month, the patient called and said, "Doc, what do I do now? I'm thirty miles from home and out of pills."

• • •

Hear about the doctor who went on a ski trip and was lost in the snow for a week? He stamped out H-E-L-P in the snow but nobody could read his writing.

• • •

"No doubt about it. You're crazy."
"I want a second opinion."
"Okay, you're ugly, too."

• • •

"Doc, I have a cold or something in my head."
"I'll bet it's a cold."

• • •

My doctor says, "I'm well aware that the cost of medical care is outrageous—but so is the price of yachts."

• • •

I could tell that my doctor was in a hurry to finish the operation by his instructions to the nurse: "Clamp, sutures, putter. . . ."

• • •

I've learned one thing about doctors. If he examines you and gives you a long, confident nod it means, "Your guess is as good as mine."

• • •

I wonder about my doctor. I mean it's okay to take out my appendix and my tonsils, but through the same incision?

• • •

He was an honest doctor. On the death certificate where it said "Cause of Death," he signed his name.

• • •

A guy said to his doctor, "My foot hurts. What should I do?" The doctor replied, "Limp!"

• • •

My doctor told me to take a hot bath before retiring. That's ridiculous. It'll be years before I retire.

• • •

I asked the doctor, "Is it anything serious?"
He said, "Only if you have plans for next year."

• • •

The very first words that Rip Van Winkle heard after awakening from his twenty-year sleep, "The doctor will see you now."

• • •

I always wanted to be a doctor but it didn't work. I could never stand the sight of golf balls.

• • •

My doctor says I shouldn't smoke, drink, overeat, dissipate or do anything else that could interfere with paying his bill.

• • •

I asked the doctor, "How do I stand?"
He answered, "That's what puzzles me."

• • •

If you are a doctor, you can always expect to face constant challenges, frustration, adversity, and yes, even heartbreak. So much for golf, now let's talk about medicine.

• • •

The doctor took out his stethoscope and carefully listened to my wallet.

• • •

(doctor in an operating room) "Phew, that was a close one! An inch either way and it would have been out of my specialty."

• • •

He went for his annual physical. After the examination, the doctor said to the wife, "I don't like the looks of him."
The wife said, "I don't either, but he's so good to the kids."

• • •

I just know that my son is going to grow up to be a doctor. He is already collecting old magazines.

• • •

There is one thing my doctor can do better than anyone else. Read his own handwriting.

• • •

My doctor gave me a four-way cold tablet, but it couldn't figure out which way to go.

• • •

My doctor says he'll give me a clean bill of health as soon as my check clears.

• • •

I have a really tremendous doctor but I have trouble getting sick between his vacations.

• • •

We need all the doctors we can get. After all, what would we do with all the old magazines?

• • •

I saw a sign in the doctor's office that said, 10 to 1. So I went home. I want better odds than that.

• • •

(at a doctors' convention) It's such a pleasure to be talking to a group of doctors without having to take my clothes off.

• • •

"I've been seeing spots in front of my eyes."
"Have you seen a doctor?"
"No, just spots."

• • •

I don't have much faith in my doctor. All of his patients are sick.

• • •

(to patient) "Let me know if that medicine works. . . . I'm having the same problem myself."

• • •

We've decided to postpone your operation until you're stronger—financially.

• • •

I called the doctor the other morning at 3 A.M. and said, "I hate to bother you, but I have a bad case of insomnia."
He replied, "What are you trying to do . . . start an epidemic?"

• • •

I told my doctor, "I'm temporarily broke, but I'll remember you in my will."
The doctor replied, "Oh, would you let me have that prescription back I just wrote for you? There's one small change I'd like to make."

• • •

My doctor told me: "First the good news. You're going to have a disease named after you."

• • •

I always wanted to be a surgeon but one thing stopped me. I just couldn't stand the sight of money.

• • •

"I can't do anything for your sickness. It's hereditary."
"Well, then send the bill to my father."

• • •

A minor operation is one performed on someone else.

• • •

I just heard the saddest story. A doctor lost all his money on the horses. In an act of desperation, he tried to rob a bank. But nobody could read the hold-up note.

• • •

A suffering patient looked at his doctor and asked, "Are you certain I'll pull through? I heard of a man who was treated for jaundice and died of diphtheria."

"Don't be silly," said the doctor, "when I treat you for jaundice you die of jaundice."

• • •

My doctor advised me that I could avoid a sharp pain in my eye while drinking coffee by taking the spoon out of the cup.

• • •

This reminder just for doctors. It's April and time to take the snow tires off your golf cart.

• • •

My brother wanted to be a doctor, but my parents just couldn't afford the golf lessons.

• • •

According to a recent study, twenty thousand surgeons in the U.S. are incompetent. It's hard to believe, but many of these doctors didn't know the difference between such basic medical terms as bogie and birdie.

• • •

I asked, "Is this operation necessary?"

The surgeon said, "Of course. I have a mortgage payment next week."

• • •

I went to the doctor and said, "Doc, I don't know what's wrong with me, but every time I look in the mirror, I want to throw up."

He checked me over and said, "Well, I don't know what's wrong with you either, but your eyesight's perfect."

• • •

My doctor was amazed to discover that I had a disease that hadn't been around for almost a century. Turned out that I caught it from one of the magazines in his waiting room.

• • •

He was suspended from medical school for having excessively legible handwriting.

• • •

Does it make you nervous when you tell your doctor your symptoms, and he starts backing away?

• • •

Patient: "How long have I got?"
Doctor: "Ten . . ."
Patient: "Ten what? Ten months? Ten weeks? Ten days?"
Doctor: "Ten, nine, eight, seven . . ."

• • •

Dogs

"Does your dog have a pedigree?"

"Listen, if this dog could speak, he wouldn't talk to either of us!"

• • •

Classified ad: Lost dog. Left ear half off, missing leg. Blind in one eye. Answers to the name "Lucky."

• • •

Dogs aren't as smart as some people think. I took mine to obedience school, and I learned to sit and speak three weeks before it did.

• • •

He's the most vicious dog I've ever seen. He ate the tire off my car. What makes him even more tough is that that tire was in the trunk!

• • •

I got rid of my watchdog. I figured what it costs to feed him and decided that it would be cheaper to get robbed every now and then.

• • •

In some ways, a dog is better than a wife. The license is cheaper, you have no in-laws, and it already comes with a fur coat.

• • •

My dog flunked out of obedience school. He claims the kids ate his homework.

• • •

My dog has three food groups: what's on the floor, what's in his bowl and what he can beg for at the table.

• • •

My dog is getting along in years and is really slowing up. Today he brought me yesterday's paper.

• • •

My dog is half Labrador retriever and half pit bull. If it bites your leg off it'll bring it back to you.

• • •

My dog is half pit bull and half French poodle. He's not much of a watch dog, but he's a vicious gossip.

• • •

My dog is just like a member of the family. He won't do what I tell him.

• • •

Nothing in the world is friendlier than a wet dog.

• • •

Our dog is so lazy that he only chases parked cars.

• • •

We sent our dog to obedience school, and in just two weeks we've noticed the difference! Now he says grace and puts on a napkin before he bites the mailman's leg.

• • •

I go to a veterinarian who is also a taxidermist. His motto is: "Either way you get your dog back."

• • •

I made a bad mistake by buying a dog from a waiter. It never comes when I call him.

• • •

A man was waiting for his date in her tenth-floor apartment. As he waited, he played ball with her small dog. Unfortunately, the door to the balcony was open, and when the ball bounced out the door and over the balcony ledge, the dog followed it.

A few minutes later, the girl appeared, and her date inquired, "Have you noticed that your dog has been acting depressed lately?"

• • •

A Christian couple was looking for a pet that reflected their conservative principles. They learned of a kennel that specialized in religious dogs, and were shown a dog that could perform religious tricks. When ordered to find Psalm 23, it pawed through the pages until it found the passage.

That evening they showed the dog to a friend. "Does your dog do ordinary tricks?" the friend asked.

The couple was unsure but decided on a test. The man commanded, "Heel!" Instantly, the dog jumped up, put a paw on the man's forehead, closed its eyes in concentration and bowed its head.

• • •

DOUBLE CROSS

I crossed a potato with a sponge. It didn't taste very good, but it could sure hold the gravy.

• • •

I crossed a praying mantis with a termite and got an animal that says grace before it eats your house!

• • •

I crossed a hermit with a seal and got a guy that was hermetically sealed.

• • •

I crossed a shark with a penguin and got an animal dressed to kill.

• • •

I crossed a turkey with a kangaroo so that next Thanksgiving the ladies will be able to stuff him from the outside.

• • •

I crossed my hen with a parrot. Now when she lays an egg she can come over and tell me about it.

• • •

I crossed a turkey with a porcupine. Now I can eat and pick my teeth at the same time.

• • •

I crossed an electric blanket with a toaster to help people pop out of bed in the morning.

• • •

I crossed a turkey with a centipede. Now everyone can have a drumstick.

• • •

I mixed gasoline with Gatorade. Now my car only does sideline patterns.

• • •

A beekeeper crossed his bees with lightning bugs so that he could develop a night shift at his hives.

• • •

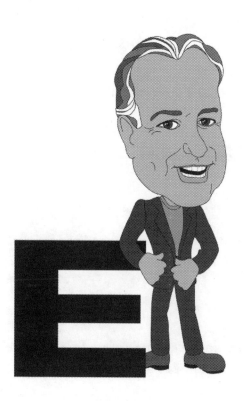

Economy

An economist is someone who didn't have enough personality to become an accountant.

• • •

What's the difference between an economist and a confused old man with Alzheimer's?
The economist is the one with the calculator.

• • •

Economists were put on this earth to make weather forecasters look good.

• • •

Fifty-five percent of economists predicted an upturn. Forty percent forecasted a decline, and the other 5 percent didn't have a coin to flip.

• • •

Food prices are astronomical! I went to a hundred-dollar-a-plate dinner last night and it was at my home!

• • •

He has figured out how to reduce the deficit and balance the federal budget. All we need to do is close twenty-nine states.

• • •

Parents and teenagers do have something in common. Teenagers listen to rock-and-roll singers and parents listen to economists— and not one of us knows what they are saying.

• • •

The economy is so bad that they're even putting anti-depressants in the Happy Meals at McDonald's.

• • •

The most serious weakness in the economic system as I can see it is that I am not rich.

• • •

Do you think there's any significance to the fact that a group photo of our economic advisors has just been published? It shows them all lined up in punt formation.

• • •

When it comes to changing the lives of millions of people, nothing beats the government's economic program. But the plague came pretty close.

• • •

There would be no economic problems today if the poor would just spend more.

• • •

I spent the weekend reading the economists' forecasts for the next few months. I also read some nonfiction.

• • •

They say that teenagers don't know the value of a dollar. They certainly do! That's why they always ask for ten!

• • •

Edison, Thomas

On this day in history, Thomas Edison invented the phonograph. It was either that or sell his record collection.

• • •

It was Edison who said that genius is 1 percent inspiration and 99 percent perspiration. I don't know about that. I hate to think of anyone with hands that sweaty handling electricity!

• • •

We can be thankful that Edison invented the lightbulb. Why if it wasn't for him, we'd all be watching TV in the dark!

• • •

EDUCATION

Never be proud about how much you know. After all, even a piece of lettuce knows more than you do. It knows if that little light really does go out after the refrigerator door is shut.

• • •

What's all this noise about silent prayer in schools? What do they think happens every time a teacher gives a test or passes out report cards?

• • •

ELECTIONS

Did you ever reflect that (losing candidate) and the earth have a lot in common? You see, the earth is flattened at the poles and so was (name).

• • •

I'll never forget the first time I voted in a presidential election. It was 1960 in Chicago. I'll never forget the second, third and fourth times I voted in a presidential election. It was 1960 in Chicago.

• • •

No one is sure what the election in Pennsylvania means, but the new state flower is hemlock.

• • •

ELEPHANTS

If we had as little on our minds as elephants, we could remember, too!

• • •

What does an elephant do when it is about to charge?
It whips out its American Express card.

• • •

When does an elephant charge?
When he doesn't have the cash.

• • •

A male elephant watching a female elephant going by . . . "Wow a perfect 250 by 210 by 400!"

• • •

Teacher: "Bobby, where are elephants found?"
Bobby: "The elephant, teacher, is such a large animal, it scarcely ever gets lost."

• • •

ETHNICVILLE

Why are there so many Italians named Tony?
When they first came to New York, they had TO N.Y. stamped on their foreheads.

• • •

An Ethnic saw a truck loaded with rolled-up sod going by. He said, "I hope I get rich enough some day so that I can have my lawn sent out to be mowed."

• • •

An Ethnic woman found her husband with a gun next to his head and screamed, "What are you doing?"
He yelled, "Shut up! You're next!"

• • •

How many Ethnics does it take to make chocolate chip cookies? Twenty. One to stir the batter and nineteen to peel the M&M's.

• • •

How do you set up an Ethnic in a small business?
Buy him a big business and wait.

• • •

An Ethnic construction worker walked into a lumber yard and announced, "My boss sent me here to buy some four-by-twos."
The clerk replied, "We only carry two-by-fours."
The worker called his boss, returned to the clerk and said, "The boss says that that'll be okay."
The clerk said, "Now I need to know how long you want 'em."
"Quite awhile, I guess," said the Ethnic. "We're building a house."

• • •

An Ethnic was in a museum when the Magna Carta was touring the United States. The guide said, "It is the source of English freedom and was signed by King John."
A tourist asked, "When did he sign it?"
"1215," replied the guide.
"Wow," said the Ethnic looking at his watch. "It's 12:30 now. I just missed it by fifteen minutes."

• • •

Two Ethnics rented reels, rods, a cabin, boat and wading suits in order to go fishing. They went out three days and caught nothing. On the fourth day, one finally caught a fish.

The one Ethnic said, "Do you realize that that one fish cost us fifteen hundred dollars?"

His partner replied, "Wow, it's a good thing that we didn't catch any more!"

• • •

An Ethnic landscaper was showing a man around the outside of a house. Every two minutes or so, he would poke his head around the corner of the house and say, "Green side up."

After awhile, the customer became curious and said, "What's this 'green side up'?"

The Ethnic boss replied, "I'm just reminding the workers out front how to lay the sod."

• • •

An Ethnic parachutist was plunging rapidly, unable to get his chute open. Suddenly he saw a man flying up toward him.

The skydiver yelled, "Say, do you know anything about parachutes?"

"No," said the sky-born. "Do you know anything about gas stoves?"

• • •

An Ethnic was caught in a power blackout and stood on an escalator for nearly two hours before it got going again.

A friend said, "You dummy! You stood on that escalator for two hours while it was being repaired? Why didn't you sit down?"

• • •

An Ethnic carpenter, working on the third floor of a building accidentally sawed off his ear. He yelled down to his fellow workers, "Did anyone find an ear down there?"

A worker held one up and said, "Is this it?"

"No," said the injured Ethnic, "mine had a pencil behind it."

• • •

He bought his wife a three-hundred-piece dinner set. It was only supposed to be twenty-four, but he slipped on the way home from the store.

• • •

A fellow walked into a coffee shop and said, "I've got the best Ethnic joke you've ever heard."

A patron stopped him and said, "Just wait a minute. I'm an Ethnic, my buddy's an Ethnic, and those two big dudes over there in the corner are Ethnics. Are you sure you want to tell the joke?"

The stranger said, "No, I'll reconsider. I'd hate to have to explain the joke four times."

• • •

The Ethnic College archery team had only one competition. They won the coin toss and elected to receive.

• • •

An Ethnic traveled to Hawaii. When he got off the plane, a cute young lady put a lei around his neck and said, "Aloha from Hawaii." He said, "Glad to meet you. Jaworski from Ethnicville."

• • •

What's the leading cause of missing persons in Ethnicville? Revolving doors.

• • •

What do Ethnics do with their old, outdated clothes?
They wear them.

• • •

Did you hear about the Ethnic Hilton? It has a revolving restaurant in the basement.

• • •

An Ethnic boy wrote his mother from camp, "This summer I've grown a foot." So his mom knitted him another sock.

• • •

At the Ethnicville symphonic concert, the musicians paused to clean the saliva from their instruments. Unfortunately, it was the string section.

• • •

An Ethnic won a gold medal in the Olympics and was so proud of it that he took it right to a shop in Ethnicville and had it bronzed.

• • •

I want to tell this joke. Are there any Ethnics in the audience? (Pause) Oh, there are? In that case, I'll tell it very slowly.

• • •

An Ethnic and his wife won a trip around the world for two, but they turned it down because they wanted to go somewhere else.

• • •

Why don't Ethnics get ten-minute coffee breaks? It takes too long to retrain them.

• • •

An Ethnic went on an elephant hunt and got a hernia carrying the decoys.

• • •

An Ethnic was in the Indy 500 and made seventy pit stops—two for gas, two for tires, and sixty-six to ask directions.

• • •

"We don't have to move to a more expensive apartment after all," the Ethnic told his wife. "The landlord just raised the rent on our apartment!"

• • •

An Ethnic once said, "I'd give my right arm to be ambidextrous."

• • •

An Ethnic was told to go to the end of the line but soon returned. "Why did you come back here? I thought I told you to go to the end of the line!" barked the officer.

"I did," said the Ethnic, "but there was someone already there."

• • •

The Ethnics football team was pitted against their arch rivals from another town. When the five o'clock factory whistle blew, the rivals walked off the field, thinking it was the end of the game. Three plays later, the Ethnic Turkeys scored.

• • •

EXERCISE

His favorite machine at the gym is the vending machine.

• • •

My wife's idea of exercise is to shop faster.

• • •

What has one hundred legs and eats cottage cheese?
My wife's aerobic class.

• • •

Why would anyone invent an exercise machine to simulate an activity that has been rendered obsolete by an elevator?

• • •

This afternoon I phoned to sign up for a fitness class and the instructor told me to wear loose clothing. I said, "Look, if I had any loose-fitting clothing, I wouldn't need the class."

• • •

It's important to remember when exercising, start slowly and then gradually taper off.

• • •

I have a couch at work that I named Nautilus. That way I can honestly tell people that this afternoon I put in two hours on the Nautilus.

• • •

I play golf for the exercise. I asked my caddie, "Do you think I can get there with a 5-iron?"
He said, "Eventually."

• • •

FARMING

Uncle Horace wanted to raise chickens, so he bought five thousand of them. They all died. He figured that he planted them too close together.

• • •

I visited a pig farm and observed a farmer in the orchard, holding his pigs up one by one to graze on apples in the trees. I asked, "Doesn't that take a lot of time?"

He said, "What's time to a pig?"

• • •

FAT

Spotted on a T-shirt worn by a three-hundred-pound man: I Conquered Anorexia.

• • •

A recent poll showed that 62 percent of American people think they are overweight. The other 38 percent didn't answer, which is easy to understand. It's hard to talk when your mouth's full.

• • •

An appetite? I once heard him call out for pizza during the middle of our Thanksgiving dinner!

• • •

As a kid he was too fat to play Little League baseball, so the coach used him to draw the on-deck circle.

• • •

Do you know how to lure him into a room? Grease the doorway and dangle a Twinkie on the other side.

• • •

Doctors removed an obstruction from his throat. It was an entire pizza.

• • •

For years scientists have told us, "You cannot put more into a container than it can hold." They have obviously never seen him in a bathing suit.

• • •

For years people said that he wouldn't amount to much. These are people who have never seen him step on a scale.

• • •

He always asks for two glasses of water with his dinner. One is to drink and the other is to cool off his fork.

• • •

He bought one of those talking scales that was made in Japan, and used it for the first time this morning. It said, "Welcome, honorable Sumo wrestler."

• • •

He complained that people call him fat. I told him, "Don't let it bother you. Just keep a stiff upper chin."

• • •

He does have a slight weight problem. Slight? Twenty more pounds and there'd be a total eclipse of his feet.

• • •

He doesn't get angry if someone calls him fat. He just turns the other chin.

• • •

He had two teeth pulled last week. They weren't decayed. They died of exhaustion.

• • •

He has a weight problem. Who else do you know who has a pork chop hanging from his rearview mirror?

• • •

He holds the distinguished scholar chair at Burger King.

• • •

He joined the neighborhood theater group and played the neighborhood.

• • •

He is on a diet where he goes horseback riding every morning. It's been partially successful. So far his horse has lost twenty-five pounds.

• • •

He is very fat but he has very tiny feet. We figured it out. Things don't grow well in the shade.

• • •

He just picked his burial site—Montana.

• • •

He pulled his chair over to the salad bar, and the manager came over to him and said, "You are welcome to eat all you want, sir, but we insist that you do it at your table."

• • •

He started eating from the six basic food groups. Sorry to say, there are now only two left.

• • •

He tried the uneven parallel bars and straightened them right out.

• • •

He was at Sea World, and when he saw Shamu jump out of the water he asked, "Does he come with vegetables?"

• • •

He was so fat as a kid that he could only play Seek.

• • •

He's so chubby that he has more chins than a Chinese phone book.

• • •

He's so fat he has to clip his toenails by memory.

• • •

He's so fat that he looks like the original mold for the Hula Hoop.

• • •

Here's a little-known fact. On this date in 1968, (large celebrity) turned down seconds.

• • •

He's a do-it-yourself taxidermist. Every night at dinner he stuffs himself.

• • •

He's the kind of guy who puts three lettuce leaves over a pizza and calls it a salad.

• • •

He's the only guy I know who owns a fork with a racing stripe on the handle.

• • •

His idea of a balanced meal is a Big Mac in each hand.

• • •

His parents always wanted twins—but not in the same body!

• • •

I bumped into him downtown the other day. Of course, he was on the other side of the street at the time.

• • •

I have the perfect build for the Oval Office.

• • •

I was so fat that when I had my shoes shined I had to take the guy's word for it.

• • •

Inside of me there is a thin person trying to get out, but I can usually sedate him with five or six doughnuts.

• • •

It's people like him who have made the world what it is today . . . crowded!

• • •

My wife told me to get in shape. I told her, "Round's a shape."

• • •

No man is an island. But (large celebrity) comes pretty close.

• • •

She was a fat ballerina. She had to wear a three-three instead of a tutu.

• • •

There used to be a skinny person inside of me screaming to get out. Now he's fat, too.

• • •

There's a thin man inside him trying to get out—in fact, maybe three or four thin men.

• • •

They named a room in the Capitol after him. It's called the Rotunda.

• • •

You know that you're overweight if you get up from a metal chair and have to fluff it.

• • •

Two tonsils lived in a fat guy's throat. "Where are we?" one asked the other.

"We must be in Capistrano," the other replied, "'cause here comes another swallow."

• • •

He walked into a clothing store and said, "I'd like to see a bathing suit in my size."
The clerk said, "So would I."

• • •

A fat man took his family to the beach. The little boy asked, "Mommy, can I go swimming?"
"Not now, dear," the mother answered. "Daddy's using the ocean."

• • •

He asked his broker, "What should I do about pork bellies?"
His broker replied, "Exercise, man, exercise!"

• • •

He was hospitalized and placed on a strict diet. The office staff sent flowers. He sent them a reply, "Thanks, they were delicious."

• • •

There was a lot of confusion during the snowstorm. I went over to help a fat lady get into a taxicab. After pushing and shoving and slipping on the ice I told her I didn't think I could help her get in.
She said, "In? I was trying to get out!"

• • •

FATHER/SON

I have two recurring dreams about my son. The first has him stretching forth his hand saying, "I am honored to accept the Nobel Prize." The other dream has him saying, "Ya want fries with this, sir?"

• • •

He even coached my Little League team. I really enjoyed it—until he traded me.

• • •

He definitely is the family patriarch. We would say something like, "Dad, next week is Thanksgiving. Is that all right with you?"

• • •

FATHER'S DAY

If you think that you are important, fathers, just remember that fathers are celebrated one day a year and the pickle gets a whole week!

• • •

I don't wish to brag, but in my family I get absolute obedience. For instance, every Father's Day I tell my family not to spend a lot of money on me—and they don't!

• • •

Father's Day is much like Mother's Day, only you get much cheaper gifts.

• • •

FIRE

A woman called the fire department and said, "My house is on fire. Can you come right over here?"
The fire chief said, "Sure, how do we get there?"
The woman replied, "Don't you guys still have that big, red truck?"

• • •

He had a fire in his house and lost all three of his books. The thing that made him mad was that he hadn't finished coloring two of them.

• • •

Our fire company bought a new fire truck. They use the old one to chase false alarms.

• • •

He had a fire at his home and while trying to escape, he ran through a screen door and strained himself.

• • •

Fishing

"I caught a twenty-pound salmon last week."
"Were there any witnesses?"
"There sure were. If there weren't, it would have been forty pounds."

• • •

A fisherman was bragging about a monster of a fish that he caught. A friend broke in and chided, "Yeah, I saw a picture of that fish and it was all of six inches long."
"Yeah," said the proud fisherman, "but after battling for three hours, a fish can lose a lot of weight!"

• • •

I catch deformed fish. The ones I get always have their heads too close to their tails.

• • •

I was glad when one fish got away. There wouldn't have been room in the boat for both of us.

• • •

First fisherman: "I went fishing and caught a 120-pound bluefish."
Second fisherman: "I was fishing from a boat when my line

snagged an old pirate ship. In working my line free, I brought up an old ship's lantern, and the candle was still lit!"

First fisherman: "I'll take a hundred pounds off my bluefish if you blow out that candle!"

• • •

Most fish would be bigger if the fisherman's arms were longer.

• • •

Fishing is simply a matter of timing. All you have to do is get here yesterday when the fish were biting.

• • •

I asked him, "What's the largest fish you've ever caught?"
He answered, "Fourteen inches."
I said, "That's not large."
He replied, "Between the eyes?"

• • •

Scientists tell us that a trout in the water grows one inch per year. However, once it is caught, it grows one inch a day.

• • •

I love seafood. My favorite is saltwater taffy.

• • •

Football

A dog was sitting at a bar watching the football game. The (poor team) kicked a field goal and the dog went into a frenzy. They kicked another and the dog repeated the action.

The bartender said to the owner, "Wow, your dog is some fan. Tell me, what does he do when the (poor team) score a touchdown?"

The owner said, "I don't know. I've only had him for four years."

• • •

A coach was hung in effigy. He remarked, "I'm just glad it happened in front of the library, because I've always stressed academics."

• • •

A referee defines the typical fan as, "A guy who screams from the bleachers because he thinks you missed a call at the center of the interior line, then after the game can't find his car in the parking lot."

• • •

A dazed halfback told the trainer, "We ran the Statue of Liberty play, and I was creamed by the huddled masses."

• • •

There was a scandal at (local university) today. Three of the football players were caught sneaking into the library.

• • •

You know that you're in trouble with the coach when he tells you, "The team bus leaves at 4 P.M. Be under it."

• • •

After a frustrating loss, a coach was asked, "What do you think of your team's execution today?"

"Sounds like a good idea," said the coach. "And the sooner the better."

• • •

Although his team was pitiful, the coach attempted to inspire them. "Look," he said, "if we receive, try your hardest to recover the fumble. And if we kick off, hang in there and try to block their extra point."

• • •

As John Madden used to say, "If you see a defensive line with a lot of dirt on their backs, they've had a bad day."

• • •

Did you hear about the world's dumbest center? They had to stencil on his pants, "This end up." On his shoes they put TGIF: "Toes go in first."

• • •

He has a nagging football injury that he got when he was moving his TV set to try to get the Eagles in better field position.

• • •

He injured himself when the coach told him to go in and run around his own end.

• • •

He knew that his playing days were over as a running back, when every time he tried to run an end sweep, he was penalized for delay of game.

• • •

He will never make the Football Hall of Fame, but there are some guys who will because of him.

• • •

How do you make football jerseys last? Make the pants first.

• • •

I asked a University of Nebraska football player what the "N" stood for on the side of his helmet, and he said, "Knowledge."

• • •

I spent weeks learning the playbook. But it didn't do any good. The groundskeeper forgot to mark those little X's and O's on the field.

• • •

I wanted to play football, but I had a handicap. I was born with a neck.

• • •

He was once a football player. He wasn't a fullback. He wasn't a halfback. He was a drawback.

• • •

He had an aversion to physical contact. When he'd dive into the line on a fake he'd yell, "I don't have it! I don't have it!"

• • •

I once got a letter in football. It was from the coach and it said, "Return your equipment immediately."

• • •

If a man watches three football games in a row on television, he should be declared legally dead.

• • •

My season seats to the Falcons were awful this year. They faced the field.

• • •

My wife says that she just doesn't understand football. She can't see why seventy thousand people would gather in one place for anything, except dollar days at Kmart.

• • •

My wife was complaining to me about football. "How can

twenty-two grown men fight over a funny-shaped ball?"

So, I proceeded to explain it to her in terms she could understand, "Imagine, dear, that that ball is on sale. . . ."

• • •

Our offensive line is so bad that our quarterback signals for a fair catch on the snap.

• • •

Our offensive line is so good that even our backs can't get through it.

• • •

Our team was slaughtered so often that our team nickname became "The Battling Lambs."

• • •

Our team was so bad that during halftime, the band would march into formation and spell the word "HELP."

• • •

Our team was so bad that we won the coin toss and elected to leave!

• • •

Our team was so bad, we had to rent cheerleaders!

• • •

Pro lineman are so huge that it only takes four of them to make a dozen.

• • •

The booster club sent a telegram to the team: "We're behind you 100 percent—win or tie."

• • •

The bus driver slammed on the brakes and said, "Look at that cow with one eye," and all the players covered one eye and looked.

• • •

The coach asked the athletic director if he would still like him if the team went 0–12 next season.

"Oh, sure, I'd like you just the same," said the athletic director, "but I'd sure miss you around here."

• • •

The coach takes all his recruits into the forest to determine what positions they should play. He tells them to run at top speed. The ones that run straight into trees he makes linemen. The ones who run around them become halfbacks.

• • •

The coach was asked why he allowed his star running back to carry the football forty times in one game.

"Why not?" replied the coach. "It doesn't weigh that much!"

• • •

The quarterback said of his teammate, "If it wasn't for the huddles, he wouldn't have any social life at all."

• • •

The winless coach was asked, "Does your team pray before games?"

"No," said the frustrated coach. "We have so many things to pray for, we'd be penalized for delaying the game."

• • •

They use their running game to set up their punting game.

• • •

We had a booster club at the beginning of the season. By the end of the year they were a terrorist group.

• • •

We were a team of losers. We used to hold victory celebrations if we won the coin toss.

• • •

We were in a really tough game. Our quarterback started praying, and we heard a distant voice say, "Please don't include me in this."

• • •

When I played, the cheerleaders would yell, "Pat, Pat, he's our man. If he can't do it, we're not surprised!"

• • •

Wife at perfume counter: "What do you have that will compete with three hours of football on TV?"

• • •

You know that your coaching job is in trouble when the marching band forms a noose at halftime.

• • •

Our football team was so bad, our homecoming was scheduled as an away game.

• • •

The team finally found a way to gain yardage. They run their game films backwards.

• • •

The football coach begged the college math professor to give his star player a makeup test. The professor agreed. The coach anxiously asked, "How did Jones do?"

"I'm sorry," said the prof. "It's hopeless. Look, he wrote '7 times 5 equals 33.'"

"Give him a break," said the coach, "he only missed by one."

• • •

"Hey, Helen," said a husband with his hand on the TV knob, "do you have anything to say before football season starts?"

• • •

We were tipping off our plays. Whenever we broke from the huddle, three backs were giggling and the other was white as a sheet.

• • •

He left his coaching job because of illness and fatigue. The fans were sick and tired of him.

• • •

One college has gotten so strict academically that it won't even give a football player his letter unless he can tell which one it is.

• • •

They recently televised a football game without announcers. Now my wife wants them to do that on radio, too.

• • •

The annual football game was held between the big animals and the little animals. The big animals led 75–0 at halftime. At the start of the second half, a centipede made three consecutive sacks on an elephant. Time out! In the huddle they asked the centipede, "Where were you in the first half?"

He said, "Oh, I was in the locker room getting my ankles taped!"

• • •

One of our neighbors is making interesting plans for the future. She says when her husband dies, she's not going to have him buried. I said, "What are you going to do?"

She said, "I'm going to have him stuffed and mounted and put on the living room couch. Then I'll turn on the TV to a football game, talk to him and he won't answer. It'll be just like he never left."

• • •

One of our linebackers can do anything with a football except autograph it.

• • •

The football captain gave his teammates a pep talk. "Today, Coach Schmidt is fifty-six. Let's go out on that field and give him something to remember on his birthday!" And they did. They went out on that field and were beaten fifty-six to nothing.

• • •

An incensed coach ran out on the field and yelled at the referee, "You stink." Whereupon the referee paced off an additional fifteen yards, looked back at the coach and said, "Okay, how do I smell from here?"

• • •

A Czech place kicker was asked to read the bottom line of an eye chart. "Read it?" he said. "I know him!"

• • •

We drafted a 5'3", 130-pound fullback, and he's having a great year. That's the exact size hole our offensive line opens up.

• • •

How do (losing football team's) fans learn to count to ten? 0–1, 0–2, 0–3, 0–4 . . .

• • •

Garden

I just bought that book called *Gardening for Beginners*. Real beginners. For instance, the chapter on lawns says that if you're planting sod—the green side goes up.

• • •

I call my vegetable garden The Garden of Weedin.

• • •

I don't have what you would call a green thumb. For instance, I have a rock garden, and last week four of them died.

• • •

My garden didn't turn out exactly as I had hoped. I didn't even know that you could raise cocktail-sized cantaloupes.

• • •

I'm not bragging, but my garden looks like a picture postcard—from the Sahara Desert!

• • •

When it comes to his lawn, he's a perfectionist. Every blade of grass is exactly two feet high.

• • •

This winter I discovered something that will make my front lawn look as good as my neighbor's—a huge snowfall!

• • •

This year I'm trying a new strategy with my lawn. I'm planting the weeds first in hopes that the grass will take over.

• • •

Nothing discourages an amateur gardener like watching the family eat his entire garden at one meal.

• • •

Girls

My girl had unusual eyes. She could watch an entire tennis match without moving her head.

• • •

One girl I know stopped playing Frisbee. She had to. It was ruining her teeth.

• • •

She's so skinny that in ballet class she couldn't wear a tutu. She had to wear a one-one.

• • •

She's bow-legged and he's knock-kneed. When they stand together in bathing suits they spell OX.

• • •

She had such affectionate eyes, they kept looking at each other.

• • •

She was so ugly that when I took her to the beach the tide refused to come in.

• • •

She had such buck teeth that she could eat an apple through my catcher's mask.

• • •

She's the only woman I know who can wear a form-fitting poncho.

• • •

Golf

He doesn't rent a golf cart. He doesn't need one. Where he hits the ball, he can use public transportation.

• • •

A handicapped golfer is one who plays his boss.

• • •

He asked the caddie, "What do you think of my game?"
He said, "It's okay, but I like golf better."

• • •

He's too fat to play. If he places the ball where he can hit it, he can't see it. If he places it where he can see it, he can't hit it.

• • •

"Did you drive from the fifteenth tee an hour ago?" an officer asked a golfer.

"Yes, I did," answered the puzzled golfer.

"Well," said the policeman, "your ball sailed out onto the fairway and cracked the windshield of a woman's car. She couldn't see where she was going and rammed into a fire truck which was on its way to a fire. As a result, a house burned down. What are you going to do about it?"

The golfer thought a minute, picked up his driver and said, "Well, I'm going to open up my stance a little and move my thumb around farther toward my right side. . . ."

• • •

Our guest of honor likes to be alone in the woods, go places where few have gone before and face challenges that are seemingly impossible. Unfortunately, he does all this in a golf cart.

• • •

As one of his retirement gifts, we wanted to get him something that he could use playing golf. But then we found out he already has a calculator.

• • •

As if life doesn't have enough heartaches, frustrations and despair; and then someone had to go and invent golf!

• • •

Do you like to meet new people? Then just pick up the wrong golf ball.

• • •

Golf tip: Never bet with a guy who you meet on the first tee who has a deep tan, a 1-iron in his bag and squinty eyes.

• • •

He cut ten strokes off his golf score. He didn't play the last hole.

• • •

His game improves during Daylight Savings Time. He has more time to hunt for his ball.

• • •

He's the only golfer I know who can play four courses simultaneously.

• • •

I don't cheat. I play golf for my health, and you see, a low score makes me feel better.

• • •

I was three-over today. One over a house, one over a patio and one over a swimming pool.

• • •

I whacked a ball 350 yards yesterday. Unfortunately I was playing tennis at the time.

● ● ●

If I'm ever stranded in the desert and need water, it's no problem.
I'll just tee up a golf ball and let 'er rip. The result is guaranteed.

● ● ●

Ladies, if your husband comes home with sand in his cuffs and
cockleburs on his pants, don't ask him what he shot.

● ● ●

The chief flaw in my game is that I stand too close to the ball
after I hit it.

● ● ●

A golfer sliced a ball onto the highway, then hooked another into
the woods, followed by a drive that landed in a lake.
"Why don't you use an old ball?" his partner asked.
"I never had an old ball," the duffer replied.

● ● ●

I had a tough round yesterday. I lost four balls. Three in the ball
washer.

● ● ●

"I've got good news and bad news," the caddie told the golfer.
"The good news is that you got a birdie on the sixth hole. The bad
news is you're playing the fifth!"

● ● ●

I worked as a caddie at a country club and they had a great
employee health plan. Every Wednesday you'd get to see the doctor.

● ● ●

When he goes golfing with the boss, he goes a little too far. This morning they were playing and the boss hit into a sand trap two hundred feet from the green and he conceded the putt.

• • •

He lost only two golf balls last year. He was putting at the time.

• • •

The golfer, whacking his way through some terribly high weeds, complained, "This is a terrible course."

The caddie replied, "No, it isn't. We left the course two or three miles back."

• • •

He has a beautiful short game. Unfortunately it's off the tee.

• • •

I used to watch golf on TV until my doctor told me I needed more exercise. So now I watch tennis.

• • •

This summer I discovered something that took ten strokes off my game. It's called an eraser.

• • •

The doctor who golfs has one great advantage over the rest of us. Nobody can read his scorecard.

• • •

A golfer drove an errant shot off the course and into a pigpen, killing one of the pigs.

An irate farmer blasted the golfer up and down until the golfer said, "Okay, I'll replace your pig."

"You ain't fat enough!" screamed the farmer.

• • •

He said to his caddie, "I bet there are thousands of people who are a lot worse at golf than I am."

The caddie said, "Sure, but they don't play."

• • •

I play with a golfer who is so accustomed to shaving his score, that once he got a hole-in-one and carded a zero.

• • •

Remember, golf is "flog" spelled backwards.

• • •

The golf pro wants me to keep my head down so I can't see him laughing.

• • •

My wife said, "You're so wrapped up in golf you don't even remember our wedding day!"

"Sure I do," I said. "That's the day I sank that thirty-foot putt!"

• • •

When he golfs, he always takes along two caddies because he always has to send one back for laughing too loudly.

• • •

The way some people play golf, the green flags at the hole should always be at half mast.

• • •

I'm not saying his game is bad, but if he grew tomatoes, they'd come up sliced.

• • •

I asked the golf pro how I could get greater distance on my drive. He said, "Simple. Just hit the ball and jump backwards."

• • •

His opponent placed the ball on the tee and took a wild swing, missing the ball badly.

The flustered guy said, "Wow, it's a good thing I discovered early in the game that this course is at least two inches lower than the one I normally play."

• • •

"How should I play this putt, caddie?"

"Try to keep it low, sir."

• • •

The golf pro walked over to two women and asked, "Are you here to learn how to play golf?"

One replied, "My friend is. I learned yesterday."

• • •

The position of your hands is very important when playing golf. I use mine to cover up my scorecard.

• • •

I took golf lessons yesterday, and I did really well. In just one lesson I was throwing my clubs as well as guys who have been playing for years!

• • •

I hit the ball so deep into the woods, I got to meet Bambi.

• • •

Shoot his age? He can't even shoot his Social Security number!

• • •

I went golfing yesterday and lost a brand-new ball on the sixth hole. I asked the caddie, "Why didn't you watch where it went?"

He said, "Sorry, sir, you just caught me by surprise when you hit it on the first swing."

• • •

Golf: A long walk, interspersed with frustration and creative arithmetic.

• • •

New book: *How to Line Up Your Fifth Putt.*

• • •

The season is upon us when we golfers must explain to our wives that we're too tired to dig up the garden, but not too tired to dig up the fairway.

• • •

He's the only guy I know who putts and yells, "Fore!"

• • •

Golfers are always complaining. One I know got a hole-in-one and moaned, "Great! Just when I needed the practice!"

• • •

He spends a lot of time in the rough. In fact, his favorite club is a wedge with a sickle attached to it.

• • •

Golfer: "This is terrible. I've never played this badly before."
Caddie: "Oh, then you have played before?"

• • •

With club memberships, the price of golf balls, clubs, greens fees, cart rentals and other accessories, isn't it ironic that golf was invented in Scotland?

• • •

One of my goals in life is to get a hole-in-one. And I'm getting there. Just yesterday I got a double-bogey.

• • •

He has benefited from playing golf. His golf game has made him an expert in the field of wilderness survival.

• • •

In New Guinea some of the tribes have the custom of beating the ground with clubs and uttering spine-chilling cries anthropologists call "primitive self-expression."
In America, we call it golf.

• • •

An aging friend said that he's given up trying to shoot his age on the golf course. Now he'll settle for his area code.

• • •

I did well on my golf outing yesterday. I got to hit the ball more than anyone else.

• • •

Golf doesn't have a fitness incentive in it. The better you get at it, the less exercise you get.

• • •

I have two handicaps—my woods and my irons.

• • •

The doctor told a patient, "You look worn out, Ed. I suggest you lay off golf and spend a few days in your office."

• • •

My eighty-five-year-old friend likes to golf, but he can't see where he hits the ball. So, he takes his eighty-four-year-old friend, Sam, along who can't golf, but his eyesight is perfect.

Bob tees off. "Did you see where the ball went, Sam?"

"Exactly," replied Sam.

"Where is it?" asked Bob.

"I forget," answered Sam.

• • •

He was a cheerleader for the golf team. His job was to walk around going, "Sh-Sh."

• • •

A girl dressed in a white wedding gown rushed toward the first tee, confronting a guy ready to tee off. The golfer turned toward her angrily and said, "I told you—only if it rains!"

• • •

A golfer looking over a 250-yard hole tells his companion, "I'm going to take this hole in two shots." He tees off and knocks the ball twenty yards. "Now," he continues, "you will witness the longest putt in history."

• • •

Golf partners were playing the sixteenth hole when a funeral procession passed. One took off his cap, placed it over his heart for thirty seconds, and resumed his putting stance. "We'd have been married twenty-five years today," he said.

• • •

Golfer: "You must be the worst caddie in the world!"
Caddie: "No, sir. That would be too much of a coincidence!"

• • •

Teacher: Remember what happens to boys who use bad language when they play marbles.
Boy: Yep, teacher, they grow up to play golf.

• • •

He does things first class. I played golf with him Tuesday, and he used suede golf balls!

• • •

"Why don't you play golf with George anymore?"
"Would you play with someone who puts down the wrong score and moves the ball when you're not watching? Neither will George."

• • •

My wife ran over my golf clubs with the car, although she did tell me not to leave them on the front porch.

• • •

GRADUATION

Commencement speaker's dilemma: "How can I tell the graduates that the future is in their hands without alarming the rest of the audience?"

• • •

Three essentials for graduation are: (1) a cap, (2) a gown and (3) ear plugs so you don't have to listen to the commencement speech.

• • •

During the graduation ceremony I helped five handicapped students by reading the commencement program to them. Two were blind and three were football players.

• • •

GRANDCHILDREN

We don't make a big deal about our grandchildren. They're only two and four years old. The surgeon is two and the Most Valuable Player is four.

• • •

How is it that the boy who wasn't good enough to marry your daughter is the father of the brightest grandchild in the whole world?

• • •

GROUNDHOG DAY

What's the difference between a groundhog and the TV weatherman?
The groundhog can make a forecast without all that hair spray.

• • •

Halloween

Halloween is the night when all the ghouls and creepy creatures come out. It's like working the nightshift at 7-11.

• • •

Last Halloween I put an "Out of Order" sign around my neck and went to a party as a pay phone.

• • •

Happiness

Happiness is having a large loving, caring, close-knit family; especially if they live in another city.

• • •

Health/Health Foods

I tried a new brand of aspirin today and nearly choked to death. The first one that came out was so big and fuzzy that I could hardly swallow it.

• • •

I went to one of those health-food restaurants and was amazed. Even the flies were doing pushups.

• • •

Pharmacist to patient: "Take one of these every three hours or as often as you can get the cap off."

• • •

There's so much hype about natural foods. The ancient Greeks ate natural foods, and where are they today? They're all dead!

• • •

History

My son failed history so I told him, "When I was your age, history was my best subject."

He said, "Big deal. When you were my age, what had happened?"

• • •

Hockey

Reporter to player: "Did you ever break your nose?"

Player: "No, but eleven other players did!"

• • •

A hockey player was asked, "How many accidents have you had in your career?"

The player responded, "None. Oh, sure, I've had two concussions, lost all my front teeth, have had my nose broken four times, but they weren't accidents. The opponents did it on purpose."

• • •

Hockey players have been complaining about violence for years. It's just that without any teeth, no one can understand them.

• • •

I knew that it was going to be a wild game when a fight broke out in the middle of the National Anthem.

• • •

I think hockey is a great game. Of course, I have a son who's a dentist.

• • •

I've created an invention that will revolutionize hockey and make it the wildest game on earth. It's a clear, Lucite hockey puck.

• • •

I took my kid to the fights the other night. It was the first time he had ever seen ice hockey.

• • •

I went to the fights the other night and a hockey game broke out.

• • •

They say there are three ways to play hockey: rough, rougher, and, "I'll help you find your teeth if you help me find mine."

• • •

The dentist complimented the hockey player on his nice, even teeth . . . one, three, five, seven, nine and eleven were missing.

• • •

In hockey you take a stick and hit either the puck or anyone who has touched the puck.

• • •

I don't know much about hockey. The coach gave me a puck and I spent the rest of the day trying to open it.

• • •

Homes

A housing development is a place where they chop down trees and then they name the streets after them.

• • •

I bought a two-story house. The real estate agent gave me one story before I bought it, and another one after.

• • •

I got a great deal on a little summer cottage. However, the first morning I was there people kept dropping rolls of film through the front window.

• • •

It's really easy to keep your home clean. Step number one: Put the children up for adoption.

• • •

My wife and I finally located a house that we can afford. Now if we can just get it down out of the tree. . . .

• • •

Statistics show that the average American home now has three things that have all the answers: a computer, an encyclopedia and a teenager.

• • •

What luck! He was digging in the backyard and he struck oil! Of course the gas station next door made him pay for the damage he did to their pipes.

• • •

My house is really cold. They say that M&M's don't melt in your hand. Big deal. In my house, neither do ice cubes!

• • •

Horses

"Bob, I can't understand how Bill can have so much luck at cards and be so unlucky with horses."

"That's easy," said Bob. "You can't shuffle the horses."

• • •

His horse lost the race, and the owner was irate. "I thought I told you to come with a rush at the end," he screamed at the jockey.

"I would have," answered the jockey, "but I didn't want to leave the horse behind."

• • •

A passerby stopped in a blacksmith shop and picked up a red-hot horseshoe that the smithy had placed on the floor to cool. The visitor quickly dropped the shoe.

"Pretty hot, huh?" said the blacksmith.

"No, it just doesn't take me that long to inspect a horseshoe," replied the stranger.

• • •

Before he goes to the track, he always talks to people who know horse flesh—the trainers, the jockey, his butcher.

• • •

He bet on a horse that had a photo finish with the truck that watered the track.

• • •

He bet on a horse that had excellent breeding. After the horse left the starting gate, he turned around to close it behind him.

• • •

He's been playing the horses for a long time. As a kid, he was the only one on the merry-go-round with a racing form.

• • •

His horse came in so late that the jockey was wearing pajamas.

• • •

I bought a horse. In its first race it went out 25-to-1. The only problem is that all the other horses left at 12:30.

• • •

It would have been a photo finish, but by the time my horse finished, it was too dark to take a picture.

• • •

My horse could have won the race, but he kept looking back for his plow.

• • •

My horse was right up there with the winning horse when the race started.

• • •

My horse was so slow that the jockey got paid time-and-a-half for overtime.

• • •

That horse was so slow that even the glue he'll eventually make won't dry quickly.

• • •

Racetrack: a place where windows clean people.

• • •

Roses are red. / Violets are blue. / Horses that lose. / Are made into glue.

• • •

That horse is so slow that the post office should buy him.

• • •

If Paul Revere had ridden this horse, we'd still be under British rule.

• • •

Two bookies were coming out of church and one said to the other, "How many times have I told you it's 'hallelujah' and not 'Hialeah'!"

• • •

The horse I bet on was so slow that he kept a diary of the trip.

• • •

Do you know how you can make a horse stand still?
Place a bet on him.

• • •

The next time that horse will run will be from a bottle of glue.

• • •

HOSPITALS

Things you don't want to hear during surgery:

- Wait a minute, if this is his spleen, what's that?
- Ya know, there's big money in kidneys, and this guy has two of them.
- Don't worry. I think it's sharp enough.

• • •

I went into the hospital last week to donate blood. On the couch directly across from me was an Apache Indian. I looked over and inquired, "Are you a full-blooded Apache?"

He answered, "I was. Now I'm a pint short."

• • •

He had heart surgery and had a turtle's heart implanted. Five days after he left the hospital, he got to his car.

• • •

Never leave a hospital until you are strong enough to face the cashier.

• • •

Never put your trust in an infectious disease specialist who is always scratching.

• • •

The colder the X-ray table, the more of your body you are told to put on it.

• • •

The first thing that you discover during a hospital stay is that you are not fully covered by your insurance or your gown.

• • •

Think twice before checking into a hospital where all the nurses wear uniforms made by Gucci.

• • •

Hotels

A tourist returned to the hotel lobby and said to the desk clerk, "Excuse me. I'm so very forgetful. Will you tell me what room I'm in?"
"Certainly," said the clerk. "You are in the lobby."

• • •

"What was the name of that hotel in San Francisco that we loved so much?"
"I don't remember. Let me go and check the towels."

• • •

I recently stayed at the Hotel Amway. The only problem was that before I could check out, I had to check two people in.

• • •

The hotel wasn't well managed. In the picture postcard of the hotel room, the beds weren't even made.

• • •

Want to get fast action in a hotel the next time the clerk tells you your room isn't ready? Unpack in the lobby, slip into your pajamas and ask the desk clerk to read you a story.

• • •

I stayed in such an exclusive hotel that room service had an unlisted number.

• • •

The clerk asked, "Would you like a room with a tub or a shower?"
He said, "What's the difference?"
"Well," said the clerk, "with a tub, you sit down."

• • •

A tip-weary tourist heard a knock at his door. "A fax, sir." Not wanting to have to tip again, the hotel guest said, "Please slip it under the door."

"I can't," was the reply.

"Why not?" asked the guest.

"Because it's on a tray."

• • •

How You Know It's Going To Be a Bad Day

- You see a *60 Minutes* news team waiting in your office.
- Your birthday cake collapses from the weight of the candles.
- Your twin sister forgets your birthday.
- Your car horn accidentally sticks when you are following a motorcycle gang on the freeway.
- Your artificial flower dies.
- The *Good Humor* man yells at you.
- Your swimming pool burns down.
- Your mother-in-law shows up at your house with six suitcases and a burial deed.
- You're in an airplane and the Goodyear blimp is gaining on you.
- You get a nasty paper cut from a get-well card.
- You come out of your memory-improvement class and forget where you parked your car.

• • •

Hunting

A hunting foursome paired off. Late at night, one returned dragging an eight-point buck.

"Where's Bill?" inquired the other two.

"He had a heart attack a couple miles back up the trail."

"You mean you left Bill to drag the deer back here?"

"Yeah. It was a tough decision, but I figured that nobody would steal Bill."

• • •

A hunter was boring his guests with tales of his safari. Pointing to a tiger rug, he related, "It was either him or me."

"It was a good thing it was the tiger, Bob," said an acquaintance. "You would've made a lousy rug."

• • •

A motorist ran over the hunter's favorite coon hound. He went to the hunter's house and told the hunter's wife what happened. She said, "He's out in the field, so you'd better tell him. But break it to him gently. First tell him it was me."

• • •

I'll never go moose hunting again. I didn't mind carrying the big gun, but the two-hundred-pound decoy was a real drag.

• • •

He's a deer hunter but none of them ever became aware of it.

• • •

A guy was out hunting, came to a fork in the road and read a sign which said, "Bear left." So he went home.

• • •

A group of hunters fully equipped with rifles, ammo and camping supplies came upon a young boy armed only with a slingshot.

"What are you hunting for?" asked an older hunter.

"I don't know. I ain't seen it yet," said the boy.

• • •

First hunter: "We've been here all day and haven't bagged a thing."

Second hunter: "Yeah, let's miss two more each and then head on home."

• • •

A greenhorn was telling his buddy what a great hunter he was. When they arrived at their cabin, the greenhorn said, "You get the fire started and I'll go shoot us something for supper."

After a few minutes, the greenhorn met a grizzly bear. He dropped his gun, headed for the cabin, with the bear in hot pursuit. When he was a few feet away from the cabin, the greenhorn tripped over a log. The bear couldn't stop and skidded through the open cabin door.

The greenhorn got up, slammed the door and yelled to his friend inside, "You skin that one, and I'll go get us another one!"

• • •

IMPOSSIBLE

The next time someone tells you that nothing is impossible, get them to try eating an ice cream cone from the bottom up!

• • •

The person who said "Nothing is impossible" never tried to barbecue pancakes.

• • •

The next time someone tries to tell you that nothing is impossible, try to get him to put his skis over his shoulder and go through a revolving door.

• • •

The next time someone says to you, "Nothing's impossible . . . ," tell him, "Go dribble a football."

• • •

Those who say nothing is impossible have never tried to get bubblegum out of an angora sweater, tried to slam a revolving door or tried to get off Jerry Falwell's mailing list.

• • •

Whoever said "Nothing is impossible" never attempted to twirl a baton in a mobile home, or to pick up a bald-headed man by the hair.

• • •

INSURANCE

His agent told him, "Yes, your policy does cover your falling off the roof, but it doesn't cover your hitting the ground."

• • •

I have a group policy that pays off if I die in a group.

• • •

I have a very dependable insurance company. In the twenty years I have been insured, they have never missed sending me a bill for my premium payment.

• • •

I have an old-age policy. When I reach ninety, they give me fifty dollars a week so I don't have to be a burden on my parents.

• • •

I have extensive earthquake and fire policies on my home. I call them my Shake 'n' Bake policies.

• • •

I have some retirement policy. If I pay my premiums faithfully, in ten years my insurance man can retire.

• • •

In the early days of our country, Patrick Henry said, "Give me liberty, or give me death." Nathan Hale said, "I regret that I have but one life to give for my country," and John Hancock said, "Have I got a policy for you!"

• • •

There are worse things in life than death. Have you ever spent an entire evening with an insurance salesman?

• • •

We have a great insurance policy at work. Have you read it? The benefit is that if we die, our families no longer have to pay the premiums.

• • •

My fire and theft insurance only pays me if I'm robbed while my house is burning.

• • •

My insurance company has a catchy slogan: "Long after you're gone, we'll still be here."

• • •

INTRODUCTIONS

And now a man who wears his heart on his sleeve, and spaghetti sauce on his tie . . .

• • •

And now, I introduce a man who has seen it all, but has understood very little of it. . . .

• • •

And now, I introduce a man who is clever and witty, and I could go on and on, except I'm having a terrible time reading his handwriting.

• • •

And now, a man who has made anonymity a household name . . .

• • •

Before we introduce our next speaker, let me remind you that no one is perfect.

• • •

Character. Integrity. Principle. People want to know why he hasn't run for public office. I just told you.

• • •

Frankly, I could stand up here for an hour and talk about our next speaker's accomplishments—but only if I talked really, really slow.

• • •

He won an award for the best business idea of 1952. He won that in 1988.

• • •

Here is a man who is ahead of his time, but let's not make a big deal over three or four minutes.

• • •

Here's a man who has done more for banquet audiences than the *Titanic* did for the winter cruise business.

• • •

Just last week he hosted a telethon for ingrown toenails. All the spectacular diseases had already been taken.

• • •

Remember, folks, I just introduce them. I don't guarantee them.

• • •

Throughout his many years, he has always taken the road less traveled. Some say it's because he's independent, creative and adventurous. His wife says it's because he never asks for directions.

• • •

On the way to the program tonight, I was stopped for speeding. I begged the officer to give me a warning. So he fired three shots over my head.

• • •

I saw a sad thing on the way to the banquet. A man locked his keys in the car and was working like crazy with a coat hanger trying to get his family out.

• • •

The program director wasn't exactly sure how I'd do tonight. When I asked him the size of the room he said, "It sleeps five hundred."

• • •

I'm glad to be here. I followed the toastmaster's instructions but I got here anyway.

• • •

Our next speaker is with the city. His brother doesn't work either.

• • •

Flattering introductions are like berths in the NBA playoffs. Everybody gets one.

• • •

He was nervous when I told him he had to speak tonight.
He said, "What if they boo me?"
I said, "Don't be silly! People can't boo and yawn at the same time."

• • •

He's done so many wonderful things in such a brief time, it's hard to exaggerate his accomplishments . . . but I'll do my best.

• • •

He's been voted one of the finest minds in (give location), which is a lot like being named to the ten best-dressed list in Russia.

• • •

READER/CUSTOMER CARE SURVEY

We care about your opinions! Please take a moment to fill out our online Reader Survey at **http://survey.hcibooks.com**. As a **"THANK YOU"** you will receive a **VALUABLE INSTANT COUPON** towards future book purchases as well as a **SPECIAL GIFT** available only online! Or, you may mail this card back to us and we will send you a copy of our exciting catalog with your valuable coupon inside.

(PLEASE PRINT IN ALL CAPS)

First Name _____ MI. _____ Last Name _____

Address _____

State _____ Zip _____ City _____ Email _____

1. Gender
□ Female   □ Male

2. Age
□ 8 or younger
□ 9-12   □ 13-16
□ 17-20   □ 21-30
□ 31+

3. Did you receive this book as a gift?
□ Yes   □ No

4. Annual Household Income
□ under $25,000
□ $25,000 - $34,999
□ $35,000 - $49,999
□ $50,000 - $74,999
□ over $75,000

5. What are the ages of the children living in your house?
□ 0 - 14   □ 15+

6. Marital Status
□ Single
□ Married
□ Divorced
□ Widowed

7. How did you find out about the book?
(please choose one)
□ Recommendation
□ Store Display
□ Online
□ Catalog/Mailing
□ Interview/Review

8. Where do you usually buy books?
(please choose one)
□ Bookstore
□ Online
□ Book Club/Mail Order
□ Price Club (Sam's Club, Costco's, etc.)
□ Retail Store (Target, Wal-Mart, etc.)

9. What subject do you enjoy reading about the most?
(please choose one)
□ Parenting/Family
□ Relationships
□ Recovery/Addictions
□ Health/Nutrition
□ Christianity
□ Spirituality/Inspiration
□ Business Self-help
□ Women's Issues
□ Sports

10. What attracts you most to a book?
(please choose one)
□ Title
□ Cover Design
□ Author
□ Content

TAPE IN MIDDLE; DO NOT STAPLE

BUSINESS REPLY MAIL
FIRST-CLASS MAIL PERMIT NO 45 DEERFIELD BEACH, FL

POSTAGE WILL BE PAID BY ADDRESSEE

Health Communications, Inc.
3201 SW 15th Street
Deerfield Beach FL 33442-9875

FOLD HERE

Comments

Our next speaker is very active in church . . . he squirms and fidgets and wiggles.

• • •

Here's a man who's world famous in certain parts of the country.

• • •

I just returned from a pleasure trip. I took my mother-in-law to the airport.

• • •

Coming up next is a man who needs no introduction. However, he insists upon it.

• • •

(when the microphone doesn't work) Aren't you glad this sound man doesn't make pacemakers?

• • •

(after a series of jokes) Are there any questions about the material we've covered thus far?

• • •

I used to have trouble remembering names until I took that great Sam Carnegie course.

• • •

He needs no introduction. What he needs is a conclusion.

• • •

I have been told that the mind cannot absorb any more than the seat can tolerate.

• • •

That's what I call a Burger King introduction. One whopper after another.

• • •

It's always a pleasure to speak to a group so sincerely dedicated to limiting the growth of the money supply, a dedication I first became aware of when I discussed my fee.

• • •

In introducing our treasurer, the good news is—he's as honest as the day is long. The bad news is that for the last five years, he's been working the night shift.

• • •

The purpose of hosting a children's party is to remind you that there are children who are worse behaved than your own.

• • •

I'd like to introduce one of the foremost jugglers of our time— our treasurer!

• • •

For dinner this evening we may have had the margarine as a butter substitute, and Sweet'n Low as a sugar substitute, and Cremora as a cream substitute—but our speaker tonight is the real thing!

• • •

Excuse me if I appear nervous here tonight. You see, I'm with the (poor ball club) and I'm not used to seeing this many people gathered together at one time.

• • •

(following a lengthy intro) First, let me thank you for adding something to this program. About ten minutes.

• • •

Thank you for those fine opening comments. I'm sure your thoughts, like tonight's dinner, will stay with us for a long time.

• • •

Our speaker can point to many amazing accomplishments in his lifetime. Unfortunately, none of them were his.

• • •

Rule number two in public speaking: After a very flattering introduction, never tell the audience you don't deserve it. They'll find out soon enough.

• • •

INVENTIONS

Always be on the lookout for new ideas. Why, the guy who invented spray paint got the idea when he sneezed while he was drinking his tomato juice.

• • •

I crossed my TV with a microwave oven, and now I can watch *60 Minutes* in eight and a half.

• • •

It was Alexander Graham Bell who invented the telephone, but it was the teenager who invented the busy signal.

• • •

Why do people think that Marconi, the inventor of the radio, was so smart? He invented it when there weren't even any stations to listen to!

• • •

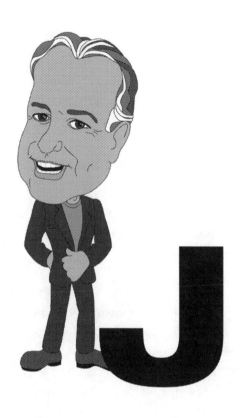

Jobs

He used to work for the unemployment office and hated it. When they fired him, he still had to show up the next day.

• • •

He's a nonskilled worker. He's a tollbooth collector in an exact change lane.

• • •

My wife says I talk in my sleep. But I'm skeptical. Nobody at work has ever mentioned it.

• • •

Our teenager lost his first job. The boss told him to report to work at eight o'clock, and our son didn't know that there were two eight o'clocks.

• • •

An ocean liner captain had a ritual for thirty years. Every morning he would start his day by going to his desk drawer, unlocking it, reading a slip of paper, then closing the drawer.

When he retired, his assistant, who had been observing this practice for years, went to the captain's drawer, unlocked it and pulled out the slip of paper. On it was written, "Port left, starboard right."

• • •

During the war he was with the Dutch underground. He collected tolls at the Holland Tunnel.

• • •

He is deeply involved with Denmark and Brazil in his work. He's responsible for bringing the boss his Danish and coffee.

• • •

He took an aptitude test at work the other day and found out that he was best suited for retirement.

• • •

I'd quit my job in a minute if it wasn't for those folks in the community to whom I owe so much . . . the orthodontist, the doctor, the plumber, the TV repairman. . . .

• • •

If you think that your job is boring, how would you like to be a proofreader in a printing shop that produces insurance policies?

• • •

The closest most people come to perfection is on an employment application.

• • •

I wanted to be a policeman, but discovered I was allergic to doughnuts.

• • •

He had to quit his last job due to illness and fatigue. The boss was sick and tired of him.

• • •

When she came to the bottom line of the application where it says "Sign Here," she wrote "Pisces."

• • •

One day I came home from work all excited and told my wife I had been named vice-president of the company. She was busy cooking dinner and replied curtly, "Vice-president. That's a big deal. A really big deal. Why, at the supermarket I shop at, they have a vice-president in charge of prunes."

I couldn't believe this, so I called the store and asked to speak to the vice-president in charge of prunes.

The voice on the other end said, "Packaged or bulk?"

• • •

JOGGING

He started jogging in the army, only then it was called desertion.

• • •

My doctor informed me that jogging could add years to my life. He's right. I feel fifteen years older already.

• • •

Who needs jogging? If I want to increase my pulse rate for twenty minutes all I need do is open my wife's MasterCard bill.

• • •

I went jogging and I was arrested for loitering.

• • •

"My brother has run ten miles a day since he was ten years old."
"He must be in great shape."
"I don't really know. He's twenty-five hundred miles away."

• • •

Before resolving to jog five miles a day, visit a cardiologist to have your heart examined, a podiatrist to have your feet examined and a psychiatrist to have your head examined.

• • •

Did you notice that people who jog in ninety-degree weather are never properly dressed for it? They should be wearing straitjackets!

• • •

I belong to Joggers Anonymous. When the urge to jog hits me, I call an associate who comes over with a pizza and a chocolate sundae and he stays until the urge passes.

• • •

If speed kills, his jogging should keep him alive forever.

• • •

If you think that fishermen are the biggest liars in the world, just ask a jogger how many miles a day he runs.

• • •

It's embarrassing. I went out for my morning run and a neighbor kid asked me if he could walk along with me.

• • •

My wife bought me a self-motivation tape that helps me when I'm jogging. It's the sound of six hungry Dobermans barking.

• • •

People who run ten miles a day with sore feet, strained muscles and a burning chest do so because they say it feels good. Those people will lie about other things, too.

• • •

The first time I see a jogger smile, I'll consider taking it up.

• • •

The reason I jog is, I just want to have a stomach that stops when I do.

• • •

I was to go out jogging this morning, but I strained my back putting on my sneakers.

• • •

Kids

Remember that as a teenager you are in the last stage of your life when you'll be happy to hear that the phone is for you.

• • •

My mother had an acute sense of hearing. She could hear a cotton ball falling on a piece of felt from fifty feet away.

• • •

Why did Abraham take Isaac to be sacrificed when he was twelve years old?
Because if he were a teenager, it wouldn't have been a sacrifice.

• • •

"I got up early to eat something before I had to use my manners."

• • •

"What's it like to raise a teenager?"
"Multiply the terrible two's by eight and add a driver's license."

• • •

We child-proofed our home, but somehow they get in anyway.

• • •

If you're having a bad day, with headaches and lots of tension, follow the advice found on an aspirin bottle: "Take two" and "Keep away from children."

• • •

Remember, kids, always share your sleds with friends. You take the sleds downhill, let the friends take them up.

• • •

Today's kids have everything. My son has his own TV, VCR, DVD, CD player, cell phone, and refrigerator in his room. When I punish him, I have to send him to my room.

• • •

There's the ongoing debate as to when life begins. In my opinion, life begins when the kids go off to college and the dog dies.

• • •

I came from a family of pioneers. My mother invented guilt in 1933.

• • •

Having three or more children is like having a bowling alley in your brain.

• • •

"Hey, Mom, you know that expensive vase that has been handed down from generation to generation? Well, this generation just dropped it."

• • •

A child's fastest period of growth is right after you purchase new school clothes.

• • •

A mother said, "When the children get unruly, I use a nice safe playpen. And when they quiet down, I get out."

• • •

A new study says that spanking is bad for kids. Experts, however, are suspicious of the findings since the entire study is written in crayon.

• • •

Cleaning your house while your kids are growing up is like shoveling the walk before it stops snowing.

• • •

Everything I tell my kids seems to go in one ear and out the other—and there is no sign that it is being slowed down by anything in between.

• • •

I know why kids always want the top bunk. That way they can look down to the floor and get an aerial view of their wardrobes.

• • •

If opportunity ever knocks on our kids' door, it better come during a commercial break.

• • •

If you have one kid, you're a parent. If you have two or more kids, you're a referee.

• • •

I'm not as smart as I used to be. But you can't stay a teenager all of your life.

• • •

I'm running away from home. Dad beats me. Mom beats me. I'm going to go live with the Detroit Lions. They don't beat anybody.

• • •

Kids spend most of their time today in a high-crime area . . . in front of the television set.

• • •

Mother: "Who started this fight?"
Son: "Well, Mom, the fight really started when Billy hit me back."

• • •

My kids are so noisy that the bowling alley next door called and asked if we could keep the noise down.

• • •

My kids served me breakfast in bed this morning. I just wish that they had put it on a plate first.

• • •

My parents couldn't tell time. When I'd come home from a date, they'd always say, "Do you have any idea what time it is?"

• • •

My son earns more now than I did on my first job. What bothers me is that he's seven years old and it's his allowance.

• • •

My son got frostbite standing in front of an open refrigerator.

• • •

Our kids' consciences are being raised. Yesterday I watched them as they were playing Cowpersons and Native Americans.

• • •

Solicitor: "We're looking for donations for the new children's home we're building."

Weary mother: "All right. I have two children I can give you."

• • •

The best way to keep kids at home is to make the atmosphere pleasant and to let all the air out of the tires.

• • •

The only way to recapture your youth is to take the car keys away from him.

• • •

We just learned that our teenage daughter doesn't have finger-prints. She wore them off dialing the telephone.

• • •

What creature is faster than a cheetah? How about a teenager when the phone rings?

• • •

When it came to orthodontia for my son, I decided that I wasn't going to spend five thousand dollars to straighten the teeth of a kid who never smiles.

• • •

You can always tell who the adults are who don't have children. They're the ones who think that the summer went by quickly.

• • •

Proud mother showing infant to neighbors: "He's eating solids now . . . keys, newspapers, pencils. . . ."

• • •

I saw a teenager who had a ring in her nose, her eyebrow, and a stud through her tongue. She looked like she had fallen face first into a tackle box.

• • •

I have three children and find it hard to believe that farmers can possibly grow a surplus of food.

• • •

A woman with many children named her last three Eenie, Meanie, Miney. She said, "There ain't gonna be no Mo."

• • •

My son keeps a hamster in his room. At first the smell was terrible—but the hamster got used to it.

• • •

I said, "Eat your spinach. Think of the thousands of kids who would love some."
My son said, "Name two!"

• • •

A man with no children misses a lot. For instance, a man with no children will never know the thrill of officiating at the funeral of a dead goldfish.

• • •

Before I got married, I had three theories about raising children. Now I have three children and no theories.

• • •

My mother read a label on an aspirin bottle that said, "Keep away from children." And we never saw her after that.

• • •

You know your children are growing up when they start asking questions that have answers.

• • •

My teenage daughter picked up the phone and only talked for thirty minutes. "Why so short?" I asked. "It was a wrong number," she replied.

• • •

I never got respect. I remember when I was a kid and played hide and seek, they wouldn't even look for me.

• • •

LAWYER

What do you call it when you walk a mile in a lawyer's shoes? Golfing.

• • •

My lawyer has never given me bad advice. He sells it to me.

• • •

The judge handed down a guilty decision. The lawyer's client said, "Where do we go from here?"
The lawyer responds, "Well, you go to jail, and I'm going back to my office."

• • •

Ah, too many lawyers, not enough ambulances.

• • •

What's the easiest way to get away from a lawyer? Get a faster ambulance.

• • •

Lawyer: "Your honor, I believe the award in this case should be more than one hundred thousand dollars. After all, my client should get something."

• • •

What do you have when you have six lawyers buried up to their necks in sand?
Not enough sand.

• • •

He's so dumb that he thinks that a legal pad is a lawyer's apartment.

• • •

He went to law school but he didn't graduate. He settled out of class.

• • •

"It says here," said the lawyer, "that you stole watches and jewelry in addition to cash. Is that right?"

"Yes, sir," answered the defendant. "I learned long ago that money alone doesn't bring happiness."

• • •

Lawyers sometimes solve a problem in such a way that you wish that you had the problem back.

• • •

As my lawyer says, "America—home of the brave and the land of the fee."

• • •

A man accused of robbing a sporting goods store asked a lawyer to defend him.

"I'll defend you if you are innocent and if you can come up with $450 cash as a retainer."

The man replied, "Will you settle for $25 and a set of matched woods?"

• • •

My lawyer is with the firm of Dewey, Cheatum and Howe.

• • •

The lawyer had his dog for ten years. He met it as a stray when they were both chasing the same ambulance.

• • •

Lawyers never smile for photos. A smart photographer corrected the problem. He said, "Gentlemen, say 'fees'!"

• • •

As a young lawyer his first client was hanged. But he didn't give up. He sued the jury for whiplash.

• • •

A convict called the family lawyer. "Look, they've shaved my head, cut a slit in my trousers, and asked me what I want for my last dinner. What should I do?"

His lawyer answered, "Don't sit down!"

• • •

Did you hear about the lawyer who was injured in an accident? The ambulance accidentally backed up.

• • •

I had a clumsy lawyer. Once he threw himself on the mercy of the court and missed.

• • •

He's such a dedicated lawyer that he even named his daughter Sue.

• • •

How can a lawyer write a document of five thousand words and call it a "brief"?

• • •

Two boys were talking on the first day of school. "My daddy's a pharmacist," said one. "What does your daddy do?"

"My daddy's a lawyer."

"Honest?"

"No, just the regular kind."

• • •

How many lawyers does it take to roof a house?
It depends on how thin you slice them.

• • •

He'd still be in jail today if it wasn't for his great lawyer. With both of them digging, he got out a lot faster.

• • •

He's a brilliant lawyer. He can look at a contract and tell you immediately if it's written or oral.

• • •

I had a feeling my lawyer might not be on top of things when I called to ask how my case was proceeding and he said, "Have you ever noticed that you always find something in the last place you look for it?"

• • •

Marriage

I must say, they do make a perfect couple. Except for him!

• • •

A husband making final arrangements for his cremation asked to have his ashes spread all over the floor at Bloomingdale's. "That way I know my wife will come and visit me," he explained.

• • •

A husband who says that he's the boss of the house will probably lie about other things, too.

• • •

A man lying in a hospital bed remarked to his wife: "When I got my draft notice, you were right by my side. When I totaled my car, you were there. When my business went bankrupt, you were there. Agnes, you're a real jinx!"

• • •

A thoughtful wife is one who has the pork chops ready when her husband comes home from a fishing trip.

• • •

Advice to brides: Burn the toast so he won't notice how bad the coffee is.

• • •

Advice to husbands: Don't try to find out who's boss of the house. You'll be happier not knowing.

• • •

All men make mistakes, but married men find out about them sooner.

• • •

For years I used to be my own worst critic, then I got married.

• • •

Being a husband is a lot like any other job. It helps if you like the boss.

• • •

Counselors will tell you that it is important to establish who's boss in the house, and I did. My problem is that every time I raise my hand, she never calls on me.

• • •

Barbara and Jim had been engaged for several months. A concerned Barbara expressed to her mother, "Jim keeps lavishing me with one expensive gift after another. How can I get him to stop spending so much money on me?"
"Easy," the mother replied. "Just marry him!"

• • •

He says he's looking for a woman whose favorite hobbies are mowing the lawn and shoveling snow.

• • •

I didn't realize how young the couple was until I learned that Gerber's catered their reception.

• • •

I have no trouble meeting expenses. My wife is always introducing me to them.

• • •

I would never be what I am today without my wife and children—broke!

• • •

If it wasn't for marriage, people could go through life thinking that they had no faults at all.

• • •

Man in a gift shop: "What do you get for a couple when it's his second marriage and her second marriage, too?"
Clerk: "Nothing monogrammed."

• • •

My wife and I like the same thing. The only difference is that I like to save it and she likes to spend it.

• • •

My wife has a great way of making a long story short. She interrupts.

• • •

My wife promised to "love, honor and obey." Right now, I'd settle for any one of them.

• • •

My wife says I only have two faults—everything I say and everything I do.

• • •

My wife says that I have a bad memory. So far this year, I've forgotten her birthday, our anniversary and who's boss.

• • •

You might say my wife gets her own way. She writes in her diary a week in advance.

• • •

Webster wrote the dictionary because of his wife. Every time he opened his mouth, she said, "Now what's that supposed to mean?"

• • •

Frustrated wife to husband: "Next Sunday we'll trade jobs. You get the children fed and dressed, and I'll go out in the car and honk the horn for ten minutes."

• • •

At license bureau: "How much does it cost to get married?"
Clerk: "It's four dollars for the license and one paycheck a week for the rest of your married life."

• • •

Now that I'm married, I know why they call English the Mother Tongue. Father never gets a chance to use it.

• • •

On our wedding day we received lots of gifts marked His and Hers. Her brother gave us something marked US. It was a green army blanket.

• • •

My wife and I have a mutual understanding. I don't try to run her life and I don't try to run mine.

• • •

Isn't it ridiculous to say to a mother at a wedding "You're not losing a daughter. You're gaining a son"? At her age, all she needs— more children!

• • •

Marriage is like twirling a baton, turning handsprings or eating with chopsticks . . . it looks easy until you try it.

• • •

You know that the couple that is getting married is too young when there are four figures on the wedding cake—the bride, the groom, his dermatologist and her orthodontist.

• • •

She was married to a banker, an actor, a minister and an undertaker. One for the money, two for the show, three to get ready and four to go.

• • •

They say that after many years of marriage, a husband and wife start looking like each other—my wife is very concerned.

• • •

The last big decision she let me make was whether to wash or dry.

• • •

The doctor told the husband that his wife needed sea air, so he fans her with a mackerel.

• • •

We divide the chores in our home. I wash the dishes, and my wife sweeps them up.

• • •

He takes his wife out every night, but she always finds her way back.

• • •

Marriage is a real grind; you wash the dishes, make the beds and two weeks later you have to do it all over again.

• • •

Wife: "I'm ready now. I thought you said you were ready awhile ago."
Husband: "I was. But now you'll have to wait for me. I've got to shave again."

• • •

I'm always the first person to admit my mistakes. But with a wife, a mother-in-law and three children, it's usually a very close race.

• • •

Midwest

I've always been fascinated by Cincinnati. No matter how you spell it, it always looks wrong.

• • •

They say it took the pioneers two months to go from the Mississippi River to California. You can still do it. Let your spouse read the road map.

• • •

Money

Americans spend $10 billion a year on games of chance—not including weddings and elections.

• • •

Don't lend money to friends. It causes amnesia.

• • •

I have enough money to last me for the rest of my life if I don't have to buy anything.

• • •

I've been saving for a rainy day, and I'm happy to report that in two more months I'll have enough to buy that umbrella I've always wanted.

• • •

I'll tell you how rich I am. I have a bank account named after me.

• • •

I've consolidated all my debts into one payment. At least now I'm paying all my bills except one.

• • •

Live within your income even if you have to borrow to do so.

• • •

My wife believes in sharing the wealth with jewelry stores, clothing stores, Bloomingdale's. . . .

• • •

Some people work all their lives and have nothing to show for it. I have that already!

• • •

Teacher: "Who's happier. A man with five million dollars or a man with five children?"
Student: "The man with five million."

Teacher: "Why?"

Student: "Because the man with five million always wants more."

• • •

Wife asking her husband for money: "Try and look at it this way: I'm an underdeveloped nation and you're the United States."

• • •

Wife to husband: "Why don't you have the same spunk that our government has? You don't see a little bit of debt keeping them from spending money."

• • •

With a wife and three children, the only chance I'll have of having folding money in my pocket is if they put hinges on nickels.

• • •

A mugger stuck a gun in a frugal man's ribs and said, "Your money or your life."

After a long pause, the tightwad said, "I'm thinking. I'm thinking!"

• • •

In the old days, men rode chargers. Now they marry them.

• • •

After looking through my bills, I think I can make it through the rest of the month if I don't eat anything or turn anything on.

• • •

Let's face it, there's only one thing money can't buy—poverty. You need credit cards to do that!

• • •

Maybe I worry too much about money, but you'd worry too, if your wife was just elected to the MasterCard Hall of Fame.

• • •

It's easy to meet expenses—everywhere I go, there they are!

• • •

How can we teach our kids the value of money in America? We can't even teach our congressmen!

• • •

Money isn't that important. After all, Henry Ford had millions and never owned a Cadillac.

• • •

My latest investment hasn't been doing too well. I put three thousand dollars into the (abrasive celebrity) Charm School.

• • •

Poverty is hereditary. You get it from your children.

• • •

My money problems are over. My investment broker just got me the Drano contract for the Alaskan pipeline.

• • •

Motels

I stayed at a famous budget motel. Not only did they leave the light on for me, they also left a half-eaten cheeseburger under the bed.

• • •

The walls at the motel were so thin, I called the manager and said, "Can you do something about my neighbor's TV set?"
He said, "Can you hear it?"
I said, "Hear it? I can see it!"

• • •

Some resort motels have towels that are so thick and fluffy that you can hardly get your suitcase closed.

• • •

They have running water in every room. I just found a spring in my bed last night.

• • •

The rooms are so small. I stuck my key in the door and broke a window. So small that the mice are hunchbacked. I closed the door, and the doorknob got in bed with me!

• • •

My motel room was so small that I had to use a folding tooth-brush. It was so small that twice a day I had to step outside just to let my mosquito bites swell.

• • •

My motel room was so small that I dropped my handkerchief and it became a wall-to-wall carpet.

• • •

We stopped in a motel outside of Miami. When we entered the room, I saw a cockroach on the bedspread. I called the desk clerk to protest.
He said, "Why, that's Florida."
I said, "You mean they've got names?"

• • •

Mother-in-Law

I first met my mother-in-law at a summer picnic where I observed her playing a game—bobbing for watermelons.

• • •

I knew that my mother-in-law wasn't exactly crazy about me. On our wedding day, when they wheeled in the cake, she bit the head off the groom.

• • •

I'm recovering from a bad fall. My mother-in-law stayed with us in October and November.

• • •

I told my mother-in-law, "My house is your house." So, she sold it!

• • •

My mother-in-law talks so much that the phone company gave her her own area code.

• • •

People could listen to my mother-in-law for hours—and have, too!

• • •

She carries her age well, and she's been carrying it for a long time.

• • •

She has a speech impediment. She has to stop once every hour to catch her breath.

• • •

I'm so shrewd. We've been married ten years, and my mother-in-law doesn't even know we have a guest room.

• • •

I just came back from a pleasure trip. I took my mother-in-law to the bus station.

• • •

Have you heard of those Indian gurus who have something profound to say about everything? They're like a mother-in-law with a beard.

• • •

I don't do mother-in-law jokes because my mother-in-law is really a wonderful woman with a lovely disposition. For those of you who have never met my mother-in-law, just picture Roseanne Barr in curlers.

• • •

I'm dedicating tonight's program to my mother-in-law—Fidel Castro in toreador pants. . . . No, I really shouldn't compare her to Castro. His speeches only take four hours.

• • •

Japanese women make the best wives. They care for you, pamper you, stay with you, and best of all your mother-in-law lives in Tokyo.

• • •

My mother-in-law speaks 140 words per minute, with gusts up to 180.

• • •

The wedding got started on a rather sour note when my mother-in-law came down the aisle and lobbed a grenade into my family's pew.

• • •

We must watch the Macy's Day Parade. This year my mother-in-law blew up three of the balloons.

• • •

My mother-in-law is so nearsighted that she nagged a coat hanger for an hour.

• • •

Mother's Day

I found the perfect Mother's Day card: "Mother, you weren't simply a cook, laundress and nurse, but you were also a taxi driver with very reasonable rates."

• • •

I called my mom on Mother's Day. I just loved the excitement in her voice as she accepted the charges.

• • •

Mom to son: "You sent me three beautiful roses, and I'm glad, but was there any special reason for sending three?"
He said, "There sure was. Twelve of them cost sixty dollars."

• • •

Movies

The Hollywood tycoon was determined to create the greatest epic ever filmed. "I will use two armies for the battle scene," he cried. "Twenty-five thousand extras on each side."
"Fantastic!" cried the director. "But how will we pay them?"
"That's the best part of my plan," replied the tycoon. "We'll use real bullets."

• • •

Movies today are terrifying. I went to one the other day and I never saw such violence, sex and vulgar language—and that was at the popcorn stand!

• • •

The movie had a happy ending. Everyone was glad when it was over.

• • •

The sign at the movie window said: "Ten dollars—popular prices." The moviegoer asked the girl, "You call ten dollars popular prices?" She said sweetly, "We like them."

• • •

He saw *Guess Who's Coming to Dinner?* twice and guessed wrong both times.

• • •

Music

A friend gave me a shower radio for my birthday. Just what I need—music in the shower. I guess there's no better place to dance than on a slick surface near a glass door.

• • •

I was listening to some rap music today. Not that I had a choice. It was coming out of a Jeep four blocks away.

• • •

A thought on the music of today: "If van Gogh were alive, he'd cut off his other ear."

• • •

Country music provides an artistic outlet, opening a special field of performance for people who can't sing.

• • •

Every time I listen to the Top 40, I shudder to think what the Bottom 40 sound like.

• • •

He has done for music what Jackie Gleason did for the sport of pole vaulting.

• • •

His voice has great range. He's gotten complaints from people as far as two blocks away.

• • •

I thought my son was playing his new compact disc, and then I discovered that it was just a spoon that was caught in the garbage disposal.

• • •

My singing got mixed reviews the other night. I liked it, but my audience didn't.

• • •

Next on the program, we will hear from the Jolly Green Giant singing his big hit, "There Will Be Peas in the Valley."

• • •

One good thing about rock songs: Kids can't whistle them.

• • •

Rap is easy to write. Just forget all you know about music.

• • •

Sure I'm familiar with the works of Chopin, Beethoven and Haydn. And someday when I have money, I'm going to buy some of their paintings for my living room.

• • •

The best thing about a popular song is that it doesn't stay popular very long.

• • •

What we now call a rock concert used to be called "disturbing the peace."

• • •

Why do bagpipers always walk when they play?
To get away from the noise.

• • •

He sings like a prisoner. Behind eight bars and looking for the right key.

• • •

I can't sing well tonight. This morning I yelled at my kids through a screen door and strained my voice.

• • •

Four carpenters formed a tuba group and called themselves The Tuba Fours.

• • •

I was in a drum and bugle corps that was so bad, the drums carried the tune.

• • •

He has a great ear for music. It looks just like a tuba.

• • •

He plays the violin just like Heifetz—under his chin.

• • •

His voice fills the hall with music. And while he was singing, I noticed some of you leaving to make more room for it.

• • •

Our high school band was terrible. The way we played, it was a good thing we kept moving.

• • •

If you want a career as a musician or songwriter, persevere. Just remember, it took Brahms five years to compose his memorable lullaby. He kept falling asleep at the piano.

• • •

The way he sings, he should play a pirate in an opera. He's murder on the high Cs.

• • •

He began his musical career as the piano player in his high school marching band.

• • •

NEIGHBORS

I've found a great way to cut down on my electric bill. It should work, unless my neighbor discovers the extension cord.

• • •

I won't say my neighbor is lazy, but for him, getting out of bed is a career move.

• • •

My neighbor tried gum to give up smoking, but he said it's no use. He just can't keep the stuff lit.

• • •

"My next-door neighbors were yelling and screaming last night at 3 A.M."
"Did they waken you?"
"No, luckily I was up playing my tuba at the time."

• • •

NEWSCAST

A man met a tragic end this Sunday morning when he picked up his newspaper. The contents slid out and he was Sunday supplemented to death.

• • •

A prison van carrying a dozen convicts collided with a cement truck. Police say to be on the lookout for twelve hardened criminals.

• • •

An appeals court has ruled that cheerleaders must have the same standards as athletes—even higher. They have to know how to spell.

• • •

Bozo the Clown died. There was a really short funeral procession—the hearse and one car. But twenty-seven mourners got out of that one car.

● ● ●

Did you ever realize that if everybody obeyed the Ten Commandments that there would be no 11 o'clock news?

● ● ●

I read that the inventor of Velcro died. It was so sad. Everyone associated with him felt so attached.

● ● ●

In Prague, doctors have successfully separated Siamese twins and have presented the proud parents with separate Czechs.

● ● ●

The State Highway Construction Commission reports that five hundred workers will be laid off. Researchers have developed a shovel that will stand by itself.

● ● ●

Pretty much the same things happened today as yesterday, only to different people.

● ● ●

Scientists have discovered the world's smallest known particle—a Denny's steak.

● ● ●

The director of the Department of Motor Vehicles resigned suddenly yesterday, marking the first time in the history of his department that anyone had done anything suddenly.

● ● ●

The United Nations has just started a campaign to wipe out hunger and illiteracy at the same time, by giving out 800 zillion tons of alphabet soup.

• • •

Two thousand pounds of human hair fell off a truck in New Jersey today and blocked the highway. Police are still combing the area.

• • •

War has broken out in Africa between Zulus and the Pygmies. Battle casualties are seven wounded, twenty captured and thirty-nine stepped on.

• • •

In Center City today, a wine truck collided with a cheese truck, resulting in a $3,000 fund raiser.

• • •

A tragic accident occurred in a sawmill today when a man lost his entire left side. He was immediately rushed to the hospital, and doctors report that he's all right now.

• • •

A new attempt is being made to wipe out malaria. I wonder what those poor Malarians have done this time?

• • •

The State Department has some good news and bad news. The good news is that last week an American on a pleasure cruise fell overboard and was rescued by an enemy sub. The bad news is that he went overboard off the coast of Florida.

• • •

In the field of medicine, Dr. Seymour Savem has announced that he will spend the rest of his medical career seeking a cure for wheat germ.

• • •

Newspapers

The *Daily Globe* is short of staff today. Two of the editorial writers are out with a good mood.

• • •

The newspaper carrier accidentally left two copies of the morning paper on my front step. As he was coming back down our street, I called to him, "You gave me an extra paper today."
He said, "That's yours. Keep it. I'm taking tomorrow off."

• • •

My paperboy must have a sore arm. This morning it took him three tries before he could get my paper on the roof.

• • •

New Year's

We received a party invitation that said, "Bring your noise-makers." But we prefer to leave the kids at home.

• • •

On New Year's Eve I call friends all around the country, but the different time zones are confusing. Like last year I was talking to the operator in New York and I said, "How far behind New York is Los Angeles?"
She said, "Literally or culturally?"

• • •

NEW YORK

A man walked into a Cadillac showroom and plunked down forty thousand dollars for a car.

"Shall we deliver it, or do you wish to drive it out?" the salesman asked.

"Leave it right here," the man said. "I'll never get such a good parking place again."

• • •

Something's happening all the time in New York—most of it unsolved.

• • •

Peter Minuit was purchasing Manhattan Island from the Carnarsie tribe, and as he surveyed the territory, he looked across the East River and remarked, "Isn't that Brooklyn over there?"

"Listen, paleface," said the chief, "for twenty-four dollars, don't expect the place to be perfect."

• • •

The crime rate is down in New York City. They're running out of victims.

• • •

A guy asks me, "Do you know where Central Park is?"
I replied, "No."
He said, "Okay, I'll mug you here."

• • •

OFFICE

We just bought a new conference table. It's nine feet wide and thirty feet long and sleeps twenty.

• • •

I don't want to complain about the size of my office, but it's a little embarrassing when you have to wheel your desk chair all the way out to the lobby just to swivel.

• • •

OIL

One oil company's public relations man said, "Of course we spilled eight hundred thousand gallons of oil in the ocean, but after all, who wants a squeaky ocean?"

• • •

OPENING

I am grateful to be invited to speak here tonight. You see, I'm married, and what I'm usually invited to do is listen.

• • •

Good evening, ladies and gentlemen. You'll be happy to know that when I gave my speech to the secretary to be typed, I asked her to eliminate all that was on the dull side. So, in conclusion . . .

• • •

Optimists

The optimist fell out a window on the top floor of a skyscraper. As he passed the tenth floor he was heard to say, "Well, so far, so good."

• • •

An optimist is a guy who goes out fishing for Moby Dick in a rowboat, carrying a harpoon, a jar of tartar sauce and a piece of lemon.

• • •

He's so optimistic that he puts his shoes on when he hears a speaker say, "Now in conclusion . . ."

• • •

When he goes fishing he takes along a camera and a frying pan.

• • •

A real optimist is a guy who pulls up in front of a shopping mall to meet his wife and leaves the motor running.

• • •

I'm not very optimistic. The horse I bet on was so late getting home, he tiptoed into the stable.

• • •

PANHANDLERS

The lady said to the panhandler, "I'm sorry, but I have a policy never to give money to someone on the street."

The panhandler asked, "Well, what do you want me to do? Open an office?"

● ● ●

Panhandlers in this city really try to make you feel guilty if you don't give them something. One said to me, "Please give me five dollars for a meal."

When I refused him, he took out his teeth, handed them to me and said, "Thanks to you I won't be needing these."

● ● ●

Next time a bum asks you for a quarter for a cup of coffee, give it to him. Then follow him to find out where you can get a cup of coffee for a quarter.

● ● ●

A panhandler asked, "May I have a dollar for a cup of coffee?"

"But I thought that coffee was only fifty cents," said the man.

"It is," said the panhandler, "but I have a date."

● ● ●

"Could I have a dollar for a cup of coffee?"

"A dollar? That's ridiculous!"

"Just tell me yes or no. Don't tell me how to run my business."

● ● ●

"I haven't eaten in four days."

"Boy, I wish I had your willpower."

● ● ●

PARACHUTES

Rule number one in parachuting is never have an argument with your wife while she's packing your parachute.

• • •

I always wanted to be a skydiver but nothing ever opened up for me.

• • •

If your primary chute doesn't open, and the reserve chute doesn't open either, well, that's what you call jumping to a conclusion.

• • •

Skydiving is like Maxwell House coffee: Good to the last drop.

• • •

PARKING

It's not as easy as you think to get parking tickets. First you have to find a parking place.

• • •

And let's have a big round of applause for the parking lot attendants. They're certainly doing a bang-up job out there. I understand that there are a lot more compacts leaving this place than ever came in.

• • •

PAYCHECK

If the boss says that he can't give you a raise, just say, "Okay, just give me the same pay more frequently."

• • •

I never get depressed with my paycheck. I never let the little things bother me.

• • •

I found a note in my paycheck which read, "Your raise will become effective as soon as you do."

• • •

My wife said she wanted to see my paycheck go further . . . so she mailed it to Australia.

• • •

Many women today are getting men's wages, but haven't they always?

• • •

PERFORMERS/PERFORMANCES

I just entertained at the:
- Bald Is Beautiful Convention in Moorehead, South Carolina
- Mystery Writers Convention in Erie, Pennsylvania
- Plastic Surgeons Convention in Scarsdale, New York
- Psychiatrists Convention in Normal, Illinois
- Accountants Convention in Billings, Montana
- Canoeists Convention in Roanoke, Virginia
- Locksmiths Convention in the Florida Keys
- Egotists Society at Lake Superior
- Weight-Watchers Convention in Gainesville, Florida
- Contortionists Convention in South Bend, Indiana
- Plumbers Convention in Flushing, New York
- Insomniacs Society at Wake Forest University
- Lawyers Convention in Sioux City, Iowa

• • •

Speaking is such a tough business. One day you are delivering a soliloquy, and the next day you're delivering a pizza.

• • •

Last week I appeared at Carnegie Hall and drew a line two blocks long. Then some wise guy came along and took away my chalk.

• • •

(if you close the show) I'm glad they finally put me on. I've been standing out there for forty-five minutes with my suit and material slowly going out of style.

• • •

His performances are always refreshing. The audience always feels good when they wake up.

• • •

A reviewer wrote of my most recent performance, "For the first time in my life, I envied my feet. They were asleep."

• • •

My publicity agent did have one other well-known client—the Unknown Soldier.

• • •

PLUMBERS

I called a plumber and he arrived two hours later than I expected. He apologized and said, "I'm sorry I'm late, but my chauffeur phoned in sick."

• • •

A plumber fixed a dripping faucet and worked an hour.

"What do I owe?" asked the homeowner.

"Two hundred seventy-five dollars," answered the plumber.

"Why, I'm a lawyer and even I don't charge two hundred seventy-five dollars an hour!" said the outraged homeowner.

"Neither did I when I was a lawyer," said the plumber.

• • •

The plumber said, "Let me put it this way. You can go on a vacation, or you can have hot and cold water in your house."

• • •

My plumber has a sign in his window that says, "Do It Yourself. Then Call Us."

• • •

Plumber to homeowner: "It's even worse than I thought. This mess is going to put me into a higher tax bracket."

• • •

A plumber at a repair job advised the housewife, "The best way to avoid future trouble is to hide your husband's wrenches."

• • •

The plumber said, "Your basement's not too bad. Just pretend you live in Venice."

• • •

A person who can laugh when things go wrong is probably a plumber.

• • •

Ladies, given the choice of marrying a plumber or a stud muffin, marry the plumber. Do you know how hard it is to get your toilet fixed on Sunday afternoon?

• • •

Politics

At one of his rallies someone yelled, "What about the powerful interests that control you?"

He shot back, "Leave my wife and children out of this!"

• • •

A little old lady from Iowa requested that she be buried in Chicago so that she could keep on voting.

• • •

All presidential candidates should undergo a stress test before being allowed to run for office. I think they should have to drive a school bus for two weeks.

• • •

You can fool some of the people all of the time, and those are the ones you should focus on.

• • •

America is a country where a person is assumed innocent until the president offers him a job.

• • •

Columbus traveled around the world at public expense and they called him an explorer. Today they would call him a congressman.

• • •

Fifty percent of the people who listened to his speech are undecided. The other 50 percent will be polled as soon as they wake up.

• • •

Grave marker: "Here lies a politician and an honest man."
Passerby: "Can you imagine? Two people in the same grave!"

• • •

He just returned from a fact-finding tour of the French Riviera.

• • •

He lost the election because of the age issue. Hardly anyone over eighteen voted for him.

• • •

He was fired from his government job on his first day at work. His supervisor caught him working.

• • •

He was followed by his usual entourage on his speaking tour. The cameraman, the sound man, the sandman . . .

• • •

He's a politician who is so afraid of the consequences of air pollution that he's canceled six of his speeches.

• • •

He's hitting the campaign trail. He has experience, and after two terms as vice-president, he should be well rested.

• • •

I asked a politician, "What is two plus two?"
He said, "What do you want it to be?"

• • •

I asked him why he was running in the gubernatorial race, and he said, "Because I want to be a gubernor."

• • •

I asked the senator, "What's your idea of a good farm program?" He answered, "How about *Hee-Haw*?"

• • •

I attended my first political dinner. Since I was unaccustomed to formal etiquette, I watched everything (local politician) did. I held my fork properly, switched my knife from hand to hand, I held out my pinky finger when I was drinking. There's just one thing I can't bring myself to do. Let's both give back the silverware.

• • •

I collect contradictory phrases such as postal service, peace-keeping missile and government worker.

• • •

I won't say how badly he was beaten, but I hope he was covered by landslide insurance.

• • •

If we didn't have elections every four years, how else would we know how bad off we are?

• • •

Isn't it too bad that all the people who know how to run the country are too busy teaching school, writing editorials, driving taxis or cutting hair?

• • •

It is not necessary to fool all the people all the time. A simple majority will do.

• • •

I've got a suggestion to make the police department more cost-efficient. Put the stations next to Dunkin' Donuts.

• • •

Late one night before an election, two campaign workers were in the town cemetery writing down the names of the deceased to put into the register of voters.

One noticed that his partner had bypassed the name Thaddeus Pulaski. "Copy it, Sam," he ordered. "This is America. He has as much right to vote as the next guy."

• • •

More and more people today are realizing the American dream, because the candidates' speeches are putting so many to sleep.

• • •

Politics is such a dangerous business, as I was saying to our waiter, (losing candidate).

• • •

The government may not cure poverty, but the way they've been raising taxes, they'll be sure to cure wealth.

• • •

There was such a poor choice of candidates in the last election that the people of Chicago only voted once.

• • •

There were so many members of royalty at the party that it looked like a live chess game.

• • •

Washington said, "I cannot tell a lie," so right after that, his advisors hired a press secretary for him.

• • •

What do you call a politician who has lost an election?
Professor.

• • •

What happens to the child who goes to the grocery store and forgets what his mother sent him there for? He grows up to be a congressman.

• • •

What's the best cure for insomnia? A government job.

• • •

What's the difference between Congress and kindergarten? Kindergarten has adult supervision.

• • •

When a constituent has a baby or gets married he sends him or her a personal card. If one dies, he sends that person an absentee ballot.

• • •

You don't have to fool all the people all the time—just the 30 percent who vote.

• • •

You'd think (losing candidate) would be over his defeat by now, but he's really acting childish. I mean, ringing the White House doorbell and running away?

• • •

I love to visit Washington—if only to be near my money.

• • •

He introduced a bill that would create 20 million jobs. He proposed to build a bridge across the Mississippi—lengthwise.

• • •

He's one of the finest representatives money can buy.

. . .

As a safety tip: Do not attempt to drive a car or operate heavy equipment after hearing one of (candidate's) speeches.

. . .

Did you ever wonder what the people of city hall do to celebrate Labor Day?

. . .

When a group of Nobel Prize winners gathered at the White House for dinner, the president declared, "This is the most extraordinary collection of talent and intelligence gathered at the White House since Thomas Jefferson dined alone."

. . .

I don't know why everyone is picking on that congressman. After all, he hasn't done anything.

. . .

I don't have to do this for a living. I have the hemlock concession at Democratic headquarters.

. . .

Election returns were forming a pattern. Mrs. (Candidate) went up to her husband and said, "I've got some good news and some bad news for you. First the good news. You won't have to buy a new suit for the inaugural."

. . .

I just picked up a marvelous bargain in a secondhand car. It was only used by (losing candidate) in inaugural parades.

. . .

In the United States, everyone's vote counts—and in Cook County, that's true many times over.

• • •

Don't be too hard on our politicians. Many of them are doing the work of two men—Laurel and Hardy.

• • •

The cheapest way to have your family tree traced is to run for public office.

• • •

As Mayor Daley used to say on election day, "Vote early and vote often."

• • •

In one of his most stirring speeches, the politician said, "For years they lied to you. For years they cheated you. For years they stole from you. Now give me a chance."

• • •

I was at city hall, and the mayor was making one of his decisions. I didn't actually see the mayor, but I did see the coin being flipped.

• • •

Our little daughter asked my wife the other day, "Mommy, do all fairy tales begin with 'Once upon a time . . .'?"
My wife said, "No, dear. Some of them begin with, 'If I'm elected . . .'"

• • •

He's not a member of an organized political party. He's a Democrat.

• • •

I ate much better during Truman's administration. I had my own teeth then.

• • •

He's an election-day taxidermist. He stuffs ballot boxes.

• • •

I like political jokes unless they get elected.

• • •

Now there's a candidate who doesn't take any chances. A reporter asked him what his favorite color was and he replied, "Plaid."

• • •

I was on the Metro in Washington and inquired, "How do I get to the White House?"
The native replied, "Well, first you've got to enter the primaries. . . ."

• • •

I always love the bobsled event in the Winter Olympics. The bobsled is said to be the fastest way of going downhill without being a part of (politician's) campaign.

• • •

I got a letter from the president in reply to one I had sent. He told me that when the time comes, he wants me to serve in an advisory capacity. Well, those weren't his exact words. It was more like: "When I want your advice, I'll ask for it."

• • •

Our chief of police has done a super job of getting crime out of the alleys and back onto the streets where we can all see it.

• • •

Why does (candidate) want to eliminate poverty? That's all most of us have left!

• • •

He's got the cleanest mind in politics, and that's because he changes it every hour.

• • •

Post Office

"Jenkins, you're the fastest letter carrier we've ever had."
"Well, thanks, boss. And tomorrow, I'll even do better. I'm going to read the addresses."

• • •

The post office has finally done something to shorten the waiting lines in the lobby. They've asked the customers to stand closer together.

• • •

I got a package in the mail the other day that had written on the front: Photographs: Do Not Bend. And underneath the postman had written, Oh, yes they do!

• • •

Post office employee to boss: "Sir, may I present Joe Johnson? He's retiring from the post office after thirty years."
Boss: "Well, Johnson, what have you learned after thirty years with us?"
Johnson: "Don't mail my check."

• • •

People usually get what's coming to them . . . unless, of course, it's mailed.

• • •

I don't want to be uncharitable to the post office, but the mailman just delivered my *TV Guide*. It has Ed Sullivan on the cover.

• • •

I saw a package in the post office that said, "Fragile: Throw Underhand."

• • •

If you are what you eat, the post office must eat a lot of escargot.

• • •

A lady at the post office purchased stamps and said to the clerk, "Shall I stick them on myself?"

"Positively not," said the clerk. "They'll accomplish much more if you put them on envelopes."

• • •

They say, "Bad news travels fast. . . ." Not if you mail it!

• • •

The other day I drove by one of those signs that say: Slow Children—and underneath it someone scrawled: Grow Up to Work for the Post Office.

• • •

PREACHER

"Our church should be air-conditioned," said a member of the congregation. "It's unhealthy to sleep in a stuffy room."

• • •

Today's sermon is entitled, "An Honest Christian." At the close of the service, we will sing the hymn, "Steal Away."

• • •

A parishioner had a tendency to read ahead of the rest of the group during congregational reading. The pastor announced, "We will now read the Twenty-third Psalm. Will the lady who is always beside the still waters, while the rest of us are in the green pastures, please pause until we catch up?"

• • •

A parishioner told the pastor, "Reverend, that sermon was like water to a drowning man."

• • •

A pastor was leaving his congregation to go to another church. He comforted a disconsolate parishioner. "Now, now, the next pastor will probably be better. . . ."

The woman was still discouraged. "That's what they said the last time," she complained.

• • •

A preacher was sharing with a friend, "It is the duty of the rich to help the poor."

The friend inquired, "Have you been successful in convincing your congregation on this matter?"

"Well, I've been 50 percent successful. So far I've convinced the poor."

• • •

As he waited in the foyer, the pastor greeted a stranger. "You didn't understand," said the pastor. "I called for a meeting of the board."

"I qualify," said the stranger. "After hearing you speak for an hour and a half, I have never been so bored in my life."

• • •

He talks in other people's sleep. He's a preacher.

• • •

He's so pre-mil and pre-trib that he won't even eat Post Toasties.

• • •

If you were to take all the people who fall asleep during his sermons, and lay them end-to-end, they'd be a lot more comfortable.

• • •

Man to preacher: "This is a nice church. How many does it sleep?"

• • •

Some gain strength from a sermon. Others wake up refreshed.

• • •

The minister confessed, "I only know a little Greek and a little Hebrew. The little Greek owns a restaurant, and the little Hebrew runs a deli."

• • •

"I've always said that the poor are welcome in our church, and judging by today's collection, I see that they have come."

• • •

He was such a great preacher that at the close of each sermon there was a great awakening.

• • •

Prison

He was given ten years for something he didn't do. He didn't run fast enough.

• • •

We'll never have prison reform until we start sending a better class of people to jail.

• • •

On the day of the execution, the warden approached the prisoner's cell and said, "You can have anything you want for your last meal."
The prisoner replied, "I want fresh asparagus."
The warden said, "Asparagus won't be here for another three months."
The prisoner replied, "I'll wait."

• • •

His mother visited him in prison and advised him not to hang around with a bad crowd.

• • •

Profound Thoughts and Questions

A man who seldom finds himself in hot water is a man with a wife, two teenagers and one bathroom.

• • •

Americans are living longer these days, which is great news unless you happen to figure prominently in someone's will.

• • •

Anything that isn't nailed down is mine. Anything I can pry loose isn't nailed down.

• • •

As Noah's wife once told him, "I'd sure feel a lot more relaxed if those termites were in a special container."

• • •

Can vegetarians eat animal crackers?

• • •

Did the "i before e" rule confuse Einstein? After all, he had it twice in his name.

• • •

Did you ever notice that in women's magazines there are thirty pages of recipes, and then thirty pages of diet tips?

• • •

Did you ever turn on your dehumidifier and your humidifier at the same time and let them fight it out?

• • •

Did it ever occur to you that stretch pants may have no other choice?

• • •

Did the Three Stooges ever reject a script?

• • •

Did you ever buy a cured ham and wonder what it had?

• • •

Do Mexicans sing, "Way Up Yonder in New Orleans"?

• • •

Do pediatricians play miniature golf on Wednesdays?

• • •

Do they have skywriting in Japan?

• • •

Do you know how to get seventy-seven shaves out of one blade? Wince.

• • •

Don't criticize a man until you have walked a mile in his shoes because then you're a mile away and you have his shoes.

• • •

Everything is within walking distance if you have the time.

• • •

Have you ever wondered what chairs would look like if your knees bent the other way?

• • •

How many successful jumps do you have to make before you join the National Skydivers' Association? All of them.

• • •

How can you tell when you're running out of invisible ink?

• • •

How come you never hear about gruntled employees?

• • •

How do "Do Not Walk on the Grass" signs get there?

• • •

How come economy-size means big in soap and small in cars?

• • •

How come fat chance and slim chance mean the same thing?

• • •

How come my garbage weighs more than my groceries?

• • •

How come we drive on a parkway and park on a driveway?

• • •

How come when you cook bacon, the fat splatters in every direction, but when you eat it, it all accumulates in one place?

• • •

How come wrong numbers are never busy?

• • •

How do they get the deer to cross at that yellow road sign?

• • •

How do you explain counterclockwise to someone with a digital watch?

• • •

How do you know when it's time to tune your bagpipes?

• • •

How does a grapefruit know where your eye is?

• • •

How does the guy who drives the snowplow get to work in the mornings?

• • •

How much deeper would the ocean be if sponges didn't live there?

• • •

I met a man who was half Chinese and half Native American who believes that a journey of a thousand miles begins when you walk a mile in another man's moccasins.

• • •

I hate Indian-givers. No, I take that back.

• • •

I take pleasure in the simple things in life, like seeing the person who cut me off on the bypass going eighty miles an hour pulled over by the police four miles down the road.

• • •

I went to a general store. They wouldn't let me buy anything specific.

• • •

I'm not a vegetarian because I love animals. I happen to hate plants.

• • •

If a man can swallow an aspirin at a drinking fountain, don't you think he deserves to get well?

• • •

If the world is getting smaller every day, as some say, why is the price of airline tickets continually rising?

• • •

If a boomerang always comes back to you after you throw it, why throw it in the first place?

• • •

If a parsley farmer goes bankrupt, can they garnish his wages?

• • •

If a woman's work is never done, how come she doesn't start earlier?

• • •

If a word in the dictionary is misspelled, how would we know?

• • •

If all the nations of the world are in debt, where did all the money go?

• • •

If Americans throw rice at weddings, do the Chinese throw hot dogs?

• • •

If ants are such hard workers, how come they always have time for a picnic?

• • •

If builders are afraid to have a thirteenth floor, then why aren't book publishers afraid to have a chapter 11?

• • •

If elbows bent the other way, what would saxophones look like?

• • •

If Gatorade is such a great thirst quencher, how come they only have it in sixty-four ounce bottles?

• • •

If man evolved from monkeys and apes, why do we still have monkeys and apes?

• • •

If olive oil comes from olives, where does baby oil come from?

• • •

If oxygen tarnishes silver, can you imagine what it does to our lungs?

• • •

If quitters never win and winners never quit, who came up with, "Quit while you're ahead"?

• • •

If seafoods are so good for us and so safe to eat, let me ask this: When was the last time anyone heard from Mr. Paul?

• • •

If the black box flight recorder is never damaged during a plane crash, why isn't the whole plane made out of the same stuff?

• • •

If the city really wants to solve its parking problems, why don't they hire the guy who squeezes twenty-five thousand units of vitamin C into those tiny little capsules?

• • •

If the post office ever went on strike, how would anybody know?

• • •

If truth is beauty and beauty is truth, how come you never see a woman getting her hair done in the library?

• • •

If we have mileage, yardage and footage, why don't we have inchage?

• • •

If you ate pasta and antipasta, would you still be hungry?

• • •

If you could have a conversation with anyone, living or dead, who would you choose?
The living one!

• • •

If you laid every jogger end-to-end around the world, 71 percent of them would drown.

• • •

If you melt dry ice, can you swim without getting wet?

• • •

If you refuse to eat the pudding, what proof do you have?

• • •

If you were arrested for loitering at a doughnut shop, could you be charged with impersonating a police officer?

• • •

Imagine how long it took Henry Wadsworth Longfellow's mother to sew his name in his clothes before sending Hank to camp.

• • •

In 1869, the waffle iron was invented for people who had wrinkled waffles.

• • •

In 1915, pancake makeup was invented, but most people still preferred syrup.

• • •

In Germany, they have the cities of Frankfurt and Hamburg. Whatever happened to grilled cheese?

• • •

Isn't it amazing that through the years headaches have managed to keep up with all these new, improved pain relievers?

• • •

Names are important. Without them, the phone book would just be a book of numbers.

• • •

Never forget: you are one of those who can be fooled some of the time.

• • •

Never invest your money in anything that eats or needs repainting.

• • •

Raisins are important. Without them, thousands of gingerbread men wouldn't be able to see.

• • •

The colder the X-ray table, the more of your body you will be asked to put on it.

• • •

Time is nature's way of keeping everything from happening at once.

• • •

Two wrongs don't make a right, but three lefts do.

• • •

Was Robin Hood's mother known as Mother Hood?

• • •

What do little birdies see when they get knocked unconscious?

• • •

What do people in China call their good plates?

• • •

What do they call the coffee break at the Lipton Tea Company?

• • •

What do you call a male ladybug?

• • •

What do you get when you place a corpse against a doorbell?
A dead ringer!

• • •

What does a farmer do if his rooster has laryngitis?

• • •

What does a mummy do to unwind?

• • •

What does cheese say when it has its picture taken?

• • •

What happens if you get scared half to death twice?

• • •

What was the best thing before sliced bread?

● ● ●

What's so great about endangered species? You never see any of them around.

● ● ●

What's the big deal about Shakespeare's plays? They're nothing but a bunch of famous quotes thrown together!

● ● ●

What's the longest distance between two points?
A taxi ride.

● ● ●

When somebody eats something that they think has gone bad, why do they always want you to taste it?

● ● ●

If golf had never been invented, how would they measure hail?

● ● ●

When a color-blind person reads the Yellow Pages, how does he know he's reading them?

● ● ●

When a person says, "I'm going outside for some air," what was he breathing inside?

● ● ●

When an octopus puts on deodorant, how does he remember where he started?

● ● ●

When a Chinese child sits at the piano, does he play "Forks and Spoons"?

• • •

When Congress goes into recess, who handles playground duty?

• • •

When the pope comes to the United States, does anyone check his passport?

• • •

When they first invented the clock, how did they know what time to set it to?

• • •

When they ship Styrofoam, what do they pack it in?

• • •

When we borrowed customs from other countries, why didn't we borrow the siesta?

• • •

Whenever I see a public map that says, "You Are Here," I always wonder, "Where else would I be?"

• • •

Whenever I wear a turtleneck, I feel like I'm being choked by a really weak person.

• • •

Where did people hang their kids' pictures before the invention of the refrigerator?

• • •

Where do contractors go in the middle of a job?

• • •

Where is this city called Charter? You see so many buses going there.

• • •

Who edits fishing shows, and who decides what's too boring?

• • •

Whose cruel idea was it to put an 's' in the word lisp and to put three 't's in the word stutter?

• • •

Why are all historical places located within one hundred yards of a souvenir shop?

• • •

Why are funeral processions allowed to go through red lights? What's the big hurry?

• • •

Why are we expected to remember history when they keep adding stuff all the time?

• • •

Why is it always the third car back that is the first to see the light turn green?

• • •

Why is it that doctors who perform delicate microsurgery can't write so you can read it?

• • •

Why is it that every time a dead shark washes ashore, scientists cut open its stomach and find a license plate inside? Who are these people who drive their cars into the ocean and why do they park near sharks?

• • •

Why is it that people who can't count to ten always seem to wind up in front of you in the supermarket express lane?

• • •

Why is it that the caterpillar does all the work, and the butterfly gets all the headlines?

• • •

Why is it that the people who forget to turn off their car headlights always remember to lock their cars?

• • •

Why is living in California like eating a bowl of Granola?
Because after you're done with the fruits and nuts there are still a lot of flakes left.

• • •

Why are boxing rings square?

• • •

Why are there five syllables in the word *monosyllable*?

• • •

Why are there interstate highways in Hawaii?

• • •

Why call it "rush hour" when no one is moving?

• • •

Why did kamikaze pilots wear helmets?

• • •

Why do banks charge you for insufficient funds fees on money they know you don't have?

• • •

Why do bills travel through the mail at two-and-a-half times the speed of checks?

• • •

Why do cat hairs stick to everything but the cat?

• • •

Why do convenience stores have twenty thousand dollars worth of cameras to watch twenty dollars worth of stale sandwiches?

• • •

Why do croutons come in airtight packages? They're just stale bread to begin with.

• • •

Why do I always turn the twisty ties in the wrong direction first?

• • •

Why do people wait for vacations to wear the tackiest things they own?

• • •

Why do the signs that say "Slow Children" have a picture of a running child?

• • •

Why do they call them apartments when they're all stuck together?

• • •

Why do they call them appetizers when all they do is spoil your appetite?

• • •

Why do they call them buildings when they're already built?

• • •

Why do they lock gas station bathrooms? Are they afraid someone will clean them?

• • •

Why do we call them "hot-water heaters" when they heat cold water?

• • •

Why do women wait until they get to Kmart to spank their kids?

• • •

Why does sour cream have an expiration date?

• • •

Why does the army issue you a duffel bag and then complain if your clothes are wrinkled?

• • •

Why don't you ever see a baby pigeon?

• • •

Why is abbreviated such a long word?

• • •

Why is it called "lipstick" if you can still move your lips?

• • •

Why is it that every person in the express lane picks up at least one item without a price tag?

• • •

Why is it that lemonade cans say, "Contains artificial lemon juice," and a can of Pledge advertises, "Contains real lemon juice"?

• • •

Why is it that the closer you get to the ocean, the more seafood costs?

• • •

Why is it that when I go to the supermarket, the woman ahead of me always has a loaded cart, no driver's license and a check drawn on the Bank of El Salvador?

• • •

Why is the alphabet in that order? Is it because of the song?

• • •

Why is the federal department that is in charge of everything outdoors called the Department of the Interior?

• • •

Why is the Miss Universe competition always won by someone from Earth?

• • •

Why is there so much pressure to spend Independence Day with other people?

• • •

Why must the phrase, "It is none of my business," always be followed by the word "but"?

• • •

Why should we care about future generations? What have they done for us?

• • •

Will designer jeans ever replace the tourniquet?

• • •

Why is it that the sun lightens our hair, but darkens our skin?

• • •

Why is the third hand on a watch called the second hand?

• • •

If four out of five people suffer from gout, does that mean that one enjoys it?

• • •

Why do people say that something is "out of whack"? What's a whack?

• • •

Why is the man with whom you invest your life savings called a broker?

• • •

If a person who plays a piano is called a pianist, why isn't a race-car driver called a racist?

• • •

PROGRAM HIGHLIGHTS

On tonight's program we will have a man shot from a cannon. He will soar two hundred feet and play a violin solo on his descent. Understand now, he's no Heifetz.

• • •

On tonight's show we have a clairvoyant ventriloquist who can read your mind without moving his lips.

• • •

Tonight we will have a juggler who will juggle ten razor-sharp knives, after which he will juggle eight fingers.

• • •

I saw the sword swallower that we had lined up for our halftime show swallowing pins and needles. He told me, "I'm on a diet."

• • •

Later on in the show, those fine Filipino contortionists, The Manila Folders! From Dover, Delaware, the remarkable Dover twins, Ben Dover and Eileen Dover, who will demonstrate their unusual hobby of twisting animals into the shapes of balloons.

• • •

Tonight we have a galaxy of international stars performing for us: from Indonesia, Mr. Frank Sumatra; from South America, the gorgeous Bolivia Newton-John; from Chile, Mr. Andes Williams; from Bermuda, the acrobatic midgets, the popular Bermuda Shorts; and the Olympic Czechoslovakian Trampoline team, the sensational Bouncing Czechs.

• • •

Tonight we will feature a sword swallower who will swallow a five-and-one-half-foot sword. What makes it really amazing is that he's only five feet tall.

• • •

We were expecting to have a man entertain us at halftime (intermission) who first jumps off a 50-foot tower into a tank of water, and then a 100-foot tower into a barrel of water, and finally a 150-foot tower into a damp rag. He'd be doing it tonight, but unfortunately, during rehearsal, somebody wrung out the rag.

• • •

Next on the show, the State Police Barbershop Quartet—the fabulous Coppertones.

• • •

PSYCHIATRISTS

"Doc, I think I'm a deck of cards."
"Go to the waiting room. I'll deal with you later."

• • •

Psychotherapy turned his life around. He used to have money.

• • •

A guy goes to his psychiatrist and says, "Doc, I have a three-way personality. I think one thing, say another and then forget what I said."
The psychiatrist says, "Excuse me, but what office did you say you're running for?"

• • •

Aspiring psychiatrists were attending their first class on emotional extremes.
"Just so we can establish some parameters," said the professor, "Mr. Nichols what is the opposite of joy?"
"Sadness," said the student.
"And the opposite of depression, Mr. Biggs?"
"Elation."
"How about the opposite of woe, Mr. Wilson?"
"I believe that that is giddy-up," said the student.

• • •

And then there's the psychiatrist who showed such poor judgment that he furnished his waiting room with a cuckoo clock.

• • •

(to patient) "By the way, two of your multiple personalities haven't paid me for their last visit."

• • •

A friend talking to a psychiatrist on an elevator said, "How can you listen to all those problems and phobias and still be fresh and alert at the end of the day?"
The psychiatrist answered, "Who listens?"

• • •

Woman: "My husband thinks he's a horse."
Psychiatrist: "I can cure him, but it will take a lot of visits and a lot of money."
Woman: "Oh, money is no object. Last year he won the Kentucky Derby."

• • •

Psychiatrist to patient: "What do you do for a living?"
Guy says, "I'm an auto mechanic."
Psychiatrist says, "Okay, get under the couch."

• • •

I've got some good news and some bad news. The bad news is that my psychiatrist says that I'm afraid of success. The good news is that he says I have nothing to worry about.

• • •

Psychiatrist to patient: "If you think you're walking out of here cured after only three sessions, you're crazy!"

• • •

There are only two things to do if you have a nervous breakdown. Go away for a long rest in the country—or get a job in the National Basketball Association where it won't be noticed.

• • •

Three Jewish mothers were talking about how much their sons love them.

The first says, "See that Mercedes in the driveway? My son Abe bought that for me."

The second says, "You know that Van Gogh that hangs on my living-room wall? That was a gift from my son Bernie."

The third brags, "That's nothing. My son, Samuel, is in therapy five days a week with the finest psychotherapist on Park Avenue. And all he can talk about is me!"

• • •

Railroads

The railroads publish a monthly joke sheet. It's called a timetable.

• • •

Timetables are so precise. They tell you that you'll arrive in St. Louis at 10:23 A.M.—give or take a few days.

• • •

I asked the ticket agent, "Is there any way I could get to Boston sooner?"
He said, "Sure, take the first car on the train."

• • •

An experienced train rider never orders soup that doesn't match his pants.

• • •

Railroads are carrying fewer and fewer passengers. I called the station and asked, "What time does your train for Richmond leave?"
The agent said, "When would you like it to leave?"

• • •

Restaurant

You should leave the restaurant immediately if:
. . . the menu spells quiche with a k.

• • •

"Waiter, there's a fly in my soup."
"I know. The cook ran out of RAID, so he had to drown them."

• • •

"Waiter, what's this fly doing in my ice tea?"
"Cooling off. It's very hot in the kitchen."

• • •

"Waiter, what's this fly doing in my soup?"
"It must have escaped from the salad."

• • •

"Waiter, what's this in my soup?"
"How should I know? I can't tell one insect from another."

• • •

"Waiter, there's a fly in my soup."
"Let's hope for his sake that he didn't swallow any."

• • •

(to waiter) "What would you eat if you were me?"
Waiter: "Prime rib, but not here."

• • •

Sushi is popular today, but it's nothing new. When I was growing up, they called it *bait*.

• • •

A child sitting down at a restaurant table said, "Boy, we ought to eat at this place more often. They leave money for your meal under the plates."

• • •

A girl ate at a Jewish-Chinese delicatessen. An hour later she was hungry and had a strong urge to marry a doctor.

• • •

A man ordered a bottle of wine. The steward said, "What year?"
"Right now," answered the man. "We'd like to have it with the meal."

• • •

The portions were so small that I had to fill up on parsley.

• • •

We went to a secluded restaurant. It was so secluded that apparently the Board of Health couldn't find it.

• • •

Ask the waitress, "Can we substitute items on the menu?"
If she answers yes, say, "In that case, I'll have the prime rib in place of the parsley."

• • •

At this restaurant you eat like a king, which means you should have someone taste the food for you first.

• • •

Customer: "My juice is warm. I wanted it cold."
Waiter: "If you wanted something cold, sir, you should have ordered soup."

• • •

Customer: "The service here is awful."
Waiter: "How would you know? You haven't had any yet!"

• • •

Customer: "Waiter, I'll have the chef's salad."
Waiter: "Really? Then what will the chef eat?"

• • •

He always orders a waffle with his alphabet soup so he can do a crossword puzzle.

• • •

I asked the waitress, "What's the soup du jour?"
She said, "I'll check." She came back a few minutes later and said, "It's the soup of the day."

• • •

I asked the waitress, "What's the chef's surprise?"
She said, "He doesn't wash his hands."

• • •

I had a steak at a restaurant that was so bad you could still see the jockey's whip marks on it.

• • •

I have discovered why waitresses always give their first names. It's in case you have to file a missing persons report a couple of hours later.

• • •

I know of a protester who went nine days without food or water. Finally he asked for a different waiter.

• • •

I suggest you try their soup du jour. It tastes different every time I have it.

• • •

My wife and I faced a tough decision at a restaurant the other night. We had to decide whether we wanted the prime rib, the lobster tail or a month of electricity.

• • •

That restaurant served the strongest coffee I ever had. I put three containers of creamer in it, and it still didn't change color.

• • •

The maître d' said, "Two waiters called in sick tonight, so we're running about an hour and a half behind. Would you care for an appetite suppressant?"

• • •

The Mexican restaurant had such a realistic motif that none of the patrons drank the water.

• • •

Waiter: "How did you find your hamburger?"
Customer: "By sheer accident. I just picked up my pickle ring and there it was."

• • •

Waiter: "Sorry, sir, our policy is no dessert unless you clear your plate."

• • •

What's today's special?
The Heimlich maneuver.

• • •

"Waiter, there's a fly in my soup!"
"That's all right. It's not hot enough to burn him."

• • •

"Waiter, there's a fly in my soup!"
"Well, there's a fly that knows good soup!"

• • •

Sign: "We not only honor credit cards, we love and respect them."

• • •

A waiter carrying a flaming shish kebab was asked by a customer, "What is that?"

"A customer who didn't leave a generous tip," the waiter answered.

• • •

The waiter said, "Your dinner will be along shortly, sir. In the meantime, would you care for another candle?"

• • •

I dined in a posh restaurant, and two men approached my table. One said, "Good evening. I am Pierre, your waiter. And this is Mr. Samuels. He'll arrange the financing."

• • •

Two fellows go into a restaurant. One says, "I'll have the iced tea and make it very weak."

The second says, "I'll have the iced tea also, but I'd like it very strong. And make sure it's in a clean glass."

The waiter returned and said, "Now I forget. Who gets the clean glass?"

• • •

I'd like to send my compliments to the kitchen crew. It's the first time I've ever been served roast beef, coffee, and ice cream all at the same temperature.

• • •

The restaurant advertised "Homestyle Breakfast." And sure enough, the waitress wore a bathrobe, had her hair in curlers, and served burnt toast, weak coffee, and lumpy oatmeal.

• • •

The waiters were independent. They took orders from no one.

• • •

The restaurant advertised "blended coffee."

I asked the waitress, "What coffees go into the blend?"

She said, "Yesterday's and today's."

• • •

I won't comment on the size of their portions. Suffice it to say that the steak I had was good to the last bite—which, incidentally, was also the first.

• • •

They're closed on Mondays. That's when they do the dishes.

• • •

Their soup du jour comes from the finest du jours grown today.

• • •

And wasn't the service at this dinner something? I didn't know that the post office catered.

• • •

I saw a cockroach in a restaurant that was really tough . . . he was bench pressing a bread stick.

• • •

I asked the waitress to warm up my coffee, and she stuck her cigarette in it.

• • •

I told the waiter that the soup was awful and asked who made it. He said, "I had a hand in it."

• • •

I saw a touching thing at the restaurant. Two of the waitresses were singing "Happy Birthday" to several of the doughnuts that had been under the plastic dome for a year.

• • •

I went to a seafood restaurant and asked, "What's the catch of the day?" and the waiter replied, "Hepatitis."

• • •

I went to one of those restaurants that advertise "Breakfast Anytime" so I ordered pancakes from the Renaissance period.

• • •

It has been said: We pass this way but once. I don't know who said it. It might have been our waiter.

• • •

When you go to a restaurant, be sure to get a table near a waiter.

• • •

It's the kind of restaurant where nobody bothers you. Not even the waiters.

• • •

Sign on a restaurant cash register: Sure we'll cash your personal check if you're over eighty and accompanied by your parents.

• • •

Restaurant sign: "Shoes are required to eat in restaurant. Socks may eat wherever they wish."

• • •

One restaurant owner stated: There will be no increase for New Year's Eve. The restaurant's normal exorbitant prices will prevail.

• • •

Just once I'd like to meet the waiter with enough courage to leave the check face up on the table.

• • •

I really impress people when I take my wife to dinner and order everything in French. The employees at McDonald's are amazed!

• • •

We go to one of those very swanky health food restaurants. Their specialty is rack of soybean.

• • •

Sign on a restaurant window: Come on in. Everything else has gone wrong today.

• • •

He claims to have gone forty-four days without food. He should have given his order to another waiter.

• • •

I said to the waiter, "What is our offense? We've been on bread and water for over an hour now!"

• • •

A fellow at a restaurant ordered a breakfast of warm orange juice with pits and pulp, two eggs sunny-side up but very lightly done and gooey, burnt toast, and cold coffee in a dirty cup with lipstick smudges on the rim. The astonished waiter said, "But, sir, we can't make such a breakfast!"
To which the man replied, "Why not? You did it yesterday!"

• • •

The restaurant even had monogrammed napkins. What class! At least I thought so until I saw my monogram crawl away.

• • •

I won't say what the size of their servings are like, but I asked the waiter to put my steak on my credit card—and it fit!

• • •

Their house specialty was Pollo con Riviera. That's a chicken that has been run over by a Buick.

• • •

Retirement

You could always find our guest of honor with his nose to the grindstone and his shoulder to the wheel. How he ever slept in that position, I'll never know!

• • •

"The people in the personnel department tell me that they're going to hire your replacement just as soon as they figure out what it is that you've been doing all these years."

• • •

This company can't begin to repay you for your many years of devoted service, as you will see when you get your first pension check.

• • •

Retirement is when you ask the hotel front desk clerk for a wake-up call at seven and he asks, "A.M. or P.M.?"

• • •

As a retirement gift, we give to you the clock from your office wall. We know you admire it, because you were always staring at it.

• • •

He elected to skip coffee breaks altogether and it enabled him to retire three years earlier.

• • •

He's always been an optimist. When he retired at sixty-five, he planted two acorns and bought himself a hammock.

• • •

His company didn't give him a gold watch, but they do call him once a week with the correct time.

• • •

It's appropriate we give him a dinner. Everyone has in the past. He hasn't picked up a check in years.

• • •

Now that he's retired, what will he stop doing?

• • •

Now that he's retiring, his friends are afraid that the sudden increase in activity will be too much of a shock to his system.

• • •

One woman defines retirement as "twice as much husband with half as much money."

• • •

Our company has a different retirement program. You work until you die.

• • •

Retirement is a slow, leisurely pace. Unless, of course, you worked for the post office, in which case, things speed up considerably.

• • •

Retirement is when your favorite piece of software is a pillow.

• • •

This will be a big period of adjustment for him. He'll have to get used to taking his afternoon naps at home.

• • •

We all chipped in to get you something that will help keep your bills down. It's a paperweight.

• • •

We all pitched in to get you a recliner with racing stripes.

• • •

When he planned his retirement, he told his wife that he would be spending much more time around the house. She immediately started making plans. I was amazed to find out that they'd let a woman her age join the Foreign Legion!

• • •

When he retired, he vowed that he would sit around and not do a thing. It's been an interesting experience for him, and even more interesting for his wife. She told me that she had never dusted a person before.

• • •

When he started working for the company twenty-five years ago, he said there was nothing he wouldn't do for this company, and in those twenty-five years, he's done just that.

• • •

When you retire, make a two-part deal with your wife. Deal one: you agree to shovel the snow, if she mows the lawn. Deal two: you move to Florida.

• • •

You are always welcome to come back to your old desk, Sam, if you need to catch up on your sleep.

• • •

You know you're retired when evening comes and you want to change into something more comfortable, and you're already in something more comfortable.

• • •

In his years with this firm, he's kept his ear to the ground. I'm told he can sleep anywhere.

• • •

Look at the crowd that has assembled to honor you on your upcoming retirement. Who was it who said, "Give the people what they want, and they come out in droves"?

• • •

He told me, "When I retire, I'll finally be able to finish the book I started thirty years ago."
I asked, "What book are you reading?"

• • •

We wanted to get something for you, Bob, but no one would start the bidding.

• • •

As a symbol of our gratitude, we have created this special gold watch to serve as a reminder of your many years with the company. It needs a lot of winding up—is always a little late—and every day at quarter to five, it stops working.

• • •

In preparation for this dinner the office staff produced a thumbnail sketch of all his accomplishments during his thirty-five years with the company. It's called a thumbnail sketch because that's what it fits on.

• • •

I hear that the biggest challenge of adjusting to retirement is sitting around and doing nothing. With Bill this won't be a problem. With our company alone he's had over twenty-five years of practice.

• • •

We have two wishes for your future—that your bowling score will be as high as your hopes, and your golfing score will be as low as your pension.

• • •

It was a little embarrassing planning this event. When Bill announced that he was going to retire, it came as a complete surprise to most of us—because most of us thought he already had.

• • •

I retired three years ago. The biggest problem is to keep the boss from finding out.

• • •

The problem with being retired is that you never know what day it is, where you're supposed to be, or what you're supposed to be doing. It's much like working for the federal government.

• • •

One big shock that comes when you retire after a lifetime of office work is that some people actually buy pencils, pens and paper.

• • •

He took an aptitude test to find out for what he was best suited, and he found out he was best suited for retirement.

• • •

Here's a person who's put in twenty-five great years with this company—thirteen if you don't count coffee breaks.

• • •

Rich

(at the reading of a will) "And to my young nephew who always said that 'Health is more important than wealth,' I leave my sweat socks and jogging shoes."

• • •

An elementary-school girl from an exclusive neighborhood was asked to write about a poor family. She wrote, "Once upon a time there was a poor family. The father was poor; the mother was poor; the sisters and brothers were poor; the butler was poor; the chauffeur was poor; they were all poor."

• • •

It seems ironic that all the people who hate the rich are the ones that are in line buying lottery tickets.

• • •

He's so rich that he considers the IRS to be a terrorist organization.

• • •

He's so rich that he gets most of his exercise from folding his money.

• • •

His neighborhood is so rich that they have Little League polo teams.

• • •

I knew that I was in a rich neighborhood when I went into the fast-food chain and they served Kentucky-Fried Pheasant.

• • •

The homeless in his neighborhood carry signs that say, "Will work for pâte."

• • •

The neighborhood is so rich that the football team's mascot is a mink.

• • •

The rich miss out on one of the greatest pleasures in life—the last payment on an installment plan.

• • •

They're suffering from a water shortage in his neighborhood. Two Perrier trucks collided.

• • •

His town is so exclusive that the Salvation Army band has a string section.

• • •

His neighbor is so rich that he has a birdbath in his backyard. Now that might not sound unusual, but his has a salad bar!

• • •

Kid: "When I grow up, I want to be a philanthropist. They always seem to have lots of money."

• • •

He's so rich that, when he flies, his wallet is considered carry-on luggage.

• • •

He's so rich that his bank gave him bookends for his bankbooks.

• • •

Their neighborhood was so rich that the girls go door-to-door selling Girl Scout croissants.

• • •

Roast

Our guest of honor is living proof that having a goal, a dream, and struggling hard to attain it don't always work.

• • •

A frugal man, he has sometimes been compared to Santa Claus. He has one suit, but he gets a lot of wear out of it.

• • •

He likes to be alone in the woods, go places where few have gone before and face seemingly impossible challenges. Unfortunately, he does all this while golfing.

• • •

He's afraid of his own shadow—and for good reason. It looks just like him.

• • •

Ancestry

He comes from a musical family. He told me that almost everyone in his family has a record.

• • •

He loves bowling—and for good reason. He was born in an alley. In fact, his parents named a gutter after him.

• • •

His family album indicates that his ancestors went west in a covered wagon. And when I saw pictures of them, I realized why the wagon was covered.

• • •

His parents were in the iron and steel business. His mother used to iron, and his father used to steal.

• • •

Appearance

After seeing your outfit, I get the feeling that somewhere in this town there's a horse that's shivering.

• • •

As a kid he was so ugly that they put him in a corner and fed him with a slingshot.

• • •

He has a great outfit on tonight. It's not often that you see a suit and toupee made of the same material.

• • •

He has the perfect face for radio.

• • •

He's so thin that he looks like an advance man for a famine.

• • •

He looks like he went to the blood bank and forgot to say when.

• • •

He was so lonely as a kid that his mother hung a pork chop around his neck so the dog would play with him.

• • •

Here is a man with his shoulder to the wheel, nose to the grind-stone and his ear to the ground. Worst posture you ever saw.

• • •

He's originally from New York. Well, at least the first 175 pounds of him.

• • •

He's really mad tonight. He spent forty minutes combing his hair and forgot to bring it with him.

• • •

His folks weren't exactly proud of him. Early home movies show his parents sneaking out of the hospital with bags over their heads.

• • •

I can truthfully say that I've been with him through thick and thin. Thick and thin—his waist and hair.

• • •

I can't imagine where he eats out, now that 7-Eleven has a dress code.

• • •

I wouldn't have recognized him, because I hadn't seen him in eight years. But I never forget a suit.

• • •

Look at that haircut! I didn't know that (famous blind person) owned a barber shop.

• • •

That photograph doesn't do him justice. It looks like him.

• • •

The City Beautification Committee has asked him to keep out of sight.

• • •

Ugly? As a kid, his parents used to feed him rock candy with a slingshot.

• • •

We were going to put a statue of him in the park, but then we figured, "Why should we scare the poor pigeons?"

• • •

What an outfit! Don't let anyone tell you that burlap won't hold a crease.

• • •

What can you say about a man who not only wears a clip-on tie, but also wears a clip-on suit?

• • •

When they made him, they threw away the mold, but it appears to be growing back.

• • •

Business

He could be rich and famous except for two things—he's broke and nobody knows him.

• • •

He couldn't wait for success, so he went ahead without it.

• • •

He has meant to his profession what waterskiing has meant to the economy of Arizona.

• • •

He robbed a synagogue in Israel and escaped with two million dollars worth of pledges.

• • •

Here is a man who turned the family business into a million-dollar business. Of course, it had been a multimillion-dollar business.

• • •

He's an inspiration to men everywhere. They figure that if he can make it, anybody can.

• • •

He's been compared to the vice president of the United States. No one can figure out what either one does.

• • •

He's just been named Man of the Year, which gives you an idea of what kind of year it's been.

• • •

I will say this for him. He has always given this company an honest day's work . . . sometimes it's taken him a week to do it.

• • •

CHEAP

He found that it cost ten dollars a year to feed a child in China, so he sent his whole family over there.

• • •

He had his name legally changed to Hilton, so that it would match the name on his towels.

• • •

He is very charitable. Every year he offers fifty thousand dollars to the wife of the Unknown Soldier.

• • •

He's so generous that he'd give you the sleeves out of his vest.

• • •

There's nothing that I wouldn't do for Bill, and there's nothing that he wouldn't do for me. And that's how we are going through life—doing nothing for each other.

• • •

Dull

Dull? His favorite hobby is waiting in line.

• • •

Dull? His life flashed before his eyes, and he fell asleep.

• • •

He reminds me of St. Paul—one of the dullest towns in America.

• • •

He's a lot of fun to be with if you like to yawn.

• • •

He's dull. He spent another exciting weekend rearranging his sock drawer.

• • •

He's so bland that when he walks into an empty room he fits right in.

• • •

His life is so dull that he actually looks forward to dental appointments.

• • •

With him, there's never a dull moment. The whole day is dull.

• • •

Education

He was a four-letter man in high school. He never learned the rest of the alphabet.

• • •

One advantage he's had in life is that he's never been pestered by the Rhodes Scholarship people.

• • •

Ego

He was adjusting his tie in front of the mirror tonight before this awards dinner and he asked his wife, "Honey, how many great men do you think there are in the world today?"
"One less than you think," his wife replied.

• • •

Here he is, a legend in his own mind . . .

• • •

Here he is, a legend in his spare time . . .

• • •

INEPTITUDE

He had an accident with a horse when he got caught in the stirrups, and the horse kept going and going until the Kmart manager came out of the store and unplugged it.

• • •

He has sometimes been called a self-made man—which just shows what can happen when you don't read the instructions.

• • •

He has sometimes been called a self-made man. This, of course, was in the days before quality control.

• • •

He has the Midas touch. Everything he touches turns into a muffler.

• • •

He's not a super athlete. I remember his sports days with people yelling, "Air ball! Air ball!" And that's when he was bowling.

• • •

He's still recovering from injuries he suffered when he went to a costume party dressed as a piñata.

• • •

Here is a person of limited skills who did not master the art of waving bye-bye until he was eleven years old.

• • •

Here's a man who helps underprivileged kids. They look at him and feel better.

• • •

He's really accident prone. Just the other day, he cut himself on his bowling ball.

• • •

You should have heard him scream when he stepped on a thumbtack. There's no telling what he would have done if he had stepped on the pointed end!

• • •

INTELLIGENCE

Childhood impressions can last a lifetime. When he was a kid, his father said, "Now, don't go getting any bright ideas . . . ," and sure enough, he hasn't.

• • •

Dumb? Someone asked him, "What's your favorite dish?" and he said, "A saucer."

• • •

He bet ten dollars on a football game and lost. Then he bet another ten dollars on the instant replay and lost again.

• • •

He is a man who has a firm grip of the obvious.

• • •

He is so proud that it took him just eighteen months to finish a jigsaw puzzle. He boasts, "The box says three to five years."

• • •

He never lets his mind wander. It's too small to go out by itself.

• • •

He said, "What kind of idiot do you think I am?"
I said, "I don't know. What other kinds are there?"

• • •

He wants to take One-A-Day vitamins, but he can't figure out the dosage.

• • •

He was like a big oak tree, standing tall, a shelter to all as we huddled under his branches. A symbol of strength and stability, but like all oak trees, he wasn't too bright.

• • •

He was so excited when he was promoted to sixth grade that he could hardly shave without cutting himself.

• • •

He won a gold medal in tennis and immediately had it bronzed.

• • •

He's no dummy. He knows plenty. He just can't think of it.

• • •

He's not exactly ready for the computer age. Last week he just figured out how to work his View Master.

• • •

He's so dumb he bought a motorcycle with an air conditioner.

• • •

He's so dumb, he thinks that Taco Bell is the Mexican telephone company.

• • •

He's so dumb. His wife asked him to change the baby and he brought home a different kid.

• • •

He's so slow that it takes him an hour and a half to watch 60 Minutes.

• • •

He's the king of the one-liners. That's because he can't remember two.

• • •

Here's a man who's educated beyond his intelligence.

• • •

He's really excited today because he made a discovery. He found out that he could play his AM radio in the evening, too.

• • •

He's so dumb. He was driving here tonight, saw a sign that said, "Draw Bridge Ahead," and he turned to go back home to get his paper and crayons.

• • •

Hey, if ignorance is bliss, this man is in paradise.

• • •

I know, Jim, that you won't take umbrage at what I say about you, because you don't know what "umbrage" means.

• • •

In all the years I've known him, no one has ever questioned his intelligence. In fact, no one has ever mentioned it.

• • •

It's a miracle he can speak to us tonight. He's recovering from an unusual accident. He was struck by a thought.

• • •

Just last year, our guest of honor won an award for originality and creative imagination. The bad news is that it was from the IRS.

• • •

Just the other day he was heard to say, "They're not making antiques the way they used to."

• • •

Not only does he not know what's going on, he doesn't suspect anything either.

• • •

Success hasn't gone to his head. In fact, not much has gone to his head.

• • •

They say that what you don't know won't hurt you, so he's a man that must feel no pain.

• • •

INTRODUCTIONS

NOBODY EVER THREW HIM A PARTY (NETHAP)
How about Alexander Graham Kowalski, the first telephone Pole NETHAP . . .

or Thomas Alva Edison, who tried twenty thousand filaments before holding the lightbulb up to his ear and saying, "Hello? Hello?" NETHAP . . .

or his friend who claims, "Honesty is one of the better policies," NETHAP . . .

or the guy who discovered slow motion by watching Bill Norton reach for a dinner check, NETHAP . . .

or Frank Perdue's charisma coach, NETHAP . . .

or George Washington, who proved reincarnation by coming back as a bridge, NETHAP . . .

or the guy who was punched out by Leo Buscaglia while Mother Teresa held his arms, NETHAP . . .

or Ponce de Leon, whose wife said, "Hey Ponce, you're going to Florida and you're not taking me?" NETHAP . . .

• • •

After a speech like that I say, "May you be a light sleeper, and may the guy upstairs take a correspondence course in polka and tap dancing."

• • •

And now a man who has done for this city what (famous fat person) has done for wicker furniture.

• • •

He is a marvelous public speaker who got his start in the business announcing the blue light specials at Kmart.

• • •

He's about as well-known as Whistler's father.

• • •

He's all excited because his name is on the front page of USA Today. There it is, right on the address label.

• • •

He's wearing his dinner jacket tonight. As you can see, his dinner is all over it.

• • •

His life has been full of trials, but so far no convictions.

• • •

His name is on the lips of many, but then again, so is Chap Stick.

● ● ●

I know the hour is late, and it's been a long evening, but I don't intend to leave this mike until I've told you every good thing I know about our guest of honor. (Pause briefly). Thank you and good night.

● ● ●

I love this place. I've come back six consecutive years and I look back on them as the best years of my life. Which gives you some idea of the miserable life I've been leading.

● ● ●

I sacrificed a lot to be here tonight. Mostly my self-respect.

● ● ●

I was asked to give a few thoughts on our guest of honor, which is very difficult since I never think of him.

● ● ●

If we fall asleep while you're talking, Bob, it's only because we trust you.

● ● ●

I'd like to thank our previous speaker, a man of many talents. As we all observed, humor isn't one of them.

● ● ●

I'll remember this evening for as long as it takes me to get to my car.

● ● ●

Let's examine our guest of honor. And let's face it. Our guest of honor should have been examined long ago.

• • •

Our next speaker needs no introduction. What he needs is an act.

• • •

Since I met him ten years ago, there hasn't been a day that I did not think of him. And I didn't think of him again today.

• • •

Thank you for that introduction. What you lacked in clarity and wit, you certainly made up for in length.

• • •

The legal definition of a roast: assault and flattery.

• • •

The reason that we subject people to a roast is because tarring and feathering is illegal.

• • •

This evening has lasted longer than a Christmas fruitcake.

• • •

This man is responsible for selling more radios than anyone I know. When he went on the air, I sold mine, my sister sold hers and all the neighbors sold theirs.

• • •

Tonight we honor a man who doesn't know the meaning of the word fear; he doesn't know the meaning of the word quit. And so we all chipped in and bought him this dictionary.

• • •

Usually we roast the ones we love, but today we break that tradition.

• • •

We came to praise (roastee), not to bury him. But the vote was mighty close.

• • •

We're truly pleased that our guest of honor is here tonight. You know how fickle parole boards can be.

• • •

You came here tonight out of affection. You also came here tonight out of material.

• • •

You have what it takes—but you've had it too long!

• • •

You've been listening to the famous Chinese toastmaster, On Too Long.

• • •

MEAN

He doesn't hate his enemies. After all, he made them.

• • •

He doesn't get ulcers, he gives them. In fact, I'm going to name my first ulcer after him.

• • •

He enjoys Super-Gluing worms to the sidewalk so he can watch robins go crazy.

• • •

He has an offbeat sense of humor. He just called the city's allergy clinic and invited everyone in the waiting room on a hayride.

• • •

He's a vicious guy. He gives 10 percent of his money to piranha research.

• • •

He's the type who likes to walk up to overweight people in the supermarket and say, "Haven't you had enough already?"

• • •

Here's a man who's been just like a brother to me. In fact, just yesterday he beat me up and took my bicycle.

• • •

His hobby is painting passing lines on mountain roads.

• • •

His idea of a fun evening is sneaking into a wax museum and turning up the thermostat.

• • •

Isn't he sweet? In his spare time he's a heckler at telethons.

• • •

I've even seen him get hate mail from Quakers.

• • •

This has certainly been an evening to remember. I say this because I want to remember everything correctly for when I talk to my lawyer in the morning.

• • •

What can you say about him that hasn't already been said about poison ivy?

• • •

Personality

Always a gentleman, as a youth he helped old ladies across the street. Which wasn't easy. He lived in Venice.

• • •

And now, here he is, (boring celebrity's) charisma coach . . .

• • •

As a youth he had lots of charisma, but lately it's cleared up.

• • •

Cautious? He was told that most accidents happen within twenty miles from home, so he moved to a town fifty miles away.

• • •

Have you ever been to the zoo? I mean as a visitor.

• • •

He belongs to a very exclusive club. In order to be accepted, you must have your name listed in the phone book.

• • •

He hasn't many faults, but he makes the most of the ones he has.

• • •

He read that just as many accidents happen in bathtubs as do in airplanes, so he hasn't been in either one since.

• • •

He used to be miserable and depressed, but he's turned that all around. Now he's depressed and miserable.

• • •

He wanted to be his own best friend, but his mother would not let him hang around with that kind of person.

• • •

He's a man who has his feet planted firmly in midair.

• • •

He's a modest man. But then again, he has so much to be modest about.

• • •

He's a real pessimist. He wears a medic alert bracelet that says, "In case of an accident, I'm not surprised."

• • •

He's more than a friend to me. He's a total stranger.

• • •

He's not an only child, but his mom says that if he had been born first he would have been.

• • •

He's paranoid and feels the world is against him. That's not true. Some of the smaller countries are neutral.

• • •

He's so cautious that he burns his bridges in front of him.

• • •

He's so narrow-minded that he can look through a keyhole with both eyes at the same time.

• • •

He's the strong, silent type because he can't talk and hold his stomach in at the same time.

• • •

His father gave him a bat for his birthday. The first day he went outside to play with it, it flew away.

• • •

I think the world of him, and you know the condition the world is in.

• • •

Intense? He hunts Easter eggs with a shotgun.

• • •

I've been asked to say something nice about him. He doesn't shed.

• • •

I've heard a lot about him. And sometime I'd like to hear his side of the story.

• • •

I've known Bill as a whining child, a petulant teen, a rebellious young man and a demanding adult . . . often on the same day.

● ● ●

I've known him all my life, but it seems longer.

● ● ●

Men like him don't grow on trees. They usually swing from them.

● ● ●

Say what you want, but there is only one [name here]. I found that out by looking in the telephone directory.

● ● ●

The psychiatrist said to him, "Here are some sleeping pills."
He asked, "When should I take them."
The shrink said, "Whenever you wake up."

● ● ●

There's no end to his talent . . . and no beginning either.

● ● ●

Unlucky? Last week his swimming pool burned down.

● ● ●

Unlucky? Today his artificial flower died.

● ● ●

We didn't expect anything from him and he came through.

● ● ●

What a personality. He had a charisma bypass operation.

● ● ●

Physique

He should go on a diet. He discovered this morning that he can still touch his toes, but only with his stomach.

• • •

He walked into a clothing store and asked, "What do you have for a man my size?"
The clothing salesman said, "Pity!"

• • •

He willed his body to science and science is contesting the will.

• • •

He's in great shape for someone his age. Of course when he was born, things were built to last.

• • •

He's so fat that he can take a shower without getting his feet wet.

• • •

He's so fat that if he gets on an elevator, it better be going down.

• • •

I didn't even know that they made designer jeans in chubby.

• • •

It has been said that the human body is the apex of human art. His is more like a cave painting.

• • •

Look at that body! If he were a building, he'd be condemned!

• • •

Our honoree has the hands of a surgeon. They're always gripping a golf club.

• • •

(short) Being short really isn't such a handicap. Do you realize that he's gone through his entire life without ever being told to duck?

• • •

(short) He recently did a benefit for Save the Shrimp.

• • •

(short) He's so short he can keep his feet warm just by breathing hard.

• • •

(short) He's so short he can swim laps in his bathtub.

• • •

(short) I don't want to imply that he's short, but yesterday I saw him playing handball against the curb.

• • •

(short) He's so short that his feet show up on his driver's license photo.

• • •

(short) Poor guy. Imagine going through life without being able to see a parade.

• • •

Popularity

He has an unlisted phone, a post office box, and a numbered bank account, which is really unnecessary since no one wants to reach him anyway.

• • •

I've been to parties where the surgeon general offered him a cigarette.

• • •

In all the years I've known him, no one has ever said a bad word about him. It usually takes several paragraphs.

• • •

In honor of you, a tree has been uprooted in Israel.

• • •

Taste

He arrived from New Jersey broke, illiterate, uncouth . . . and nobody has ever been able to take that away from him.

• • •

Unusual Characteristics

He has unusual hobbies. For instance, in the summer he likes to build sand castles out of cement. Then he sits on his beach chair about twenty-five yards away and waits for kids to run by and try to kick them over.

• • •

He's so uncoordinated that I once saw him get tangled up while using his cordless phone.

• • •

As a kid, he always had his nose in a book. He never had a handkerchief.

• • •

He likes to reminisce with people he doesn't know.

• • •

He starts mystery novels in the middle, so he won't have to only wonder how it will end, but also how it began.

• • •

He sleeps like a baby. Every two hours or so he wakes up crying.

• • •

He's the outdoor type. He just loves nature in spite of what it did to him.

• • •

He's got a really strange mind. He told me, "Lightning would probably be even faster if it didn't zigzag."

• • •

What a practical joker! He lives to send people telegrams that read, "Ignore previous telegram."

• • •

Salary

An employee found a note in his paycheck which read: "Salary is your personal business, a confidential matter, and should not be discussed."

Signing his receipt, one of the workers added: "I won't mention it. I'm just as ashamed of it as you are."

• • •

Sales

Somebody once did a painting of our sales department. It was a still life.

• • •

I'm good at making excuses for our sales department. It could be that we have such a great product that we hate to part with it.

• • •

"We appreciate your business, but your account has been overdue for ten months now. Already we've carried you longer than your mother did."

• • •

Have you ever had the feeling your sales department couldn't sell batteries on Christmas morning?

• • •

Talk about a super salesman! He could sell carbon paper to the Xerox Company.

• • •

Did you ever get the feeling that your sales force couldn't peddle pickles in a maternity ward?

• • •

SALESMAN

"I got three orders today: 'Get out! Stay out! and Don't come back!'"

• • •

(customer weeping to salesman) "It's such a great deal, I don't think I'm worthy of it."

• • •

A good salesman is a guy who can convince his wife that she looks fat in a fur coat.

• • •

A shoe salesman assigned to Africa filed this report: "Impossible territory. Everyone here goes barefoot."
He was replaced by an optimistic salesman whose first report was, "Piling up orders by the bushel. Nobody here has shoes."

• • •

A very successful Bible salesman had a severe stuttering problem. When he was asked how he did it, he replied, "I just show them the Bible and ask, "W-W-W-ould y-y-you like to b-b-buy a B-B-Bible from m-m-me, or w-w-would y-y-you j-j-just l-l-like me to r-r-read it t-t-to y-y-you?"

• • •

At the hunting lodge, they had a dog named Salesman, a great hunter. The next time the hunter went to the hunting lodge, he asked for Salesman. The owner had renamed him Supersalesman.

The hunter went back a third time and asked for Supersalesman. "You can't have him," the lodge owner said. "We named him Sales Manager and now all he does is sit on his tail and bark."

• • •

Did you hear about the traveling salesman who died and left his family fifteen hundred towels?

• • •

He discovered that he had an aptitude for sales work in elementary school when he talked his fourth-grade teacher into giving him an oral exam in penmanship.

• • •

He has that typical sales personality. He's the kind of person who would call King Henry VIII "Hank."

• • •

He just made his first two sales—his car and his home.

• • •

He's such a good salesman that if you were shipwrecked and treading water, he could swim over to you and sell you an anvil.

• • •

Married men make the best salesmen because they are used to taking orders.

• • •

One of our salesmen is really excited. He just sold the fiction rights to his expense account.

• • •

The greatest salesman in the world is the guy who convinced restaurant owners that those hot-air hand dryers really work.

• • •

He's such a great salesman that he could:

- sell a MacIntosh to Bill Gates
- sell soap to an Amway salesman
- sell a double bed to the pope
- sell an anvil to a drowning man
- sell carbon paper to the Xerox company
- sell a Toyota to Lee Iacocca
- sell crowd control insurance to an indoor lacrosse league

• • •

Lady to a salesman: "I am not in the market for a vacuum cleaner. But the Smiths next door are. We borrow theirs all the time, and it's in terrible condition."

• • •

A judge said to a salesman: "Do you mean to tell me you need to get off jury duty because your company can't do without you?"

Salesman: "No, sir, I know they can do without me. I just don't want them to find out."

• • •

A salesman began his pitch to a housewife: "I want to show you a product that several of your neighbors told me you couldn't afford."

• • •

This weekend I read some light fiction. Last week's expense accounts.

• • •

Our salesmen have great imaginations. The trouble is that they put it all in their expense accounts!

• • •

Salesman: "If you buy this freezer, you could save enough on food bills to pay for it."
Housewife: "But we're buying a car on the bus fare we save, paying for a washer on the laundry bills we save and paying for a house on the rent we save. We just can't afford to save any more right now."

• • •

I was a brush salesman, and a woman opened the door in her negligee, which is kind of an odd place to have a door.

• • •

He's received offers from four publishers for the fiction rights to his expense accounts.

• • •

The salesman claimed, "This encyclopedia will tell you just about everything you need to know."
"I don't need one," replied the man of the house. "I'm married and have three teenage daughters!"

• • •

SCHOOL

"Beethoven wrote music even though he was deaf. He was so deaf that he wrote loud music."

• • •

"Dad, I think I flunked my science test today."
"Oh, son, don't be so negative."
"Okay. I'm positive I flunked my science test today."

• • •

"Mom, why am I the tallest kid in third grade. Is it because I'm Irish?"
"No, it's because you're eighteen."

• • •

"No wonder Claudette gets straight A's in French," one teen said to another. "Her parents were born in Paris and they speak French in their home."
"In that case I ought to get an A in geometry," said the other. "My parents are squares and always talk in circles."

• • •

"Please excuse my son from Spanish class. His throat is so sore that he can hardly speak English."

• • •

"Well, Jerry," said Father, glancing at his report card, "one thing that's in your favor is that with grades like these, you couldn't possibly be cheating."

• • •

"What is 13 and 12?"asked the teacher.
"Twenty-five," answered Tommy.

"That's very good, Tommy," said the teacher.

"Good? That's perfect!" said Tommy.

• • •

I won't say what kind of student I was, but teachers used to give me extra credit for being absent.

• • •

(A rural school district) has been forced to cancel drivers' education. The mule died.

• • •

A mother recently told me that she thinks that summer vacations are subsidized by Extra-Strength Excedrin.

• • •

A neighbor boy of ours is really confused. He was kicked out of parochial school for swearing, and he was suspended from public school for praying.

• • •

A student missed every question on an aptitude test. His counselor told him, "Don't be discouraged. You can always become an economic forecaster."

• • •

A wise school teacher sent this note home on the first day of school, "If you promise not to believe everything that your child says happens at school, I'll promise not to believe everything he says happens at home."

• • •

Don't take the high school years for granted. They go by so quickly. I know my six years did.

• • •

Don't you think that we should change Mother's Day to the day that kids go back to school following summer vacation?

• • •

"Encyclopedia" comes from a Latin phrase meaning to paraphrase a term paper.

• • •

He does well with questions. It's the answers he has trouble with.

• • •

He doesn't understand Roman numerals. He asked, "When did we fight World War Eleven?"

• • •

He finished school in half the time. He was expelled in sixth grade.

• • •

He got an "America the Beautiful" report card. You know—from "C" to shining "C".

• • •

He missed his tenth high school reunion. He was at home still doing his homework.

• • •

He walked six miles to school and six miles back. That's strange, too because the school was right across the street from his house.

• • •

He was a sensitive and emotional student. He cried in math class when the teacher told him that parallel lines never meet.

• • •

He was kicked off the high school debating team because he kept agreeing with the other side.

• • •

Here it is: September again and another school year begins, with name calling, petty bickering and childish behavior. But enough about the school board meetings.

• • •

His best subject is recess. Maybe he'll be a congressman when he grows up.

• • •

A boy came home from school looking forlorn. His mother asked why. Her son replied, "Today when I told my teacher I was an only child, she said, 'Thank goodness!'"

• • •

The student complained to his teacher, "I don't deserve an F on this test." "I know," answered the teacher, "but school policy dictates that that's the lowest grade I can award."

• • •

His teacher didn't like him much. Even during fire drills she would tell him to stay in his seat.

• • •

History repeats itself, especially if you fail the course.

• • •

I had a conference with my son's teacher and she said that it was really helpful. She said that after meeting me, she understood why my son had problems.

• • •

I had four years of Latin in college, which comes in very handy when I run into a pharmacist or a very old Roman.

• • •

I wanted to be a doctor but I couldn't stand the sight of blood, so I became a teacher because I couldn't stand the sight of money.

• • •

I was not a good artist in elementary school. When I'd bring home pictures from school, my mom used to hang them on the inside of the refrigerator door. "I'm just trying to keep them fresh," she would tell me.

• • •

I wasn't a slow learner. It's just that teaching came hard to most of my instructors.

• • •

Kids eat lunch in the school cafeteria, and it's only fair. It's one of the few ways that the school can get back at them.

• • •

I made straight A's in school. Of course, my B's were a little crooked.

• • •

Most Americans haven't read the United States Constitution. And the simple reason is that it doesn't fit on a bumper sticker.

• • •

My teacher did bird imitations. She watched me like a hawk.

• • •

My teacher told us biology was important because when we got out of school we never knew when an important client might ask us to dissect a crayfish.

• • •

Only one thing kept him from going to Harvard—high school.

• • •

Principal: "Are there any abnormal kids in your class?"
Teacher: "Yes, there are two with good manners."

• • •

She signed up for shop class because she thought it meant visiting different malls.

• • •

She took her lipstick, mascara and eye shadow to school yesterday because she heard the teacher say that she'd be taking a makeup test.

• • •

Teacher: "What do you think was the worst job during the Stone Age?"
Pupil: "Delivering newspapers."

• • •

Teacher: "Use 'counterfeiting' in a sentence."
Student: "My mother was worried about her new counter fitting in the kitchen."

• • •

Teacher: "What's a supervisor?"
Student: "It's something that Superman wears to keep the sun out of his eyes."

• • •

Teacher: "What's an example of wasted energy?"
Student: "Telling a hair-raising story to a bald-headed man."

• • •

Teacher: "Who was George Washington Carver?"
Student: "He was the first president to whittle in the White House."

• • •

Teacher: "Why are you late?"
Student: "I overslept."
Teacher: "You mean you sleep at home, too?"

• • •

Teachers are fortunate to get summer jobs that are school-related. Unfortunately, there just aren't that many openings for lion tamers.

• • •

Teachers complained about my attendance problem. I was always present.

• • •

The attention span of a teenager is now over.

• • •

The first American school opened in 1635. Of course, the easiest subject back then was American history.

• • •

The instructor in the high school etiquette course said, "Girls, give your escort every opportunity to be polite. Stay seated in the front seat of the car until he has had time to step around to open the front door for you. Of course, if he has already gone into the restaurant and started to order, there's no need to wait after that."

• • •

The lion tamer at the circus who steps into the cage full of lions impresses everybody except a school bus driver.

• • •

The teacher says that my son has original ideas, but most of them are in spelling.

• • •

Two boys were walking home from school, and they began talking about their schedule of activities for the evening.

"I've got an idea," said one. "Let's flip a coin. If it lands on heads, we'll go bowling. If it lands on tails, we'll go to the movies. And if it lands on its side, we'll study."

• • •

When he was in eighth grade, he wasn't like any of the other eighth grade boys, and that's because he was eighteen years old at the time.

• • •

When I was in school there was prayer in the classroom. But it didn't work. The teacher still called on me.

• • •

When I was in school, I read mystery books—algebra, geometry. . . .

• • •

When they sent back my SAT scores they included an application blank and a map to the nearest McDonald's.

• • •

Parent to teacher: "We realize our son is hyperactive. We just don't know what to make of him."
Teacher: "How about a nice rug?"

• • •

The three best things about teaching? Motivating young people, shaping the next generation and opening up young minds. Or perhaps it's June, July and August.

• • •

Teacher: "Who was the smallest man in history?"
Student: "I suppose it was the Roman centurion who fell asleep on his watch."

• • •

It's a wise father who burns all his old report cards.

• • •

A student wrote on his exam paper, "Views expressed on this paper are my own and not necessarily those expressed by the textbook."

• • •

An elementary student wrote in an essay, "We get our parents when they are so old that it is very hard to change their habits."

• • •

The boy's report card read, "Alan is a fine student, but he talks too much."
The father's written reply read: "You ought to meet his mother!"

• • •

I know that a lot of you envy teachers, but any teacher will tell you that ten weeks in the summer is not nearly enough time to allow their eardrums to heal.

• • •

Principal to second-grader: "It's very generous of you, Tommy. But I don't think that your resignation would help relieve our over-crowded situation."

• • •

Teacher: "What happens to the human body when it is immersed in water?"
Student: "The phone rings."

• • •

Teacher: "If your father made three hundred dollars a week and gave half to your mother, what would she have?"
Student: "Heart failure!"

• • •

A third-grader going through the cafeteria line on a day when peanut butter and jelly sandwiches were being served: "Finally, a home-cooked meal."

• • •

A parent asked his child what a zero was doing at the top of his paper. The lad said, "Mrs. Fisher ran out of stars so she gave me a moon."

• • •

At our high school, the guy voted most likely to succeed didn't graduate.

• • •

Thinking back on my school days, words fail me. In fact, so did half of my teachers!

• • •

Has your boy's education been of any value?
Yeah, it's cured his mother of bragging about him!

• • •

Not all Texans are fabulously wealthy . . . someone has to teach school.

• • •

His latest report card reveals that he's courteous, attentive, prompt and dumb.

• • •

My nephew prefers young teachers. He thinks it's fun to watch them age.

• • •

A boy walked into the living room and announced, "Dad, I've got good news for you. Remember when you promised me five dollars if I passed school this year? Well, I'm sparing you that expense."

• • •

A teacher asked her students to list the nine greatest Americans of all time. Albert was taking a long time. His teacher asked, "Are you almost through, Albert?"

"Yes," Albert replied, "but I'm having a really tough time picking the shortstop."

• • •

When your children come home from school and you ask them what they've learned that day, do you ever get the idea that they're majoring in shrugging?

• • •

Teachers really need more money to do their jobs. Do you realize what a gun, whip and chair cost these days?

• • •

Principal says, "What would you do if you were in my shoes?" A kid answered, "I'd polish them."

• • •

He was in high school for two terms . . . Bush's and Clinton's.

• • •

Not all kids are smart. They need role models, too. That's why schools have gym teachers.

• • •

September is when millions of bright, shining, happy faces turn toward school. They belong to mothers as they wave good-bye to their children.

• • •

My teacher told me that I'd never grow up to be president, but with my absentee record I might make it to the Senate.

• • •

Wife to husband: "Sam, you'd better help Johnny with his homework while you can. Next year he goes into the fourth grade."

• • •

"Nobody likes school," he complained. "The teachers don't like me, the kids don't like me, the superintendent wants to transfer me, the school board wants me to drop out and the custodians have it in for me. I don't want to go to school."

"But you have to go to school," replied his mother. "You are healthy. You have lots to learn, you have something to offer others. You are a leader. And besides, you are forty-five years old and you are the principal."

• • •

A report card convinces parents that they don't have to be weight lifters to raise a dumbbell.

• • •

I can't say that I was in the top half of my class, but I was in the group that made the upper half possible.

• • •

The only fella whose problems are all behind him is a school bus driver.

• • •

Can you tell me anything about the great philosophers of the nineteenth century?
Yeah, they're all dead.

• • •

Where are the tenth-graders? I spent the three happiest years of my life in tenth grade.

• • •

Adult education will continue as long as kids have homework.

• • •

He was such a bad kid in school that his parents used to attend PTA meetings under an assumed name.

• • •

If a little learning is a dangerous thing, most kids in school today have nothing to fear.

• • •

A first-grade teacher was filling out her district's annual medical questionnaire. She came to the question, "Have you ever had a nervous breakdown?"

She wrote in, "No, but watch this space for developments."

• • •

A school troublemaker was in the principal's office for the fifth straight day. The principal said, "This is the fifth day in a row you've been in my office to be paddled. What do you have to say for yourself?"

"I'm sure glad it's Friday," the kid replied.

• • •

An elementary class was on a field trip to a museum. "Don't look," advised one of the pupils. "If we look, we'll have to write about it tomorrow."

• • •

"Did you make the debating team?"

"N-n-n-o. Th-th-they s-s-aid I w-w-wasn't t-t-tall enough."

• • •

When he was in school, the teacher told him to stand in the corner and his head fit perfectly.

• • •

A teacher was lecturing her class on the importance of truthfulness and honesty. She illustrated her point: "Now children, if I put my hand into a man's coat pocket and took all his money—what would I be?"

"You'd be his wife!" shouted a youngster.

• • •

"The teacher really must like me," a boy reported to his father. "I heard him tell the principal, 'I wish he were my kid for just ten minutes.'"

• • •

The school I went to had thirty-seven students—thirty-six Indians and me. One time we had a school dance, and it rained for thirty-six straight days.

• • •

Discussing a recent fire at school, one first-grader said, "I knew it was going to happen. We've been practicing for it all year."

• • •

The school I attended was really advanced. One day I dropped my notebook on the floor, and by the time I bent down to pick it up I had missed a year of calculus.

• • •

"Don't blame me for flunking history!" cried the boy. "They keep asking me about things that happened before I was born."

• • •

The government has a student loan program. Now who do you know that wants to borrow a student?

• • •

It's a little discouraging to send your kid through high school and college and find a parrot has a greater vocabulary.

• • •

If you think things improve with age, attend a class reunion.

• • •

You know you've reached your fiftieth reunion when it looks like an archaeological dig.

• • •

You know you're at your fiftieth reunion when you look at your diploma and it's written in Latin—because that's what people were speaking at the time.

• • •

She's very proud of the fact that she has a daughter and they're often mistaken for sisters. Oldest-looking kid you've ever seen.

• • •

Reunions can be confusing. You look at the girl that you took to the senior prom and can't decide whether there's still some love-light in her eyes, or whether it's just the reflection from her trifocals.

• • •

The difference between a twenty-five-year class reunion and a fifty-year class reunion is that at the fifty-year reunion, even the name tags have wrinkles.

• • •

SECRETARY

"How long was your last secretary with you?"
"She was never with us. She was against us from the start."

• • •

A secretary in the hospital was visited by a coworker. "Don't worry, Denise," said her friend. "We are all sharing your work. Mary makes the coffee. Sally is filing her nails, and Meg is watching TV while Diane is doing the crossword puzzle."

• • •

My secretary asked me, "Why don't you ever compliment me on the things I do well?"

I said, "All right, you erase beautifully!"

• • •

My secretary is a slow typist. The last time she typed a letter, she had to change the date on it four times.

• • •

My secretary is not a good typist. Every afternoon by 3 P.M., she's light-headed from sniffing correction fluid.

• • •

My secretary makes two types of coffee—regular and crunchy.

• • •

My secretary says that a filing cabinet is a place where you can lose things alphabetically.

• • •

She didn't get the secretarial job she applied for. The personnel director asked, "Can you take dictation?"

She said, "Absolutely not! I believe in democracy!"

• • •

One morning, our single secretary passed out cigars in the office.

I asked, "What's this for?"

She flashed a big diamond and announced, "It's a boy! Six-feet-three, two hundred pounds!"

• • •

She types sixty words per minute—many of them recognizable!

• • •

She's the first secretary I ever had who buys White-Out in the gallon spray can.

• • •

The new secretary said, "I've added these figures three times."
"Great!" said the boss.
"And here are my three answers," she said.

• • •

He asked a secretarial applicant, "How many words can you type per minute?"
"Big or little?" she questioned.

• • •

(to boss) "I'm not late. I took all my coffee breaks before coming in."

• • •

A new secretary complained: "My boss is really bigoted. He thinks that words can be spelled only one way."

• • •

I don't think our new secretary is too bright. Two hours ago, I asked her to look up the phone number for Zaleski's Flower Shop. When I passed her desk she looked up at me as she was thumbing through the phone book and said, "I'm already up to the 'G's'."

• • •

He's always trying to impress visitors to the office. He said to his secretary, "After this meeting, I want you to call my broker."
The secretary replied, "Stock or pawn?"

• • •

Boss: "You should have been here at nine o'clock."
Secretary: "Why, what happened?"

• • •

Boss: "Do you realize the importance of punctuation?"
Secretary: "Yes, sir, I always get to work on time."

• • •

Your typing is improving. Only three mistakes. Now type the second word.

• • •

My new secretary is really sharp. Just the other day, she discovered that the dictionary is in alphabetical order. . . . She said, "Boy, this is great. This is really going to save some time!" One time she took three weeks to look up the word *zoology*.

• • •

Every day the secretary was twenty minutes late. Then one day she slid snugly into place only five minutes tardy. "Well," said her boss, "this is the earliest you've ever been late."

• • •

My secretary stopped answering the phone. She said, "It's always for you."

• • •

I have a secretary who files seven hours a day. She has the most beautiful nails. . . . She's so organized she files her nails under "N."

• • •

She's very thorough. I mean, who proofreads Xeroxes against the originals?

• • •

My secretary had an awful accident last week. She broke her typing finger.

• • •

She has a perfect attendance record. She hasn't missed a coffee break in five years.

• • •

She never makes the same mistake twice, but she has a great knack for making new ones.

• • •

SENIOR CITIZENS

You know you're getting old when . . .

- you need a permit to light your birthday candles.
- you find yourself beginning to like accordion music.
- your underwear starts creeping up on you and you enjoy it.
- you discover that your measurements are now small, medium and large . . . in that order.
- your insurance company has started sending you their free calendar one month at a time.
- when you do the Hokey Pokey you put your left hip out . . . and it stays out.
- one of the throw pillows on your bed is a hot-water bottle.
- you have come to the conclusion that your worst enemy is gravity.
- the waiter asks you how you like your steak and you say pureed.
- your little black book contains names that only end in "M.D."
- you get winded playing chess.
- you sit in your rocking chair and can't get it going.
- your knees buckle, but your belt won't.
- dialing long distance wears you out.
- your back goes out more than you do.
- you sink your teeth into a good steak and they stay there.

• • •

"Do you participate in sports?"

"No, my parents won't let me."

"Your parents?"

"Yeah, Mother Nature and Father Time."

• • •

"You must have had some exciting times in your life," someone remarked to a centenarian.

"Well, to tell the truth," said the old-timer, "everything is usually over by the time I find my glasses."

• • •

(to another) "I'll be eighty-four years old next week and I did it without jogging."

• • •

A seventy-five-year-old man went to a doctor for a physical.

Doctor: "You're in great shape. How do you do it?"

Patient: "I exercise by jogging, swimming and playing tennis."

Doctor: "You must have excellent genes. How old was your father when he died?"

Patient: "Died? Why he's 103 and I played tennis with him three times last week."

Doctor: "How old was your grandfather when he died?"

Patient: "My grandfather is 125. I play golf with him every Saturday. However, this Saturday I can't because he's getting married."

Doctor: "Why would a 125-year-old man want to get married?"

Patient: "His mother's making him."

• • •

A census taker asked a homemaker, "What is your age?"

She replied, "Have the Hills next door given you their ages?"

"Yes," said the census taker.

The homemaker said, "Well, I'm the same age."

"Good," said the census taker. "I'll just write down that you're as old as the Hills."

• • •

A hairpiece might take ten years off your appearance, but it doesn't mean anything to a long flight of stairs.

• • •

A man was explaining how he lived to be one hundred. "Every morning I get up at six. I drink twelve cups of coffee. I jog five miles a day."

"I had a friend who did that, and he only lived to be eighty," a listener interjected.

"Well, I guess he just didn't keep at it long enough," said the old-timer.

• • •

A reporter asked a centenarian to what he attributed reaching the milestone of his one-hundredth birthday.

"Well, I guess the main reason is that I was born in 1902," he drawled.

• • •

A vacationing senior friend sent me a postcard, "Wish you were here. Where am I?"

• • •

A woman was determined to get her newly retired husband some attractive leisure clothes. She went into a men's clothing store and told the salesgirl, "I'm looking for something youthful, something wild in a men's pair of slacks."

"Oh," sighed the salesgirl. "Aren't we all?"

• • •

Age is contagious. You get it from birthday candles.

• • •

As a boy, he read everything that Shakespeare wrote. But when he was a boy, Shakespeare hadn't written very much.

• • •

His birthday party was cancelled on account of rain. The candles on his cake set off the sprinkler system.

• • •

At the home they just sit around to see whose foot falls asleep first.

• • •

At the retirement home, the happy hour is any hour that you complete.

• • •

There is not a thing I could do at eighteen that I can't do now, and that gives you an idea of how pathetic I was when I was eighteen.

• • •

Birthdays are nice, but too many of them will kill a person.

• • •

By the time you're eighty, you've learned everything. All you have to do is try to remember it.

• • •

Deep breathing will add longevity if you do it for eighty-five years.

• • •

He discovered the secret of eternal youth. He lies about his age.

• • •

He knew Alexander the Great when he was just Alexander the Mediocre.

• • •

He seems to be living in the past. And why not? It's a lot cheaper!

• • •

He's at the age that when he goes into a restaurant and orders three-minute eggs, they make him pay in advance.

• • •

He's so old that he can remember when fast food was an antelope.

• • •

He's so old, he knew the first of the Mohicans.

• • •

He's so old, he remembers Absorbine Senior.

• • •

His mother started running five miles a day when she was sixty. Now she's eighty-seven and he has no idea where she is.

• • •

I personally don't mind growing old, but my body's taking it badly.

• • •

I saw a T-shirt worn by a senior citizen: "It's hard to be nostalgic when you can't remember anything."

• • •

If he dressed his age, he'd be wearing a pelt.

• • •

If he were a car, he'd be tough to get parts for.

• • •

I'm at the age where when I bend over to pick up the newspaper, I'm not sure it's going to be a round-trip.

• • •

My hair is receding, my waist is expanding, my arches are flattening, my hips are widening and my mind is narrowing. I may be getting older, but at least you can't say my body isn't busy.

• • •

Old? When you say, "Remember the Alamo!" he does!

• • •

Older man to young girl: "Where have you been all my life?"
Girl: "Teething."

• • •

One advantage of being sixty-five and getting a Social Security check is that the paperboy can cash it.

• • •

One of the first signs of old age is driving at least two hundred miles with your left turn signal on.

• • •

She loves to wear antique jewelry. Of course, when she got it, it was new.

• • •

She says, "I've had a crush on him for years. He's my kind of guy. He's handsome, successful and breathing."

• • •

She told him, "Look, at this point in my life, I don't even buy green bananas anymore."

• • •

She's still looking for Mr. Right. I'm not sure whether it's Orville or Wilbur.

• • •

Social Security agent to applicant: "Feeling sixty-five is not enough. You've got to be sixty-five."

• • •

The first sign of old age is when you hear snap, crackle and pop, and it isn't coming from your breakfast cereal.

• • •

The great thing about being eighty-five is that there is not a lot of peer pressure.

• • •

There have been a lot of changes since he was in the service. For one thing, the British are now our allies.

• • •

There's nothing wrong with getting old, just as long as you keep on doing it.

• • •

When he speaks of memories of Washington, people ask, "The city, the state or the general?"

• • •

When you reach one hundred, you're a good insurance risk, because very few people die past the age of one hundred.

• • •

When you're twenty-five, fishing is a challenge. When you're forty-five, it's relaxation. When you're sixty-five, fishing is exercise.

• • •

You know that you're getting old when everything you want for Christmas can be purchased at a drugstore.

• • •

You know that you're getting old when somebody compliments you on the lovely alligator shoes you are wearing, and you're barefoot at the time.

• • •

You know that you're getting old when somebody refers to a piece of furniture as an antique—and you bought it new.

• • •

You know that you're getting old when the Cream of Wheat tastes too spicy for you.

• • •

You know that you're getting old when the first candle on your cake burns down before the last one is lit.

• • •

You know that you're getting old when you can relate to more things in a museum than you can in a shopping mall.

• • •

You know that you're getting old when you need glasses—to put your teeth in.

• • •

You know you're getting old when you can remember when bacon, eggs, milk and sunshine were good for you.

• • •

You know you're getting older when they have to stick the birthday candles in the side of the cake, too.

• • •

You're starting to get old when your kids come home from school and tell you what they're studying in history, and you remember studying that as current events.

• • •

They don't make mirrors like they used to. The ones I buy now are all full of wrinkles.

• • •

Old age is nice. That's the perfect period in life when people come to your birthday party just to stand around the cake and get warm.

• • •

You know you're getting old when you stoop to tie your shoelaces and ask yourself, "What else can I do while I'm down here?"

• • •

A highlight of the senior citizens' Halloween party was the game "Bobbing for Dentures."

• • •

You're getting old if your feet hurt before you get out of bed.

• • •

On his last birthday, he went to blow out the candles, and the heat drove him back.

• • •

He's ninety-three years old, and he still has that gleam in his eye. And that's because he keeps missing his mouth with his toothbrush.

• • •

You know you're getting older when you have to put tenderizer on your puffed rice.

• • •

They say that old age is in your head—as anyone with bifocals, dentures, a hearing aid and a toupee already knows.

• • •

You know you're getting old when you try to straighten the wrinkles in your socks, and you aren't wearing any.

• • •

She's been pressing forty so long it's pleated.

• • •

You know that you're getting old when they light the candles on your birthday cake and the air conditioner automatically switches on.

• • •

You know you're getting old when the birthday candles cost more than the cake.

• • •

His doctor told him to slow down, so he got a job with the post office.

• • •

You know you're getting old when they start grilling hamburgers over your birthday cake.

• • •

One thing nice about being seventy, at least you're not constantly being bothered by insurance salesmen.

• • •

"How do you live to be a hundred?"

"Well, first you get to ninety-nine and then you live very carefully for a year."

• • •

A newspaper reporter ended his interview of the ninety-nine-year-old man with, "Well, I hope I can come back next year and interview you on your one hundredth birthday."

The senior citizen said, "I don't see why not. You seem in pretty good health."

• • •

She was named after Betsy Ross, and not very long after, either.

• • •

Old? I had a slice of her birthday cake, and on my slice alone there were twelve candles.

• • •

SHORT

He has a job posing for the guy that they put on the tops of trophies.

• • •

He was playing shortstop and a grounder went right over his head.

• • •

He's so short that he once won a limbo contest standing up.

• • •

SIGNS

I saw a sign that proclaimed, "Ten Years at the Same Location." Now most businesses would be proud of such an achievement, but this was a road crew!

• • •

I saw a strange sign in a jewelry shop window: "Ears pierced while you wait."

• • •

SKIING

Given a choice, I prefer skiing in the winter to skiing in the summer. I don't have to hold my stomach in when I'm wearing a ski jacket.

• • •

Here's my thought on skiing: The only reason that they give you ski poles is to help you get accustomed to crutches.

• • •

I don't ski. I refuse to participate in any sport that has an ambulance waiting at the bottom of the hill.

• • •

Skiing is a great sport, but there must be a cheaper way to break your bones.

• • •

A small girl watching a water-skier said to her father, "That man is silly. He'll never catch that boat."

• • •

A guy learning to ski remarked, "By the time I learned to stand up, I couldn't sit down."

• • •

Ski jumping is where you race down a steep hill and fly three hundred feet through the air. There's just got to be a better way to meet nurses.

• • •

Skinny

He's so skinny that he has only one stripe in his pajamas.

• • •

He's so skinny that he has to run around in the shower just to get wet.

• • •

He's so skinny that he can't keep his seat down at the movies.

• • •

Small Towns

In Salunga, no mail had been delivered for seven months. The postal service in Washington contacted the postmaster for an explanation.

"The bag ain't full yet," was his reply.

• • •

It's so dull in Salunga that the roosters sleep until noon.

• • •

Our new art museum was going to open, but the frame broke.

• • •

Our town is so small that they carry cottage cheese in the gourmet section of the market.

• • •

Salunga held a rock festival last week and my rock took first place.

• • •

Salunga sponsored a slogan contest. The winning entry was, "You've Got to Live Somewhere."

• • •

The key to the city is from a canned ham.

• • •

The Salunga Zoo is closed today. The pigeon is sick.

• • •

The town was so small that the "Welcome to" and "You Are Now Leaving" signs were on the same pole.

• • •

I grew up in a small, flat Midwestern town, the kind of town where you could watch your dog run away for three days.

• • •

Our town is so small that the Masons and the Knights of Columbus know each other's secrets, so they formed a coalition, and they call themselves the Masonites.

• • •

Our McDonald's has a sign that reads, "Over four sold."

• • •

Our library burned to the ground last week and we lost both books in the fire.

• • •

Our town is so small that our Ben & Jerry's has only one flavor.

• • •

Our town is so dull that the tour bus doesn't even have windows.

• • •

The only heavy industry in Salunga is our 250-pound Avon lady.

• • •

The Salunga Aquarium was forced to close. Our clam died.

• • •

The bully in our high school always used to pick on me. But I got even. I married her!

• • •

Smoking

Do you realize that if it wasn't for coughing, some smokers wouldn't get any exercise at all?

• • •

Snow

I just can't stand to see my wife shovel snow—so I pull down the shades.

• • •

There's no chance that my car will be snowed in this winter. I've got front wheel drive, snow tires, antifreeze, a shovel for the driveway and a son with a girlfriend downtown.

• • •

Soccer

Millions of people play soccer because that way they don't have to watch it on TV.

• • •

Who are the most indispensable men in international soccer competition?
The riot police.

• • •

Solar Energy

I'm not so sure about the potentials of solar energy. My son has spent most of his life on the beach, and he has less energy than anyone I know.

• • •

Speaker

(substitute speaker) "Our next speaker needs no introduction . . . an explanation, maybe. . . ."

• • •

I also want to mention the handsome suit he is wearing. It's a tribute to the quality of the cloth, the skill of the tailor and the generosity of the Salvation Army.

• • •

After a long-winded speaker had gone on for fifty minutes, he concluded by saying, "And now I call on Mr. Smith for his address."

Smith rose and said, "My address is 75 Sturbridge Road, and I'm going home!"

• • •

As a kid, he wanted to be an after-dinner speaker, but he had to give up his dream when it was discovered that he was allergic to stuffed chicken breast and cold mashed potatoes.

• • •

He got his fast-talking skills from his parents. His father was an auctioneer and his mother was a woman.

• • •

He's a great speaker to listen to, particularly if you have just twenty-four hours to live and you want time to drag on forever.

• • •

He's got a great ten-minute speech. Unfortunately, it takes him half an hour to give it.

• • •

He's the oratorical equivalent of a blocked punt.

• • •

Some speakers rely on professional speechwriters to prepare their remarks. Not me! I depend on my own thoughts, delivered in my own way. "Four score and seven years ago, our fathers . . ."

• • •

I'll never forget my first speaking engagement. It was for a group "on a tight budget that can't afford much for an honorarium." But they more than made up for it by not listening very closely.

• • •

Unfortunately, our speaker, who was to have spoken on the topic, "How to Solve World Problems," cannot be with us this evening. He couldn't find a baby-sitter.

• • •

I gave a speech last week that will be remembered for a long, long time. It was to a group of elephants. . . .

• • •

He's got rapid delivery. He can tell six jokes in one minute. That's true because he never has to stop for laughs.

• • •

An American on business in Hong Kong was seated next to a Chinaman. During the course of the meal, the American inquired, "Likee soupee?"
The Chinaman grunted, "Yes."
Next he asked, "Likee meatee?" Same response.
After the meal, the Chinaman got up and gave an eloquent speech for half an hour, using perfect English. When he sat down, he turned to the American and asked, "Likee speechee?"

• • •

I don't mind when people look at their watches while I'm speaking, but it does bother me when they start to shake them.

• • •

I'd rather hear him speak than eat. I just heard him eat.

• • •

"The speaker we had last year really made a hit."
"Oh, really? What did he speak about?"
"Oh, about ten minutes."

• • •

(after speech) Well done, Bill. Those of us still awake salute you.

• • •

Thank you. He just always seems to have so many words left over after he has run out of ideas.

• • •

Thank you. Whatever that speech lacked in content, you more than made up for in length.

• • •

(when room is too hot) They said that this room would be air-conditioned, and they were right. I've never seen air in such condition.

• • •

Speaker to audience: "As I understand it, it's my job to speak and your job to listen. If you get finished before I do, please let me know."

• • •

Speakers are a lot like mushrooms. You never know if you're getting a bad one until it's too late.

• • •

The other night I overheard a woman say to her husband, "That certainly was an inspirational speech, wasn't it?"

Her husband said, "Yeah, but thirty minutes of rain would have done us a lot more good."

• • •

(when you have a laugher in the crowd who laughs prematurely) "Not yet, Evelyn, wait till the punch line."

• • •

I was up all night thinking about this speech. Wouldn't it be ironic if the speech that kept me awake puts you to sleep?

• • •

The world's best after-dinner speech is, "Waiter, I'll take both checks."

• • •

(after speech) Of all the speakers we've ever had, he's certainly one of them. . . .

• • •

(after speech) Of all the speakers we've ever had, you're certainly the most recent.

• • •

You're much better than our last speaker. He talked for over an hour and a half and never said anything. You only took fifteen minutes.

• • •

I've practiced this speech all week and I feel pretty good about it. So, if you can just manage to look a little more like the bathroom mirror, we'll get on with it. . . .

• • •

There are only two things more difficult than making after-dinner speeches. One is climbing a wall leaning toward you, and the other is kissing a girl leaning away from you.

• • •

Before coming to speak tonight, we negotiated a price and settled on fifteen hundred dollars. So I wrote a check for fifteen hundred dollars to your organization, and they let me speak to you.

• • •

I have two talks, a fifteen-minute talk and a half hour talk. They're both the same speech. I lose my place a lot.

• • •

(if the microphone is low) Who were you expecting? (short celebrity)?

. . .

(take a drink of water) As you can see, this is an instant speech. All you add is water.

. . .

I love this place. I've come here for the last six years, and I look back on them as the best years of my life. Which will give you some idea of what a miserable life I've been leading.

. . .

Whenever I hear a speaker say, "I just don't know where to begin!" some small voice within me says, "Near the end."

. . .

He couldn't get a standing ovation if he finished his speech with "The Star-Spangled Banner."

. . .

At my first speech I was so nervous that I bit my nails so often my stomach needed a manicure.

. . .

The most difficult thing a speaker needs to learn to do is not to nod while the toastmaster is praising him.

. . .

Always remember the first rule of public speaking: Be brief, no matter how long it takes.

. . .

There's a 1978 Buick in the parking lot with its headlights on and the radio blaring. Would the owner please report to the parking lot attendant? They want to hold a memorial service for your battery.

. . .

After the meeting we're all going to get together and toast marshmallows on the air conditioner.

. . .

I don't know what it is that makes our meetings so dull, but whatever it is, it works.

. . .

Always remember that being able to express your opinion without fear of reprisal is what distinguishes democracy from marriage.

. . .

It's a great honor to be here tonight having satisfied the two philosophical requirements of the program chairman: (1) He believes in free speech, and (2) He believes in free speeches.

. . .

A speaker stopped abruptly during the course of his speech to arouse a sleeping man in the audience who was snoring loudly. "Just how long have you been sleeping?" asked the speaker.
"Just how long have you been speaking?" came the reply.

. . .

I told the program chairman, "Sure, I believe in free speech."
He said, "Good, because that's what you're going to be giving."

. . .

He's not going to bore you with a long speech. He can do it with a short one.

. . .

I predict that tonight's speaker will be interesting and entertaining. I also predicted that the (losing team) would win the Super Bowl.

• • •

When your entertainment chairman first phoned me to do this, I gladly accepted the charges.

• • •

You may not agree with what this man has to say, but I can assure you of one thing. Nobody says it longer.

• • •

Thank you for that speech. Those were words that needed to be spoken . . . but not necessarily in that order.

• • •

The text of my speech tonight is available for those of you who have trouble falling asleep at home.

• • •

Sports

I was a nonathletic child. My parents had to hire a stunt double for our home movies.

• • •

"Bullfighting is the number-one sport in Latin America."
"That's revolting!"
"No, that's the number-two sport."

• • •

Coach: "I don't mind turning fifty. It's just that at the beginning of the year, I was forty-three."

• • •

Men forget everything; women remember everything. That's why men need instant replays in sports. They've already forgotten what happened.

• • •

The doctor told him, "You've got six months to live. But invest in (losing team's) season tickets, and they'll be the longest six months of your life."

• • •

You know that your coaching job is in jeopardy when the booster club gives you a gift certificate to the U-Haul company.

• • •

The swimming coach summed up the season: "We had a semi-successful season. We didn't win any meets, but nobody drowned either."

• • •

During the mid-season break, we got the team together for the team picture. And believe me, getting twelve big guys inside one of those little booths at Kmart is no easy task.

• • •

Fast? When he's through sprinting, he has to wipe the bugs off his goggles.

• • •

(coach after a loss) "I feel like the guy in the javelin competition who won the toss and elected to receive."

• • •

Coach: "The only time my player didn't run up the score was when he was taking the SATs."

. . .

(losing team) This team loses so much that they have a (losing political party) for a mascot.

. . .

A coach should have a wife because sooner or later something is going to happen that you can't blame on the officiating.

. . .

At halftime an angry coach went up to the ref to complain.
"Oh, you're just angry," said the ref, "because we're beating you by ten points."

. . .

Contrary to what he believes, parallel bars are not two taverns across the street from each other.

. . .

He gave up his last job due to exhaustion. He was a play-by-play man for Ping-Pong matches.

. . .

He threw the javelin two hundred yards. Actually, he only threw it one hundred yards. The guy he hit crawled the other hundred yards.

. . .

He was an avid water polo player until his horse drowned.

. . .

He attended the Indianapolis 500 and remarked, "If they just started earlier, they wouldn't have to drive so fast."

• • •

The trouble with officials is that they don't care who wins.

• • •

His coach gave him a letter that year, and that letter said he should try out for the croquet team.

• • •

I asked the hot dog vendor why his hands were all yellow. "People keep telling me to hold the mustard," he said.

• • •

I spoke at a meeting of the (losing team's) fan club. Two of the nicest people I've ever met.

• • •

I was talking to my wife the other day. You know how it is when the only thing on TV is *Bowling for Dollars.*

• • •

Fan to player: "Hey, I was you for Halloween, but I strained my back carrying the bench."

• • •

We didn't have a great season. Instead of a highlight film, we had a highlight slide.

• • •

What a sprinter! He can really burn up a track. In fact, I looked at the track after his trial heat and it was all cinders.

• • •

Rowing has to be the worst sport. You sit down while playing and go backwards to win.

• • •

We lost ten in a row and then went into a slump.

• • •

The fat coach kept his players in peak condition by having them run laps around him.

• • •

Being a track coach would be so simple. All I'd have to say is, "Okay boys, keep to the left and get back as soon as you can."

• • •

"If you were the coach, how would you have played the final quarter of the last play-off game?"
"Under an assumed name."

• • •

I've always been quite an athlete myself—big chest, hard stomach. But that's all behind me now.

• • •

I've decided to cut back on Sunday TV snacks. My wife saw me getting ready with Pepsi, chips, chip dip, peanuts and pretzels, and said, "Well, here he comes. The wide world of sports."

• • •

Guys begged him to join the team. He was a wide receiver on the archery team.

• • •

How can a guy who signs a contract for $3 million be called a free agent?

• • •

The coach's wife yells to her husband, "It's *Sports Illustrated* on the phone. The coach falls all over himself, racing to the phone. "Hello?" "For just 75 cents an issue . . .

• • •

The best three years of a sportswriter's life are usually the third grade.

• • •

He's an exciting guy. After the big win he went out and painted the town beige.

• • •

I quit the javelin team when our coach elected to receive.

• • •

The tickets he got me were so high up in the stadium, I didn't have an usher. I had a stewardess strap me in my seat before the game.

• • •

We lost fifteen in a row and then went on a one-game winning streak.

• • •

I asked the recruit, "What do you run the mile in?" He said, "Shorts and a T-shirt."

• • •

The rookie was so young that he autographed everything in crayon.

• • •

Our team is so young that we have a team orthodontist and dermatologist.

• • •

I told one of the players, "You smell good. What do you have on?" He said, "Clean socks."

• • •

He played a key role in the pennant drive. He got hepatitis. The trainer injected him with it.

• • •

What can a coach say after his team's lost twenty straight games, "Way to shower, men. Nice sweating, fellas"?

• • •

Our track team had a cross-eyed discus thrower. He wasn't that great, but he kept the crowds loose.

• • •

A kid ran cross-country for a college in Texas, and they practiced in prairie land.

The coach said, "The only problem with that is, it's so hard to explain to a mother that a coyote got her son."

• • •

He got me seats for the game. From where I sat the game was just a rumor. I turned to the guy sitting next to me and said, "What do you think of the game?"

He said, "How should I know? I'm flying the mail to Cleveland."

• • •

Before bed at night I eat a bowl of Rice Krispies and read (sportswriter's) column in the (newspaper). That way, before sleeping I won't have anything on my mind or stomach.

• • •

I wasn't much of an athlete in college, but I was waterboy for the swim team.

• • •

My doctor advised me to stay away from crowds, so I followed his advice. Now I spend weekends at (losing team's stadium).

• • •

If a tie is like kissing your sister, then losing is like kissing your mother-in-law with her teeth out.

• • •

A youngster was explaining to another what the term "no-cut contract" means.

"It means," he said, "getting paid your allowance if you don't clean your room."

• • •

Stock Market

He made a tremendous impact on his company's profits this year. For the first time in the firm's history, they will be able to file as a nonprofit organization.

• • •

My broker said, "Remember that stock we bought which we said would enable you to retire at age fifty-five? Well, your retirement age is now 105."

• • •

Times are really tough. I just got a letter from my Wall Street brokerage, and they're having a bake sale.

• • •

What is the best way to call your financial consultant these days?

"Oh, waiter . . ."

• • •

Wall Street just voted my broker Man of the Year—for 1929!

• • •

One broker told me, "You'd be surprised how many people drive to my office in a Mercedes to take advice from a guy who came to work on the bus."

• • •

And now, here's the latest market report. Empire hemlines are up. 7UP is down. International Harvester is stable, and Pampers remain unchanged.

• • •

I invested half my money in paper towels and the other half in revolving doors. . . . I was wiped out before I could turn around.

• • •

SUMMER

I always worry about dumb things at a picnic. Like how many calories are in an ant?

• • •

If you don't believe that this is the land of the free, just let your neighbors know that you own a summer cottage.

• • •

Hurricanes do a lot of damage, make a lot of noise, and man hasn't learned how to control them. No wonder they're named after women!

• • •

Sunday School

"What are the Epistles?"
"The wives of the apostles."

• • •

Sunday school teacher: Now who decreed that all the world should be taxed?
Student: The Democrats.

• • •

Small boy: Mom, the Sunday school teacher told us that we came from dust and go to dust.
Mother: That's right, dear.
Small boy: Well, I looked under the couch in the living room, and somebody's either coming or going.

• • •

The teacher asked her Sunday school class, "If you found $1 million in the street, what would you do?"
Billy replied, "If it belonged to a poor person, I'd be sure to give it back."

• • •

Tax

(auditor) "Thank you for your estimated tax return. Now, would you like to hear your estimated prison sentence?"

• • •

(IRS executive) "Before we send out these new tax forms, let's run them through quality control to make sure that no one understands them."

• • •

A democratic government is one that will let you make all the money that you want. They just won't let you keep it.

• • •

A man wrote to the IRS: "I feel guilty. I owe back taxes, and I'm sending $150. If I still feel guilty a month from now, I'll send you another $300."

• • •

He owes a lot to this country, and someday the IRS will catch up with him.

• • •

He tried to deduct thirty cases of Dr Pepper as a medical expense.

• • •

He's a man of daring, determination, initiative, imagination and creativity—at least that's what the IRS said when they looked at his tax return.

• • •

He's a man of untold wealth, and that's because he never reports it on his income tax.

• • •

I am ready to do my income tax this year. I took an adult education course in creative writing.

• • •

I get my taxes done at the new firm Loopholes-R-Us.

• • •

I got in trouble with the IRS last year. At the top of the page it said, "Return this blank." So I did.

• • •

I have a sneaking suspicion that the persons who wrote up these new tax forms are the same individuals who write the easy-to-assemble directions that come with your children's Christmas toys.

• • •

I have great respect for rich people who don't squander their money on things like taxes.

• • •

I have the perfect tax shelter. It's called poverty.

• • •

I invest in taxes. They're backed by the government, and they're sure to go up.

• • •

I love those instructions on the back of IRS envelopes:

- "Did you remember to affix your computerized sticker?"
- "Did you remember your W-2 forms?"
- "Did you remember to enclose the shirt off your back?"

• • •

I think we poor people should be proud to pay our taxes. I mean, just look at all the rich folks who can't afford to.

• • •

I wrote to the IRS and inquired, "What did you do with all that money I sent you last year?"

• • •

IRS auditor to taxpayer: "The trick is to stop thinking of it as your money."

• • •

If Patrick Henry thought taxation without representation was bad, he should see what it is like with representation!

• • •

If you're late with your taxes, the IRS will give you more time . . . like ten years.

• • •

I'm concerned about the national debt. I got my income tax refund check with a note attached to it that said, "Please hold this check until next Thursday."

• • •

I'm proud to be an American taxpayer, but I'd be just as proud for half the money.

• • •

I'm taking the family to Washington, DC. I want them to meet the folks I'm working for.

• • •

My accountant tells me that if we're called in by the IRS, we're safe. He's insured by a large company—Leavenworth Mutual.

• • •

My tax accountant just gave me a copy of his new book, *All You Ever Wanted to Know About Plea Bargaining*. He has also contributed to another title, *500 Easy Exercises to Do in the Privacy of Your Own Cell*.

• • •

The IRS admits that they send out some erroneous tax bills. In fact, last week they really slipped up and accidentally sent one to a millionaire.

• • •

The IRS knows what to give the man who has everything—an audit.

• • •

The IRS refused to accept his claim for a deduction. He said that he had donated ten thousand dollars to the wife of the Unknown Soldier.

• • •

The IRS has a new tax form. Actually it's an envelope and all you do is put your paycheck in it.

• • •

The Russians have a weapon that can wipe out 200 million Americans. Sadly, the IRS has already beaten them to it.

• • •

The super-rich should not complain about paying taxes, at least not until they've tried it.

• • •

What's the difference between the long and the short form? If you use the short form, the government gets the money. If you use the long form, your accountant does.

• • •

My tax accountant is an understanding man. He has an office with a recovery room.

• • •

It's getting harder and harder for me to support the government in the style to which it is accustomed.

• • •

"We live in such a great country, we should pay our taxes with a smile."

"I'd love to. But the government insists on money."

• • •

I asked a famous author, "Which of your works of fiction do you consider best?"

He said, "My last income tax return."

• • •

He lied on his income tax form last year. He listed himself head of the household.

• • •

I feel there should be a better deadline for our taxes than April 15. How about February 31?

• • •

They say that by April 15, sixty million tax returns will have been filed—not to mention all those that have been chiseled.

• • •

Fear is taking your kids to remedial math class and seeing your tax accountant there.

• • •

Name one person who has money left after April 15. Henry R. Block.

• • •

This year the government is really simplifying the form. It reads, "What did you earn last year? Send it!"

• • •

TEENAGERS

I don't really need this job. I can always go back to my old job of explaining what clothes hangers are to teenagers.

• • •

Hungry? This kid eats like a baby-sitter.

• • •

TELEVISION

I don't need to watch TV game shows. If I want to see someone make a lot of money, I just call the plumber.

• • •

Reading makes for a well-rounded person. So does sitting in front of the TV with a tray full of snacks.

• • •

Warning! Before retiring, take a week off and watch daytime television.

• • •

Television is very educational. Just think of all the TV repairmen's children it has put through college.

• • •

TEXAS

I heard of a rich Texan who bought his kid a chemistry set for Christmas—DuPont!

• • •

A Texan called his insurance agent and said, "I need you right away. I just hit a Cadillac, bounced off a Corvette, sideswiped a Porsche and hit a Rolls head-on.

The agent said, "My goodness. Was anyone hurt?"

"Just me," said the Texan. "I was parking in my own garage."

• • •

THANKSGIVING

Advice: Never accept a Thanksgiving dinner invitation from anyone who's standing in the supermarket express checkout line.

• • •

To counter the weight gain of a typical Thanksgiving dinner, we recommend you get up from the table and jog—to Anchorage, Alaska.

• • •

Wow, can my relatives eat! Last Thanksgiving I bowed my head to say grace, and when I looked up, my cousin was handing me an after-dinner mint.

• • •

We had a wild Thanksgiving last year. I won the wishbone pull and my mother-in-law came down with food poisoning. I never knew those things worked.

• • •

My neighbor was complaining: "Grateful? What have I got to be grateful for? I can't pay my bills."

I told him, "Well, be grateful you aren't one of your creditors."

• • •

This year's Thanksgiving dinner was an educational experience for me. I didn't know that Black & Decker made turkeys.

• • •

Tough Neighborhood

I asked a policeman for directions to the theater. He said, "First you go to Forty-third Street, and if you make it. . . ."

• • •

Our high school was so tough that after our football players sacked the quarterback, they went after his family.

• • •

Our neighborhood is so tough that Mike Tyson (or other tough character) drives the Welcome Wagon.

• • •

Our neighborhood was so tough that the supermarket cashiers would always ask, "Will this be cash, check or stickup?"

• • •

Our neighborhood was tougher than a Waffle House steak.

• • •

You know that you're in a tough neighborhood when you see nine police cars on the block and there is no doughnut shop.

• • •

We had eleven kids in our family and had to wear each other's clothes. It wasn't funny either. I had ten sisters.

• • •

Somebody moved into our neighborhood the other day and they were fired on by the Welcome Wagon.

• • •

The first thing that you notice about the guy who comes to collect for the loans is that he's really big. I mean how often do you see someone wearing barbells as cufflinks?

• • •

He had his nose broken in four places, and you can bet he won't go to those places again.

• • •

I had my hubcaps stolen, which isn't unusual, but I was going forty-five miles an hour at the time.

• • •

Our neighborhood was so tough, the Welcome Wagon was a tank. We used to bowl . . . overhand!

• • •

Every morning I would make two lists: things to do . . . and the other was who I'm going to do them to.

• • •

We were so poor as kids we couldn't afford X rays. The doctor just held us up to the light.

• • •

My neighborhood was so tough, our Avon lady was Warren Sapp.

• • •

My grandmother used to sit on the front porch knitting bullet-proof shawls.

• • •

In my neighborhood we had kids' names like Rocco and Spike. And those were the girls' names!

• • •

Tough? Our high school had its own coroner. We used to write essays like "What I'm Going to Be If I Grow Up."

• • •

I come from a tough neighborhood. I was a pretty good fighter. I used to be able to take a good punch. The only problem was I'd take it thirty or forty times a round.

• • •

Undertakers

Did you hear about the undertaker who closes all of his letters, "Eventually yours"?

• • •

Never go golfing with an undertaker. He's always on top of the last hole.

• • •

United Nations

Anytime there's trouble, countries call the United Nations. And the UN is doing something about it. They're getting an unlisted number.

• • •

VACATION

Disney World is such a friendly place. A little boy I had never met before came up to me and wrapped his arms around me, and gave me a great big hug as his mother took our picture. It was thrilling—that is, until his mother smiled and said, "Thanks, Goofy!"

• • •

He'd tell his restless son, "Count telephone poles."
His son would reply, "How can I when I'm in the trunk?"

• • •

How can they call it "getting away from it all" when you start your vacation by loading your car with children, pets, toys and suitcases?

• • •

I called the hotel and asked if they take children. The desk clerk said, "Only if your check bounces."

• • •

I enjoy great fiction. So, on many evenings I curl up with a good travel brochure. Those brochures are filled with so many promises that they must be written by politicians.

• • •

I visited the most popular site at Disney World, the ATM machine.

• • •

I wondered why it was so cold in Miami and found out that my wife had been reading the road map upside down.

• • •

If you ever want to locate missing relatives, rent a cottage at the beach for the summer!

• • •

If you take a European vacation, it doesn't prove that you have money. It proves that you had money.

• • •

In Europe, we spent most of our time studying ruins—our wallets, credit cards, checkbooks, budgets. . . .

• • •

In order to settle disputes once and for all as to where to go for vacation, what this country needs is an ocean in the mountains.

• • •

It has been said, "We pass this way but once." Please disregard this message if your wife is reading the road map.

• • •

My wife leaves nothing to chance. When we go to the beach, she even packs sand!

• • •

Next year I'm going to spend my vacation somewhere near my budget.

• • •

Our neighbors came back from a trip to the Grand Canyon and one said, "I stood at the rim of the canyon and realized how insignificant man is." My wife said that she didn't even have to leave the living room to realize that!

• • •

Our vacation memories linger on months after the experience. We used our credit cards the whole trip.

• • •

Our vacation was great. My wife did all the driving, and all I did was sit behind the wheel and steer.

• • •

Remember that a journey of a thousand miles begins with an argument about how to load the car.

• • •

Rule number nine of vacationing is to always tell the paperboy not to deliver the paper while you're away. Nothing tips off the burglar that a house is unoccupied like a pile of newspapers on the roof.

• • •

Rule number six of vacationing is no matter how beautifully your kids sing together, you will always regret teaching them "John Jacob Jingleheimer Schmidt."

• • •

The boss encourages family vacations. He feels it keeps workers from taking more time off.

• • •

The ideal vacation is one where you're away long enough for the boss to miss you, but not so long that he has time to figure out that he can do without you.

• • •

The kids played a quiet game. It's called "Count the Number of Cars and Trucks That Are Doing Sixty-five Miles Per Hour."

• • •

The lines have been so long at Disneyland that by the time I reached Tomorrowland it was yesterday.

• • •

Vacationing at Disney is a form of brainwashing. I was reminded of that last night when I had dinner with my two sons, Donald and Pluto.

• • •

The only reason he's going on vacation is that he needs new towels.

• • •

The thing I like most about roller coasters is to be able to sit down for a minute and a half after standing in line for an hour.

• • •

There's a book that tells you where you should go on your vacation. It's called your checkbook.

• • •

This summer, one-third of the nation will be ill-housed, ill-fed and ill-clothed. But they'll call it vacation.

• • •

This vacation tip: If you see a gas station with a sign that says Clean Rest Rooms, it means one thing—the door is locked and no one can find the key.

• • •

Travel is educational. You learn how to get rid of your money in a hurry.

. . .

Vacations can be enlightening. Unless you actually see it for yourself, you'll never believe what a hotel will charge for a little glass of orange juice.

. . .

Vacations can last for months. You travel in August, return in September, get your bills in October, get your health back in November, and your luggage back in December.

. . .

We don't have to worry about burglars when we go away on a trip. My wife packs it all.

. . .

We had to trim our vacation budget. This year we're just going to subscribe to National Geographic.

. . .

We stopped at a motel that had a sign that said "Children Free," and they tried to give us two kids!

. . .

We were having a great vacation, but that quickly came to an end when the kids found their way back to our car.

. . .

We've had so much rain lately that I thought I was on vacation.

. . .

What a cheap motel! After we left, I discovered that they had stolen our towels.

. . .

When we returned, the customs man at the airport asked, "Anything to declare?"

I replied, "Yes. Bankruptcy."

• • •

While on vacation, a gentleman was impressed by our young daughter and he bought her a candy bar.

I prompted, "And what do you say to the man, dear?"

She replied, "Are you going to be here tomorrow?"

• • •

Why is it that we travel hundreds of miles to get away from everyone at home and then send them postcards that say, "Wish you were here"?

• • •

You can still vacation in California on twenty-five dollars a day, provided that your day ends at 6 A.M.

• • •

The ship we took on our cruise was really old. It was insured against fire, theft, and falling off the edge of the world.

• • •

Rain is caused by big, high-pressure areas; cold fronts; warm, moist air; and the first day of your vacation.

• • •

A couple on a safari was going through Africa when a lion leaped out, attacking the husband. As the lion was about to put the man's head in his mouth, the victim yelled to his wife, "Shoot! Shoot!"

The wife called back, "I can't. I'm out of film!"

• • •

Vacations are no problem for me. My boss decides when I go, and my wife decides where.

• • •

My wife is like Noah. When she packs for a vacation, she takes two of everything.

• • •

Never go on a vacation when the kids outnumber the car windows.

• • •

A fool and his money are soon parted. We smart guys wait until we go on vacation.

• • •

A true vacationer is one who travels one thousand miles to get a picture of himself standing beside his car.

• • •

A native Californian asked, "Well, isn't California the most beautiful vacation state you've ever visited?"

"Not really," said the tourist. "Take away your lakes, mountains and climate, and what have you got?"

• • •

If you're traveling with three young kids in the back seat, it really isn't a vacation. It's more like World War III with coloring books.

• • •

I don't want to seem harsh, but I am convinced that all vacation slides are processed in a solution consisting primarily of Sominex.

• • •

I had an unusual vacation that lasted two weeks. I got in an elevator in a seventy-story building right after a kid had pressed all the buttons.

• • •

My wife has a different philosophy about vacations. Most people try to get away from it all—she packs it all!

• • •

Whenever we go away on vacation, we want to make sure that the house looks lived in. We hook up an automatic timer to a tape deck and then we pre-record an argument.

• • •

I'm still a little puzzled about our vacation. How is it possible to visit eight different countries and every one of our souvenirs is from Hong Kong?

• • •

On my European vacation I saw so much poverty, I brought some home with me.

• • •

Travel agent: "Aren't you afraid that the tropical climate might disagree with your wife?"
Traveler: "It wouldn't dare!"

• • •

Nothing is quite so upsetting on a vacation as getting a call from the house sitter who asks, "Is it the custom to tip firemen?"

• • •

The perfect resort is where the fish bite and the mosquitoes don't.

• • •

I was saying that this summer I'd like to get away from it all and go some place where no one would ever think to find me. The boss suggested my desk.

• • •

The resort we stayed at was so dull that one day the tide went out and never came back.

• • •

Who will ever forget those immortal words of Sir Winston Churchill: "We will fight on the byways, we will fight on the beaches, we will fight at sea!" Forget them? That sounds like our last family vacation.

• • •

Most passport photos look like you really need the trip.

• • •

In Florida they use alligators to make handbags. Isn't it wonderful what they can train animals to do these days?

• • •

We put mistletoe over the door of our summer cottage so that when we see relatives coming we can kiss our vacation good-bye.

• • •

Happiness is having a neighbor go on a vacation and take four hundred slides with the lens cap on.

• • •

We were going on a seven-island tour, but had to cancel. I couldn't afford the first part of the trip—the one to the bank.

• • •

Last year, we wanted to go to the Bahamas in the worst way—and this year we did. We took the kids.

• • •

I'm so proud of our new compact car. Last year, we drove it to Florida during the hurricane season and got 550 miles to the gallon.

• • •

We spent last night sleeping at the neighbor's. It wasn't that there was anything wrong at our house. We were just watching slides of their vacation.

• • •

VALENTINE'S DAY

"You're my one and only" valentine cards are now available in multi-packs.

• • •

His wife hinted that for Valentine's Day she would like something on her wrist that would last forever, so he's making arrangements to have her tattooed.

• • •

If Valentine's Day were really that important, they'd have a bowl game or something.

• • •

She asked for something that comes in a little box and goes around her finger. So I got her a box of Band-Aids.

• • •

On Valentine's Day I always try to do a little more for my wife—like holding the door open when she goes out on her paper route.

• • •

Washington, George

George Washington never told a lie, proving that he neither liked to golf or fish.

• • •

George Washington never told a lie, because in those days, presidents didn't hold press conferences.

• • •

I have a son who's a freshman and he's already following in George Washington's footsteps. He went down in history.

• • •

George Washington never lied because he had no campaign promises to keep.

• • •

George Washington never told a lie. But then again, he never had to fill out an income tax form.

• • •

Weather

I just saw the first sign of spring. There is a list on the refrigerator door of things to do.

• • •

In dry weather like this, I could never understand when there is a water shortage, why we aren't allowed to wash our cars. After all, isn't that what causes rain?

• • •

It was so hot that I fed the chickens cracked ice so they wouldn't lay hard-boiled eggs.

. . .

Summer is here and of course there are three things in my home that don't work: my air conditioner, my refrigerator and my kids.

. . .

Thanks to the drought, we just discovered land on the property I bought in Florida.

. . .

We all turn to (weatherman) when we want the latest dope on the weather.

. . .

We needed this rain. There were far too many taxis in town.

. . .

Forget the millions of dollars television stations are spending on Super Dopler to enhance their weather forecasts. All I need to report weather conditions is my weather rope. It hangs from a tree in my backyard. If it's wet, it's raining. If it's white, it's snowing. If it's swaying, it's windy, and if it's gone, there's been a hurricane.

. . .

Weather forecasting is the only profession where you can be wrong all the time and not worry about losing your job.

. . .

Weathermen make so many mistakes, you would think they were elected to the job.

. . .

I have an idea that's going to increase the accuracy of the weather bureau 100 percent. It's called a window.

• • •

Don't complain about the weather. Without it, most of us wouldn't be able to start a conversation.

• • •

Let a smile be your umbrella and you'll get a mouthful of rain.

• • •

The water shortage is so bad in Iowa that they can't even take baths. My son wants to move there.

• • •

It was so cold last night that my teeth chattered all night. And we don't even sleep together.

• • •

The weatherman predicted showers last night and he was right. I know, I took one.

• • •

A day without sunshine is like a day in Seattle (or other rainy town).

• • •

The smog was so bad that I opened my mouth to yawn and chipped a tooth!

• • •

It was so hot yesterday that I saw a dog chasing a rabbit and they were both walking.

• • •

(following a wicked tornado) "Joe, was your barn damaged badly in the tornado?"

"We don't know. We haven't found it yet."

• • •

WEDDING

I went to a vegetarian wedding last week. It was a very touching moment when the bride fed the groom the first slice of her bouquet.

• • •

They got married. Dad spent twenty thousand dollars on the wedding and they say, "He gave the bride away."

• • •

WIFE

My wife said to me, "Do you have a good memory for faces?"
I replied, "I guess so. Why?"
"I just broke your shaving mirror," she said.

• • •

"That's a beautiful mink you bought your wife. Does it keep her warm?"

"I didn't buy it to keep her warm. I bought it to keep her quiet."

• • •

"To show how considerate I am, I'm going to take out the garbage."

"Good, show it a good time."

• • •

(before birthday) "Remember, with me it's not the thought that counts. It's what you give me."

• • •

(returning from shopping spree) "I was just out spreading confidence in the American dollar."

• • •

A good listener is anyone who has a TV, stereo, radio, VCR and a wife.

• • •

His wife has so many pairs of shoes, he believes that she must have been a centipede in a previous life.

• • •

I always hold hands with my wife. If I let it go, she shops.

• • •

I was once kidnapped and my wife didn't want to pay the ransom. She said she didn't want to have to break a ten.

• • •

My wife goes to a sale and buys everything marked down. Yesterday she came home with two dresses and an escalator.

• • •

My wife is doing a better job of keeping her bills down. She bought a heavier paperweight.

• • •

Husband 1: "My wife is struggling to keep up with the Joneses."
Husband 2: "You're lucky. Mine tries to keep up with the Gateses!"

• • •

(auctioneer) "Sold to the lady with her husband's hand over her mouth!"

• • •

My wife would make a great congressman. She's always introducing new bills in the house.

• • •

(looking over bills) "The only thing to do is flip a coin. Heads I spend less, tails you earn more."

• • •

My wife is a cleanliness nut. At dinner she ties a pigeon around my neck so there won't be any crumbs.

• • •

(in fur store) "Will a small deposit hold it until my husband does something unforgivable?"

• • •

My wife called, desperate for help. She said, "The car is stalled and I am now in a phone booth at the corner of Walk and Don't Walk."

• • •

My wife suffers in silence louder than anyone I know.

• • •

I walked into the stationery store and said to the clerk, "I'd like a nice fountain pen. This is my wife's birthday."
The clerk responded, "A little surprise, huh?"
I said, "Yeah, she's expecting a mink coat."

• • •

She thinks she's Teddy Roosevelt. She runs around everywhere yelling, "Charge!"

• • •

My wife recently had plastic surgery. I cut all her credit cards in half.

• • •

She's always complaining that she has nothing to wear. Friends, she has more clothes in her closet. It's packed so tight that there are moths in there that still haven't learned how to fly.

• • •

She said, "Next Christmas, let's get practical things like ties and furs."

• • •

A wife went to a missing persons bureau and reported her missing husband. "Have you found someone short, thin and bald with false teeth? In fact, most of him was missing before he was."

• • •

He hasn't spoken to his wife for three weeks. He doesn't want to interrupt her.

• • •

My wife keeps me in touch with reality. The other night, I came home from a speech and she said, "How did you perform?"
I said, "I brought down the house."
She said, "So do termites."

• • •

It amazes me that airport security would take the time to check through my wife's purse. After all, if she can't find anything in there, how could they?

• • •

My wife never repeats gossip. You've got to listen the first time she tells you.

• • •

She's very strange with a checkbook. Once she's started one, she can't put it down till it's through.

• • •

My wife has been with the kids too much lately. I took her out to dinner with my boss. I looked up from my plate, and there she was cutting his roast beef and wiping his mouth with a napkin.

• • •

My wife always keeps a bowl of wax fruit on the table just in case a couple of mannequins drop in unexpectedly.

• • •

My wife has two closets full of nothing to wear.

• • •

She'll never find my extra money. I hid it in a sock that needs mending.

• • •

My wife went to the bank to cash my paycheck. "It needs an endorsement," the teller explained.
My wife thought for a minute and then wrote on the back of the check, "Pat is a wonderful husband."

• • •

My wife uses her credit cards so often that she's using money that hasn't even been printed yet.

• • •

My wife treats me like a baby. I wanted to discuss it at dinner the other night and she said, "I'm not going to discuss anything with you until you've finished all your carrots!"

• • •

My wife is really neat. The other night I got out of bed to get a drink and when I got back, my side of the bed was made.

• • •

He drives his wife crazy. He talks in his sleep in a foreign language.

• • •

My wife keeps complaining about headaches. So I told her, "Look, when you get out of bed in the morning, it's feet first."

• • •

I bought my wife a new dress. She claimed that every time she wore the other one people threw rice at her.

• • •

Look for subtle signs that your wife might be dissatisfied . . . like when she vacuums up your stamp collection.

• • •

My wife is always buying clothes. I think that as a child she was once frightened by an empty clothes hanger.

• • •

He got his wife a gift certificate for her birthday, and she went out and exchanged it for a larger size.

• • •

My wife ran out of the house in her house robe and curlers, and yelled to the trash collectors, "Am I too late for the garbage?"

"No," replied a worker, "hop right in."

• • •

My wife gave me two neckties for my birthday. To please her, I wore one the following day.

She said, "What's the matter? Don't you like the blue one?"

• • •

I can tell you men how you can always remember your wife's birthday. Just forget it once.

• • •

Wife's Cooking

I said, "Let's eat out tonight and give the smoke detector a rest."

• • •

If you don't like my wife's hamburger, you can always play hockey with it.

• • •

My wife says that my problem is that I judge food too much by the taste.

• • •

My wife took a microwave cooking class. It started at 8 P.M. and ended at 8:05 P.M.

• • •

My wife's cooking is so bad that in school when kids trade sandwiches, my children have to throw in an article of clothing.

• • •

The first breakfast that my wife cooked for me was scrambled eggs, toast and hash blacks.

• • •

We've had leftovers in our house for years. The original meal has never been found.

• • •

I told her I wanted to be surprised for dinner, so she took the labels off the cans.

• • •

It's important to compliment your wife's cooking. For example: "I suppose it's a matter of taste, but I like the burnt part better than the frozen part."

• • •

My wife idolizes me. She serves me burnt offerings every meal.

• • •

My wife has just one problem with cooking. She burns everything. We were married three years before I realized there were other flavors besides charcoal.

• • •

The day after we were married my wife cooked her first meal. She said to me, "Honey, I have a confession to make. I've only learned to cook two things: beef stew and banana pudding."
I said, "That's all right, dear. Just one question. Which is this?"

• • •

My wife told me to take her some place on our anniversary she's never been before, so I took her to the kitchen.

• • •

My wife burned the Thanksgiving turkey so badly that it could only be identified through dental records.

• • •

My wife doesn't need to call the family to dinner. We know it's ready when the smoke detector goes off.

• • •

I'm not bragging, but my wife can make ice cubes that just melt in your mouth!

• • •

Wife's Driving

My wife has frequent accidents in the car, but they're really not her fault. Like the other day she was driving down the street, minding her own business, when a telephone pole cut right in front of her.

• • •

It gives me a real thrill to see my wife pull our new car into the carport. Relief is felt as well. You see, our carport started out as a garage.

• • •

My wife doesn't panic when she gets lost. She just changes where she wants to go.

• • •

A traffic cop pulled my wife over for driving her car too slowly on the highway. "This is a 65 mph highway," he said. "How come you were doing less than 25?"

"I'm sorry, officer," she answered, "but I saw a lot of signs that said 22, not 65."

"That's not the speed limit," said the officer. "That's the route number."

Just then he looked in the back seat and saw two of my wife's friends trembling in fear. "What's the matter with them?" he asked. My wife explained, "We just got off Highway 120."

• • •

WILLIAMS, PAT

I was with the Phillies and was compared to Yogi Berra. My name came up and someone said, "We're not exactly talking about another Yogi Berra."

• • •

I was the only man to have my glove bronzed at the height of my career—and then I played with it.

• • •

I was so nervous my first game, the manager came and told me, "In the pros you wear your underwear on the inside of your uniform."

• • •

Each time I was traded, the newspapers read, "This is a deal that will hurt both teams."

• • •

I had deceptive speed. I was slower than I looked.

• • •

Ferguson Jenkins was asked, "Who's the toughest person you have to pitch to?"

Jenkins replied, "My catcher, Pat Williams!"

• • •

He's in the twilight of a very mediocre career.

• • •

A nonviolent player, I could go months without hitting anything.

• • •

WINTER

Our crack snow removal team has been removing snow around the clock. And now that the area around the clock is clear, they can start to work on the streets.

• • •

This is the time of year when people start going to places where they can pay two hundred dollars a day to experience the same kind of heat they were complaining about in August.

• • •

One nice thing about weather like this. It's easy to find a picnic table.

• • •

It was so cold out there today he wore his toupee upside down.

• • •

It was so cold today, I saw hens laying eggs from a standing position.

• • •

Our state has a great snow removal system. It's called August.

• • •

If you want to avoid colds this winter, take plenty of vitamin C— and take it to Orlando and stay there.

• • •

It was so cold last night, I took all my fan mail from this year and started a fire. I never knew that one postcard could create so much heat.

• • •

Women

Anyone who says that a woman could not stand the stress of combat has never been to a Presidents' Birthday sale.

• • •

Sure, Fred Astaire was a great dancer, but remember, Ginger Rogers did everything Fred did except she did it backwards and in high heels.

• • •

Women have a tougher time in business than men, and it's probably because they have no wives to advise them.

• • •

You know how to drive a woman crazy? Put her in a room with five hundred hats and no mirror.

• • •

A woman has to do twice as much as a man to be considered half as good. Fortunately, it isn't difficult.

• • •

Most women live longer than their husbands because they have three closets full of clothes that they wouldn't be caught dead in.

• • •

Women's Liberation

They keep saying that women are smarter than men. But have you ever seen a man's shirt that buttons down the back?

• • •

I am glad there is sexual equality in all areas these days. Just this morning my wife was discussing this very issue with her Avon man.

• • •

Work

There must be some truth in reincarnation. Just look at the way some office workers come back to life after quitting time.

• • •

Fathers, remember to teach your sons a trade. That way they'll always know what kind of work they're out of.

• • •

I don't have too large an office. People keep coming in and asking for brooms.

• • •

Remember, work like a dog. Eat like a horse. Think like a fox. Run like a rabbit. And visit your veterinarian twice a year.

• • •

WORLD CONDITIONS

My plan to eliminate nuclear war is to make missiles so complicated that they can't be fired. This can be accomplished by having the instructions written by the same guys who write the tax forms.

• • •

Why can't nations solve their problems like husbands and wives? Just get mad, pout and don't talk to each other for a couple of weeks.

• • •

I always read "Dear Abby" columns. It's wonderful to know that with all the problems in the world there are still some people whose biggest worry is how they should acknowledge a wedding present.

• • •

Zoo

Visitors to the zoo were surprised to see the exhibit labeled "Coexistence" containing a lion and some lambs. The zookeeper explained there was nothing to it. "All I have to do every now and then is add a few fresh lambs."

• • •

"Dad, will you take me to the zoo?"

"Son, I've told you fifty times, if the zoo wants you, they'll come and get you."

• • •

Dolphins are so smart that in only a few weeks of captivity, they can train people to stand at the edge of a pool and throw them fish.

• • •

Afterword

Winning with One-Liners is truly an eclectic work. The material presented is not original with me, but has been drawn from the finest comedians, speakers, books and humor services. It is a distillation, if you will, of the purest, funniest lines I have encountered in the past forty years from among the millions I have read and heard. I am confident that this book has provided you with much more than your minimum daily dose of laughter, and that it will prove to be the ultimate humor resource for you as you plan your presentations.

About the Author

Pat Williams is senior vice-president of the Orlando Magic and is a popular motivational speaker. He helped found the Orlando Magic in 1987, and then to guide it, as general manager, from an expansion club to one of the top teams in the NBA in just a few short years.

Pat was general manager of the Philadelphia 76ers for twelve years, including the 1983 championship season. He was also general manager of the Atlanta Hawks and the Chicago Bulls.

Pat is one of the country's top motivational and inspirational speakers. He has written twenty-five books on a variety of topics, including the popular *How to Be Like Mike*.

Pat and his wife, Ruth, live in Florida, and are the parents of nineteen children, fourteen of whom were adopted from four foreign countries.

To contact Pat Williams, phone (407) 916-2404 or e-mail him at *pwilliams@rdvsports.com*. Mail can be sent to:

Pat Williams
c/o RDV Sports
8701 Maitland Summit Boulevard
Orlando, FL 32810

To book Pat Williams for a speaking engagement, please contact his assistant, Melinda Ethington, at the above address, or phone (407) 916-2454. Requests can be faxed to (407) 916-2986 or e-mailed to *methington@rdvsports.com*.

Pat Williams is delighted to recommend his friend, comedian Ken Hussar, if anyone is looking for hilarious entertainment. Ken will bring his banjo, guitar, funny songs and arsenal of clean one-liners, that will have your audience convulsing with laughter. To book Ken Hussar for his comedy show, (west of the Mississippi River) contact Clean Comedians, attention Paul Brown, P.O. Box 1027, La Mirada, CA 90637, phone: 1-800-354-GLAD; fax: (714) 670-1990; (east of the Mississippi) A Time to Laugh Productions, Stephen Brubaker, (714) 951-8070 or (717) 898-8883, or contact Ken directly at (717) 898-0024, e-mail: *ridingsway@netzero.net*.

If you have a clean joke that you haven't found in this book, we would love to hear from you. Please use any of the contact methods above.